ISAAC ASIMOV
presents
FROM HARDING TO HIROSHIMA

ISAAC ASIMOV
presents

FROM HARDING TO HIROSHIMA

An anecdotal history of the United States from 1923 to 1945 based on little-known facts and the lives of the people who made history—and some who didn't

BARRINGTON BOARDMAN

DEMBNER BOOKS • New York

DEMBNER BOOKS
Published by Red Dembner Enterprises Corp.,
80 Eighth Avenue,
New York, N.Y. 10011

Distributed by W. W. Norton & Company, Inc.,
500 Fifth Avenue,
New York, N.Y. 10110

Copyright © 1988 by Barrington Boardman.

Library of Congress Cataloging-in-Publication Data
Boardman, Barrington.
    Isaac Asimov presents From Harding to Hiroshima.
    Includes index.
    1. United States—History—1919–1933.   2. United
States—History—1933–1945.   I. Asimov, Isaac, 1920–
II. From Harding to Hiroshima.   III. Title.
E784.B59 1988   973.91   87-14359
ISBN 0-934878-94-3

Designed by Antler & Baldwin, Inc.

To my wife, Sandy, and to my children—Sean, Brooke, Mela, and Lee—who indulged this lengthy project with good-humored support

CONTENTS

PREFACE

My thanks to Red Dembner and Isaac Asimov for their constructive criticism and enthusiasm, to Peter Schwed for his guidance and counsel, to Anne Griswold and Ann Finlayson for their editing skills, to Ellie Filanowski for preparing the manuscript, and to the Ellens—Boynton and Pemberton—for typing the research notes and early chapters. Also, special thanks go to my partners, Bill Ballard and Lynn Rotando, for their encouragement.

Finally, I am indebted to literally hundreds of authors, too many by far to name each one here—historians, biographers, journalists, commentators, among others—for providing an abundance of informative and highly entertaining source material.

The period covered in this book was particularly rich in noteworthy events and interesting people. One of the sad realities of this endeavor was the harsh fact that a single volume could not contain all that the author would like to have included; much had to be left out so that this book would not rival the Bible in word content. To those who will be disappointed not to find a favorite anecdote or reference to a particular person, I offer my apologies.

B. B.

BY FLASHES
OF LIGHTNING

There are various ways of writing history books. The old-fashioned histories were very heavy on politics and war. They included many battles, especially those that involved resounding triumphs and disasters. There were court intrigues, especially those that ended with heads being lost, or kings overthrown, or both. This makes for good, exciting stuff when written well, but it can become tedious and hard to follow when written indifferently.

Until quite recently, it was not thought necessary to go beyond rulers and the nobility. The deeds and thoughts of the lower classes were not considered of importance; history was the tale of the powerful. Nor was it thought necessary to describe everyday life, because it was assumed that everyone knew about that. It was not quite clear in people's minds that ways of eating, fashions of clothing, methods of amusement changed with time.

Even Herodotus, who carefully outlined in most entertaining form the habits, ways, and customs of foreigners such as Egyptians, Persians, and Scythians did not bother going into detail concerning the way of life of his own Greeks, since he took it for granted his readers would know all about that, and would be impatient with any attempt to teach them what they already knew.

This calm assumption that everyday things did not change accounts for the fact that in medieval paintings of scenes from the Bible, the characters involved are usually shown as being dressed in impeccable medieval garb. It is as though some modern painter painted a scene representing Charlemagne's court and had everyone dressed like Wall Street brokers.

Nowadays, it is, of course, quite understood that the course of history is more often decided by economic factors rather than by the brilliance of generals. Napoleon won a myriad victories, but the British had worked out a system of finance that left them able to grow rich while they were fighting Napoleon. Napoleon ran out of soldiers long before Great Britain ran out of cash with which to support every anti-Napoleonic move on the Continent.

You might look for reasons for the decline and fall of the Roman Empire, or the decline and fall of pre-Revolutionary France, and your search for military defeats and incapable rulers would be meaningless. Actually, neither Rome nor eighteenth-century France figured out an efficient way of taxing their subjects without destroying them, and that led to bankruptcy, alienation, and torpor. Both fell as a result of economic rot from within.

Consequently, modern histories are strong on economic factors. This presents a much more valid sort of history but it has a serious defect. It is dull. It is enormously and overpoweringly dull. A good history stressing economic factors is liable to destroy the brain of any reader who is not an economist, and there are those who say economists are immune only because they were brain-damaged to begin with.

Modern histories also recognize the fact that ways of life change, and these books frequently try to explain how ordinary people lived. This is never dull, but it is hardly ever tightly focused, either. There is a tendency to deal with people impersonally and generally as though the historian were distancing himself from them.

Here, though, in *From Harding to Hiroshima*, we have a special history. It deals with the twenty-three-year period from the death of Warren Harding to the dropping of the atomic bomb on Hiroshima, and does so in terms of specific people, from presidents and kings to movie actors and speakeasy hostesses, from singers to criminals, all identified by name and given personalities.

What a twenty-three-year period it was, too. It included the hectic and carefree years of speculative prosperity in the 1920s, the dreary and deadly blasting of hope in the depressed 1930s. It deals with the years of the rise of Hitler and the years of bitter war we had to pay for having watched that rise indifferently.

All of it is told anecdotally, with background material on some of those who made news—not the kind, perhaps, that will fill the history books of the next century, but the kind that did fill the newspapers of the time—and small illuminating snapshots of hundreds of others. It is history told by flashes of lightning, and it is uniformly fascinating. For those readers who are in their later years (as I am) there will be a strong tug of nostalgia, too.

And you will find that almost everything this book tells you is something you didn't know. You get details of the career of Rudolph Valentino, whose death in 1926 devastated American women. (Believe me, Clark Gable and Robert Taylor were merely pale imitations.) You get others of Charles A. Lindbergh, whose solo flight to Paris roused much more excitement than anything that has happened so far in space. (The ticker tape parade he received when he returned to the U.S.A. *still* holds the record for frenzy.)

Much of the material in the book is admittedly trivia, but trivia is almost always interesting precisely because it is not the sort of thing you can easily find in books. And, trivia or not, the details are so carefully organized here that they build a picture that is more illuminating, at times, than an orthodox and straightforward account might be.

Thus, you will find, in the appropriate place, the saga of the *Weekly Letter* put out by no less an august group than the Harvard Economic Society. From the time of the stock market crash in 1929, it unfailingly predicted from month to month that the worst was over and that prosperity would soon return. After about a year and a half of this steady diet of optimism and reassurance, the *Weekly Letter* stopped doing it. The reason was that it had managed to go broke in the midst of all this "returning prosperity" and had been forced to suspend publication.

That is surely the epitome of the mindless reaction of so many to the onset of the Depression—just leave things alone and they will get better. And meanwhile, from their bastions the well-off watched, with glazed and uncaring eyes, the helpless suffering of millions. Once Roosevelt was elected, however, and once he began to move rapidly to try to improve conditions for those hit by the Depression, the well-off were finally moved to emotion. They *hated* helping the unemployed and considered Roosevelt a "traitor to his class" for the vile crime of having compassion.

Here's another: In 1935, a New York state senator opposed legislation designed to curb syphilis. He felt that the very mention of the name of the disease would "corrupt the innocence of children, and . . . create a shudder in every decent woman and man." So let syphilis rage—rather than mention its name.

But that was fifty years ago, right? Then ruminate on the fact that in

1987 there are people who object violently to any mention of the use of condoms as a means of lowering the chance of contagion of AIDS. Far better, they think, to let AIDS kill thousands or millions than ever to corrupt youth by mentioning that dirty word, c–nd–m. (And this, even though I seriously doubt there is any youth or maiden in America who is so dumb as not to know what a condom is.)

Undoubtedly, the flashes of lightning that permeate this book by Barrington Boardman will serve to illuminate the human condition quite effectively, and give you pleasure—sometimes uproarious and sometimes sardonic—in the process.

Isaac Asimov

1923

I will make it a felony to drink small beer.
—William Shakespeare, *King Henry IV*, Part II

If your concern was paternal, the flapper was a problem. Otherwise, she was a pleasure. Jauntily feather-footed in her unfastened galoshes, her flesh-colored stockings rolled below the knee and her skirt barely touching it, slender and boyish, the flapper came in to the tune "I'll Say She Does"—and frequently she did.
—Lloyd Morris

☞ NATIONAL NEWS

Late in 1922, the eminent physician Emanuel Libman saw President Warren G. Harding at a reception. Shocked by his appearance, Dr. Libman predicted that the president would be dead within six months from "a disease of the coronary arteries," a diagnosis that proved to be uncannily accurate when Harding, fifty-eight, died of an embolism on August 2, 1923, during a trip to the West Coast. The physician of such disparate celebrities as Albert Einstein, Harpo Marx, and Sarah Bernhardt, Libman later predicted the death of President Franklin Roosevelt and the cause (cerebral hemorrhage) after seeing him in a newsreel in 1941.

When Harding died in room 8064 of his suite at San Francisco's Palace Hotel, he became the fifth consecutive president to die in office who had been elected in a year ending in zero. This chain of untimely

1

1923 deaths has claimed two more presidents since Harding and remains unbroken:

PRESIDENT	ELECTED	DIED
William H. Harrison	1840	1841
Abraham Lincoln	1860	1865
James A. Garfield	1880	1881
William McKinley	1900	1901
Warren G. Harding	1920	1923
Franklin D. Roosevelt	1940	1945
John F. Kennedy	1960	1963
Ronald Reagan	1980	--

Senator Warren Gamaliel Harding had gone to the 1920 Republican Convention as the darkest of horses. He had done poorly in the primaries, was not particularly eager to be president, and only his campaign manager, Harry Daugherty, took Harding's candidacy seriously. Daugherty had amused reporters four months earlier with this melodramatic scenario of the upcoming convention:

> I don't expect Senator Harding to be nominated on the first, second, or third ballot, but I think about eleven minutes after two o'clock on Friday morning of the convention, when fifteen or twenty men, bleary-eyed and perspiring profusely from the heat, are sitting around the table one of them will say, "Who will we nominate?" At that decisive time the friends of Senator Harding can suggest him and can afford to abide by the result. I don't know but what I might suggest him myself.

The press would later resurrect Daugherty's statement and shorten his words to "fifteen men in a smoke-filled room," which would become an enduring symbol of boss-controlled politics American-style.

The results of the first convention ballot found Harding a distant fifth in the voting. Nevertheless, at around 2:00 A.M. on Friday, June 11 (historians differ as to the exact time, but it was close to Daugherty's 2:11 A.M. prediction), Warren Harding was summoned to room 401 in Chicago's Blackstone Hotel, where party leaders pondered a deadlock between Leonard Wood and Frank Lowden after ten ballots had been cast. Publisher George B. Harvey posed a question to Harding that has become indigenous to the American political process: "We think that you should tell us, on your conscience before God, whether there is anything that might be brought up against you that would embarrass the party, any

2

impediment that might disqualify you or make you inexpedient, either as **1923**
a candidate or as a president." After having been left alone for ten
minutes, Harding affirmed that there was "nothing, no obstacle to his
nomination," and a day later he became the Republican presidential
candidate.

American political history suggests that there have been few office
seekers whose pasts are pristine enough to withstand totally the
microscope of political scrutiny. Yet those ten minutes of soul searching
must have given Warren Harding particular pause:

• Married to an older, dominating woman whom he called the
Duchess, Harding had had a long affair with Mrs. James (Carrie) Phillips,
the wife of a Marion, Ohio, neighbor. Harding had written the beautiful
Carrie over 100 love letters, which she had carefully preserved, in a
cardboard shoe box. Fortunately for the two lovers, these letters would
not be discovered until 1964, when Mrs. Phillips would have mercifully
joined Harding in the hereafter. Harding's letters left little doubt of his
ardor, causing his heirs to bring suit to prevent their publication until the
year 2014, fifty years after Mrs. Phillips's death. Historian Francis Russell
had read the letters before their impoundment in the Library of Congress
and recalls a poem in a letter dated Christmas 1914:

> I love you more than all the world
> Possession wholly imploring
> Mid Passion I am ofttimes whirled
> Ofttimes admire-adoring
> Oh, God! If fate would only give
> Us privilege to love and live!

• If Harding overlooked his affair with Mrs. Phillips in his delibera-
tions, it is difficult to believe that a more recent liaison failed to qualify in
his mind as a potential embarrassment to self and party. Nan Britton,
twenty-four, had given birth to Harding's child just eight months earlier in
Asbury Park, New Jersey, and was in Chicago as a spectator at the
convention.

Many Republicans felt disenfranchised by their party's selection of
such an inexperienced and little-known candidate; they would soon be
joined by large numbers of dissident Democrats. When that party's
convention ended three weeks later in San Francisco, the delegates had
convened for eight days, cast forty-four ballots, and consumed forty
barrels of whiskey supplied, despite Prohibition, by the Democratic
National Committee. Their compromise candidate, James Cox, was
another Ohioan (the state had supplied six of the last ten presidents) and,
like Harding, a newspaper publisher. A Harding-Cox campaign inspired

3

1923 this bit of doggerel from New York newspaper columnist Franklin P. Adams:

> Harding or Cox?
> Harding or Cox?
> You tell us, populi,
> You've got the vox.

Harding spent most of the campaign on the front porch of his Marion, Ohio, home, shaking hands with visitors for several hours each day. ("It is the most pleasant thing I do," said Harding.) Senator Boies Penrose advised, "Keep Warren at home. Don't let him make any speeches. If he goes on tour, somebody's sure to ask him a question, and Warren's just the sort of damn fool that'll try to answer them."

The campaign proceeded smoothly for the Harding forces. While Harding vacillated on the desirability of joining Wilson's League of Nations (he had twice voted for it in the Senate), the public hardly noticed. Harding's "Back to Normalcy" credo, while repugnant to English teachers, was in tune with a war-weary nation distrustful of foreign alliances. (Harding had actually misread the word "normality" in a speech and unintentionally created the word "normalcy.")

The press had heard stories of Harding's philandering, and the wife of a reporter covering the campaign in Marion added one of her own: "Three newsmen invited to dine at the home of one of Harding's widow neighbors were, during the evening, taken upstairs by an innocent eight-year-old member of the widow's family, and proudly shown Harding's toothbrush. Said the child, 'He always stays here when Mrs. Harding goes away.'" But none of these stories surfaced in the press, and his luck held until an unforeseen political land mine exploded in the Harding camp. William Estabrook Chancellor, a professor at Wooster College, published two pamphlets making the astonishing claim that Warren Harding was black.

Professor Chancellor stated that Harding's great-grandmother, Elizabeth Madison, had been a Negress and that his great-grandfather, George T. Harding, had Negro blood. He described Harding as "big, lazy, slouching, confused, ignorant, affable" and added that he was lax in sexual morals "like all Negroes." He made his accusations available to the Democrats and, to their credit, ailing President Woodrow Wilson and candidate James Cox did not use the material to their party's advantage; newspapers also refused to publish it. But soon this incredible accusation was whispered across the land, inspiring "jokes" like this:

SAMBO: Did yo' heah de big news, Ephrum? Dey done nomi-
    nate Mistah Harding in Chicago.
EPHRUM: Sho! Who'd de white folks nominate?

But Chancellor's charge did not come as a surprise to Harding's Marion, Ohio, neighbors because the thick-lipped, dark-skinned Harding had long been haunted by this rumor. Harding's engagement had been marred by a confrontation between the groom-to-be and his future father-in-law, Amos H. Kling, who called him a "Goddam nigger" and suggested that he should not darken his doorstep again. Kling would not speak to his daughter and son-in-law for seven years.

Reactions from the Harding camp varied. Senator Penrose saw the bright side: "From what I hear we've been having trouble holding the nigger vote lately." Others were more circumspect, and the consensus was that Harding should not acknowledge the accusation, hopefully leaving the public to conclude that the charge was so completely without foundation as to be undeserving of comment. But was it true? A Cincinnati reporter took the bull by the horns and asked Harding point-blank: "Do you have any Negro blood?" Harding answered, "How do I know, Jim? One of my ancestors may have jumped the fence."

Meanwhile, Daugherty assured the press that the Harding clan was of "a blue-eyed stock from New England and Pennsylvania, the finest pioneer blood, Anglo-Saxon, German, Scotch-Irish, and Dutch." One cynic noted that only the Scandinavians and French had not made the list.

Chancellor's accusations provided the juiciest campaign issue since Democratic candidate Grover Cleveland had admitted to siring an illegitimate son three months before the 1884 election. ("Ma! Ma! Where's my Pa?" "Gone to the White House. Ha! Ha! Ha!") But Cleveland had weathered the storm and so did Harding, who easily defeated Cox, taking thirty-seven states and 60 percent of the popular vote. Socialist Eugene Debs (inmate 9653 at the federal prison in Atlanta) polled nearly a million votes while serving a ten-year sentence for publicly denouncing prosecutions under the federal espionage acts.

Harry Daugherty's first impression of Harding had been, "Gee, what a great-looking president he'd make," and that appears to have been his principal qualification for the Oval Office. The congenial Harding was true to his friends and party, awarding hundreds of government jobs to loyalists like Harry Daugherty, whom he made attorney general. They repaid him by creating one of the most corrupt administrations in American history. But the times were uncomplicated, and Harding's inability to make decisions was not public knowledge at the time of his death, nor were his moral shortcomings, although those of his associates were beginning to emerge.

Harding died a very popular president, causing an outpouring of grief unmatched by the death of any president since Lincoln. Alas, numerous damaging revelations since Harding's death account for his current standing in history's rating of American presidents. Historian

1923 Arthur M. Schlesinger, Jr., commented, "His country would remember him affectionately as the worst president ever." Other quotes:

• Harding enjoyed drinking whiskey, chewing tobacco, and playing poker, and his first comment upon hearing of his nomination for the presidency was in the words of the gambler: "We drew to a pair of deuces and filled."

• "If you were a girl, Warren, you'd be in the family way all the time. You can't say no." (Dr. George T. Harding, the president's father)

• "The only man, woman or child who wrote a simple declarative sentence with seven grammatical errors." (e.e. cummings)

• "In this job, I'm not worried about my enemies. It's my friends, my Goddam friends, who are keeping me awake nights." (Warren G. Harding)

• "Always have an icebox full of food, and never let him travel without you." (Mrs. Warren G. Harding's advice to wives on how to prevent their husbands from straying)

• "I am not fit for this office and never should have been here." (Warren G. Harding)

On the night of August 2, 1923, Calvin Coolidge walked into the general store in Plymouth Notch, Vermont, and ordered a Moxie, a popular soft drink, originally called Moxie Nerve Food. "Hot night," observed the vice president, who was a man of few words. After finishing his drink, Collidge strolled back up the hill to his father's farm and retired for the night at 9:00 P.M.

Just after 2:00 A.M., a messenger arrived at the Coolidge farm with a telegram and awakened the vice president's father, Colonel John Coolidge. "What's wanted?" asked Colonel Coolidge. "President Harding is dead," replied the messenger. "I have a telegram for the vice president."

Calvin Coolidge later recalled, "I was awakened by my father coming up the stairs calling my name. I noticed that his voice trembled. As the only time I had ever observed that before was when death had visited our family, I knew that something of the gravest nature had occurred."

After learning of Harding's death, Coolidge had dressed in a black suit, and his father, a notary public, administered the presidential oath. The ceremony was held in the sitting room lighted by two kerosene lamps, and when it was over at 2:47 A.M., the president went back upstairs to bed. (Coolidge would learn shortly that his father's authority was restricted to swearing in state officials, and the ceremony was repeated in Washington several days later.)

When painter Charles Hopkinson later did a portrait of Coolidge, he questioned him on his reaction of Harding's death:

6

HOPKINSON: Mr. Coolidge, what was the first thought that
      came into your mind when you were told that Mr. Harding
      was dead and the presidency was yours?
COOLIDGE: I thought I could swing it.

In 1923, automobile sales were booming. More cars were built that
year than had been built in the first fifteen years of the automobile
industry in the United States.

Installment buying was a key factor in increasing sales. Americans
were overcoming their aversion to buying on credit, and by 1927 two
thirds of American automobiles would be bought on time payments.
Credit buying in conjunction with an improved economy brought large
numbers of lower income purchasers into the market for the first time.

Sales were also buoyed by the initiation of annual model changes by
several motor companies, including fast-growing General Motors, and
this "planned obsolescence" was said to create faster turnover among
style-conscious motorists. Many car manufacturers could not afford the
expense of yearly capital outlays for retooling and would go out of
business over the next fifteen years. Some of the casualties were as
follows:

Case	1927	National	1924
Chalmers	1923	Paige	1927
Crawford	1924	Peterson	1924
Davis	1928	Peerless	1932
Detroit Electric	1938	Pierce-Arrow	1938
Dorris	1926	Pilot	1924
Elcar	1930	Premier	1927
Flint	1927	Pullman	1925
Kissel	1931	Star	1928
Locomobile	1929	Stearns-Knight	1930
Marmon	1933	Stevens-Duryea	1927
Maxwell	1925	Stutz	1935
McFarlan	1927	Velie	1928
Mercer	1925	Willys-Knight	1932
Moon	1930	Winton	1924

To many Americans, Henry Ford *was* the automobile, and one out of
every two cars sold in the United States in 1923 was a Ford. Born the son
of an Irish immigrant farmer in 1863, Ford had dropped out of school at
fifteen and became a mechanic, rising to the position of chief engineer at
Detroit's Edison Illuminating Company. But his hobby was internal-
combustion engines, and in 1899 Ford, thirty-six, left Edison to try to
make a go of it in the fledgling automobile business. In his spare time he
had already built and sold his first three "Fords."

7

1923   In 1902, Ford completed his Ford 999 racing car and persuaded professional bicycle racer Barney Oldfield to become his test driver, undismayed by one drawback: Oldfield did not know how to drive an automobile. Ford taught him in two weeks, and in 1903 Oldfield became the first person to drive 60 miles an hour, the seemingly unattainable "mile a minute," giving birth to a new expression for describing speed— "going like sixty."

Henry Ford founded the Ford Motor Company in 1903 with $28,000 raised from selling stock. The company had twelve workers and a factory just 50 feet wide. Preparations for the introduction of the Model T exhausted Ford's capital, bringing the company dangerously close to bankruptcy. A friend's sister lent Ford $100 to tide the company over, and her $100 worth of Ford stock would later be repurchased by Ford for $260,000, a return of 2,600 times her original investment.

The Model T was first sold in 1908. Priced at $850, it was offered in "any color you choose as long as it's black." The 4-cylinder, 20-horsepower engine was capable of speeds up to 40 miles per hour. Ford adopted the most modern manufacturing techniques, learned from Raymond Olds and Frederick Winston Turner, father of the assembly line. By 1916, improved efficiency and high volume sales had brought the price of the Model T down to $360, and it was being produced in less than half the time of the original.

Ford had made headlines in 1914 when he had horrified fellow businessmen by offering a minimum wage of $5 per day when $2 was considered generous and $5 was the weekly wage of English workers. He said that by increasing the pay of the American laborer, a whole new market would emerge for his automobiles, composed of people who had previously not been affluent enough to afford them. A more likely reason for Ford's largesse was the terrible boredom that workers suffered on the assembly line. Ford workers were "forbidden to sit, whistle, sing, lean against the machinery, smoke or talk while working." The typical job was described as having to "put nut 14 on bolt 132, repeating, repeating, repeating until their hands shook and their legs quivered—emerging finally to doze on streetcars on the way home, hands jerking on reflex, and brains waking into the fear that they would 'go crazy.'"

By 1923, Ford had bought out all his stockholders, and his 1922 income had been estimated at $264,000 per day. Ford made his son, Edsel, president of Ford in 1919, but he continued to run the company while his son worked primarily on acquisitions that would later include both Lincoln and Mercury.

Up until 1927, Ford refused to change the Model T while other companies had made improvements in design, handling, and perform- ance, and offered a variety of colors and options. It won the ultimate

8

accolade of affectionate derision. Stories about its idiosyncrasies were the "Polish jokes" of their time:

QUESTION: Does this car always shake like this?

ANSWER: Only when it's running.

Its lightweight metal body brought it the nickname Tin Lizzie, and when it slithered out of mudholes that could trap a heavier car, owners liked to recite a popular parody:

> Oh, it was Tin, Tin, Tin!
> Though I constantly degrade you,
> By the Henry Ford who made you.
> You're better than a Packard, Hunk o' Tin!

Author Frederick Lewis Allen gives us this account of driving the Model T:

> If Mr. Smith's car is one of the high, hideous, but efficient Model T Fords of the day, let us watch him for a minute. He climbs in by the right-hand door (for there is no left-hand door by the front seat), reaches over to the wheel, and sets the spark and throttle levers in a position like that of the hands of a clock at ten minutes to three. Then, unless he has paid extra for a self-starter, he gets out to crank. Seizing the crank in his right hand carefully, for a friend of his once broke his arm cranking, he slips his left forefinger through a loop of wire that controls the choke. He pulls the loop of wire, he revolves the crank mightily, and as the engine at last roars, he leaps to the trembling running-board, leans in, and moves the spark and throttle to twenty-five minutes to two. . . .
>
> Finally, he is at the wheel with the engine running as it should. . . . Now his only care is for that long hill down the street; yesterday he burned his brake on it, and this morning he must remember to brake with the reverse pedal, or the low-speed pedal, or both; or all three in alternation.

Ford was a hero to workers all over the world. His popularity had caused him to run for the Senate in 1918, and he had been only narrowly defeated. As rumors of corruption in Washington began to surface, Ford became the popular choice for the presidential nomination in 1924. But if he was the champion of the working class, the intelligentsia regarded him as a bigoted, illiterate crackpot:

• Ford believed that there was a Jewish plot to rule the world through business. His newspaper, the *Dearborn Independent*, "accused the unhappy race of plotting the subjugation of the whole world." Ford and Hitler would soon admire one another's talents.

• In 1915, Ford decided personally to bring about the end of World War I and, without the government's support, hired a "peace ship" to carry leading Americans to Europe to petition for "continuous mediation." The ship attracted more eccentrics than "leading Americans," and Ford received two squirrels in a cage from some wag to symbolize the number of "nuts" on board, while the press ridiculed his efforts as a peacemaker.

• "History is bunk," said Ford. "I don't like to read books; they muss up my mind." During a libel trial, he was asked who Benedict Arnold was. "A writer, I think," answered Ford.

• Ford despised alcohol and tobacco, and published a pamphlet castigating cigarette smoking, entitled "The Little White Slaver." An excerpt: "Study the history of almost any criminal and you will find an inveterate cigarette smoker."

• A diet faddist, Ford championed both the carrot and the soybean. He once enjoyed a twelve-course meal prepared entirely from carrots— from carrot juice to carrot ice cream. On another occasion, he demonstrated the commercial potential of the soybean by appearing at a convention dressed in a wardrobe made totally from that vegetable, with the exception of his shoes.

• Appalled by acrobatic dances like the Charleston, Ford attempted to rejuvenate nineteenth-century dancing, holding dances for his workers that featured anachronisms such as the Virginia reel and the minuet.

• A lover of the comic strip "Little Orphan Annie," Ford despaired when Annie fell on hard times. Once when Annie's dog Sandy was missing, Ford sent this wire to *Chicago Tribune* publisher J. M. Patterson: "DO ALL YOU CAN TO FIND SANDY."

Black labor was migrating north in huge numbers. Some reasons cited were (1) the dwindling cotton crop, ravaged by the boll weevil, which had crossed the Rio Grande from Mexico at the turn of the century, (2) northern recruiting agents offering higher wages, (3) resentment because of unfair treatment, (4) discontented veterans returning from World War I, who would no longer accept the poor living conditions existing in black communities. Georgia was particularly hard hit, losing 32,000 farm workers. The *New York Globe* supplied one Yankee newspaper's reaction: "the wonder is that the Negro did not walk out long ago."

U.S. Steel agreed to go from a twelve- to an eight-hour day, a boon to the labor movement, which would eventually lead to a standardized forty-hour week in American industry. But U.S. Steel's decision was the only ray of sunshine for American labor in 1923:

10

• The Supreme Court declared unconstitutional a minimum wage for women and children in the District of Columbia, ruling that it was a form of price fixing and, as such, an abridgment of the right of contract. The proposed law called for a wage for women of no less than $16.50 per week, representing an annual wage of $858.

• The National Child Labor Committee reported that 67 percent of the workers in Michigan's sugar beet fields were between the ages of five and sixteen.

☛ PROHIBITION

Prohibition was in its fourth year in the United States. America was not the first country to attempt what President Herbert Hoover later called "a great experiment, noble in motive" as Russia had initiated Prohibition in 1904, Iceland in 1908. Like the United States, neither was successful in legislating abstinence from alcoholic beverages.

The Eighteenth Amendment to the Constitution had gone into effect on January 16, 1920, with only two states failing to ratify it—Connecticut and Rhode Island. Strangely enough, the Prohibition law did not ban the consumption of alcoholic beverages, nor was it a crime to buy, possess, or drink liquor. It was only the manufacture, sale, or transport of alcoholic beverages that was illegal.

In 1923, Prohibition received several setbacks:

• Judge John Knox ruled that prescriptions for whiskey were not limited under Prohibition, making physicians an important source for those seeking alcoholic beverages. An average of 10 million prescriptions were issued each year during Prohibition.

• Congress defeated a bill to make the purchase of alcoholic beverages a crime.

• A Prohibition agent toured major American cities posing as a would-be drinker, to find out how difficult it was to purchase spirits. Here is how long it took the agent to buy illegal alcohol in each city:

New Orleans	35 seconds
Detroit	3 minutes
New York	3 minutes, 10 seconds
Boston	11 minutes
Atlanta	17 minutes
Baltimore	18 minutes, 20 seconds
Chicago	21 minutes
St. Louis	21 minutes
Cleveland	29 minutes
Minneapolis	31 minutes
Washington	2 hours, 8 minutes

1923

• The state of New York repealed its Prohibition enforcement act because it was being so broadly circumvented.

☞ FOREIGN NEWS

Germany

• Rampant inflation destroyed the value of the German mark. Prices escalated so rapidly that by the end of the year, workers were being paid several times a day.

MONTH	NUMBER OF MARKS TO THE U.S. DOLLAR
January	7 thousand
July	160 thousand
September	13 million
November	130 billion
December	4 trillion

• A riot occurred when German brewers increased the foam in their beers in an attempt to keep prices at reasonable levels.

• Animals in the Berlin zoo were so underfed that their anguished cries kept many Berliners awake at night.

• The National Socialist German Workers' Party, a name later reduced to "Nazi," attempted to capitalize on unemployment and social unrest by trying to take over the Munich city government. Led by Adolf Hitler, thirty-four, they failed ludicrously in the attempt, and Hitler was sentenced to five years in jail. He was paroled after only nine months in cell 7 in Landsberg Prison. He passed the time writing a book called *Mein Kampf*.

• "There is no doubt that he [Hitler] had become a much more quiet and thoughtful individual during his imprisonment than he was before and does not contemplate acting against existing authority." (Otto Leybold, warden of Landsberg Prison.)

• "Upon completion of his term, Hitler, who is not a citizen [of Germany—he was an Austrian by birth], will be expelled from the country. Further nationalist activity on his part, for the present at least, appears to be excluded." (Robert Murphy, American diplomat in Germany)

12

England

• Citizens under eighteen were forbidden to drink in the pubs.
• Englishwomen for the first time were permitted to divorce their husbands on grounds of adultery. Most European women had not been granted the right of divorce under any terms until the nineteenth century.
• The second marquess of Ripon dropped dead on a grouse moor at seventy-one after shooting his fifty-second bird that day. The marquess had shot a lifetime total of 566,000 game birds, including 241,000 pheasants, a record that bird lovers hoped would never be broken.

France

A Chicago newspaper reported that a leading Paris couturier, whose clientele was chiefly American and English, had been forced to place signs in his fitting rooms stating that all customers must wear underwear. His dress measurers and saleswomen had complained that many society women were dispensing with undergarments, following the latest styles demanding supple, smooth lines.

Soviet Union

The Russian government recognized prostitution as a legitimate profession. Soviet Health Commissioner Semashko said that increased prostitution was the result of economic policy and urged the police to be polite to the prostitutes.

Andorra

• World War I had not come to an end in this small republic in the Pyrenees mountains between France and Spain. Despite having declared war on Germany in 1914, Andorra had not been invited to sign the Treaty of Versailles in 1919. Irritated by this snub, Andorra would not declare War I officially over until 1958, thirteen years after World War II had ended.
• Under an ancient treaty, Andorra was ruled jointly by the bishop of Spain and the president of France. Andorra paid two dollars to the French president every other year, while the bishop of Spain biannually received eight dollars, twelve hens, six cheeses, and six hams.
• Andorra recently reported an expenditure of $4.90 for blank cartridges to be fired on national holidays. This amount represented the country's total defense budget for one year.

Egypt

George Molyneux, fifth earl of Carnarvon, died of an insect bite. The year before, he and archaeologist Howard Carter had discovered and

1923 opened the tomb of Pharaoh Tutankhamen, the only such royal tomb ever found virtually intact. (Grave robbers had rifled all the others.) The death, so soon after the triumphal discovery, inspired rumors that an ancient curse had been laid on those who would disturb the king's bones. Unfortunately for romance, Carter lived until 1939.

Japan

An earthquake struck Tokyo and Yokohama, exploding gas mains and causing a fire that was spread rapidly by high winds. Over 100,000 people were killed or missing, and 575,000 dwellings were destroyed in what would be described as the "greatest disaster the world had ever known." Loss of life would not be substantially exceeded even by the two atomic explosions in 1945. Tokyo's Imperial Hotel survived, enhancing the reputation of its designer, American architect Frank Lloyd Wright.

☛ REGIONAL NEWS

Oklahoma

Governor J. C. Walton placed the State of Oklahoma under martial law because of the "night riding" activities of the Ku Klux Klan. He was impeached and lost an appeal to the state's supreme court for reinstatement.

• The first year during which no American black would be lynched would not come until 1949.

• The Klan's motto: "Not for self but for others."

Kansas

A bill came before the Kansas legislature making the possession of cigarettes punishable by imprisonment. The state already had a law prohibiting the selling or giving away of cigarettes, although smoking them was not an offense.

Connecticut

The lower house of the Connecticut legislature rejected a bill to legalize Sunday baseball and football by a vote of 139–86.

☛ ART

French Impressionist painter Claude Monet, eighty-three, regained his eyesight through surgery after having been blind for several years. He had been working on a series of three hundred separate paintings of a lily pond in his garden when he lost his sight.

14

Time, a weekly magazine, first went to press, the brainchild of two former Yale classmates and *Baltimore Sun* reporters, Henry Robinson Luce and Briton Hadden—both twenty-four. Inverting sentences and coining new words such as "socialite," "tycoon," "cinemaddict," and "sexational," Luce had chosen the name for the magazine after seeing a subway poster reading, "Time to Retire or Time for a Change." Originally conceived as a magazine called *Facts,* Luce and Hadden had raised $86,975 to publish *Time* from seventy investors, forty-six of whom were Yale men. Early editorial contributors were Stephen Vincent Benet, twenty-five, and Archibald MacLeish, thirty-two, both future Pulitzer Prize winners. MacLeish worked during the day as a lawyer and wrote the Education section in his spare time for $10 a week.
- The highest salary at *Time* was $40 a week.
- The first person on the cover was Congressman Joseph G. Cannon.
- The first woman on the cover was actress Eleanora Duse.
- The woman who would appear most on the cover was the Virgin Mary—ten times.

☞SPORTS

Governor Al Smith threw out the first ball as a sellout crowd of 74,000 people watched the first baseball game held at Yankee Stadium, built at a cost of $2.5 million by Colonel Jacob Ruppert. The Yankees defeated the Boston Red Sox 4–1, sparked by a three-run homer by George Herman "Babe" Ruth, former Red Sox pitcher, and the stadium became known as The House That Ruth Built. While Ruth's slugging alone would earn him admission to baseball's Hall of Fame, as a pitcher the left-hander led the league in 1915 and had a career record of 94 wins against 46 losses, with an earned run average of 2.28. Ruth had pitched 29⅔ scoreless innings in the 1918 World Series, a record that would not be broken until 1961.
- "Ruth made a great mistake when he gave up pitching. Working once a week, he might have lasted a long time and become a star." (Tris Speaker, 1921)

Jack Dempsey knocked out Luis Angel Firpo, the Wild Bull of the Pampas, at the Polo Grounds in New York City in the second round of their heavyweight title bout. Eleven knockdowns took place, and Firpo knocked Dempsey completely out of the ring in the first round. Dempsey's landing totally destroyed the typewriter of *New York Times* reporter Jack Lawrence.

1923   Canadian flyweight boxing champion Gene LaRue defended his title against Kid Pancho. Both unleashed hard lefts, which reached their destinations simultaneously. The referee counted out both boxers.

Notre Dame football coach Knute Rockne made dancing lessons mandatory for his players "to develop a sense of rhythm essential in the timing of shift plays." In 1922, Rockne had advocated compulsory football and boxing for college students as a means of eliminating "the male effeminate."

☞ ENTERTAINMENT

The Charleston was featured in the all-black musical *Runnin' Wild* and would rapidly become young America's favorite dance. Originating with Southern blacks, this fast fox-trot had four hundred different steps, and instructions for the basic moves were as follows: "You have to learn to toe in . . . then stand on the balls of your feet, pigeon-toed . . . your body swings from side to side . . . the knees knock when they come together . . . make it very snappy." Most adults considered the dance overly physical and lacking in grace, and it would be banned by many colleges. Later in the year, the dance floor of Boston's Pickwick Club collapsed under the stress of 1,000 gyrating Charlestoners, and forty-four dancers were killed.

The Miss America Pageant was in its fourth year at Atlantic City, New Jersey, having been conceived in an effort to emulate the success of fellow resort Asbury Park's baby contest in attracting visitors to the town. A committee headed by a local dry cleaner, Thomas P. Endicott ("When you see a spot, call Endicott"), asked newspapers from nearby mid-Atlantic states to select local entries, and Washington, D.C., representative 5 foot 1 inch Margaret Gorman won the first contest. Her vital statistics were a flapperish 30–25–32.

The Richard Strauss opera *Salome* was banned in Boston for the second straight year as a "danger to public morals." *Time* protested, "The scene of John the Baptist's head is moderately horrible, but is certainly not the sort to lead youth astray. Mary Garden's stilted dance might be witnessed by the frailest virtue without danger."

Rubber diaphragms were first manufactured, by Holland Rantos, providing females with a contraceptive alternative to the condom used by males.

EDUCATION

Yale University's faculty voted to abolish Latin and Greek as admission requirements.

Until the early 1800s, Hebrew had been a required language for freshmen at Yale. In a surge of anti-British feeling during the American Revolution, Hebrew was seriously considered as a replacement for English as the language of the new republic. Religious American colonists regarded Hebrew as the "mother of all languages," important to one's understanding of the Bible, and many children and towns had been given Hebrew names.

Henry Cashman of the University of Wisconsin's Board of Regents spoke out against sending American Rhodes scholars to Oxford: "The object of Rhodes scholarships is to extend British rule and ultimately recover the United States. The scheme makes traitors of some of America's finest young men."

Cecil John Rhodes (1853–1902), founder of DeBeers Consolidated Mines, had headed a syndicate that controlled the Kimberley mines in South Africa, at one time virtually monopolizing the world's diamond supply. Cashman's claim that Rhodes had created his scholarships for political purposes was an accurate one. In his will, Rhodes had made clear that his estate was to be used to secure British world domination, and the "recovery of the United States of America as an integral part of the British Empire" was fundamental to his goal. Scholarships were created for males from British colonies and the United States—as well as for Germans who spoke English—and recipients were to strive to unify English-speaking people. But following his death, trustees of Rhodes's estate took some liberties when executing his will. Scholarship awards were based solely on scholastic achievement and leadership potential. In 1975, they would be granted to female as well as male candidates.

☛ ARMED FORCES

A potential navy enlistee was rejected because the picture *September Morn* was tattooed on his arm, navy regulations banning "obscene and indecent tattooing."

September Morn was a fairly innocuous painting of a naked young woman that became famous after a press agent had it placed in the window of a New York art gallery. He had then hired two young men to gape at the painting and called police to protest violation of obscenity laws. Attendant publicity had resulted in sales of over 1 million copies of the painting.

☛ BEHAVIOR

Parents decried the rebelliousness of youth who were enjoying newfound freedom brought about in large measure by the automobile. Prohibition, instead of curbing their appetite for alcoholic beverages, seemed to make drinking more attractive. "Sheiks" were taking their "shebas" to local roadhouses, which "nice girls" had seldom frequented.

The parents of college-age boys were concerned, while those of girls in their late teens and early twenties were in a state of total disarray. Women's liberation was in full flower. Women had voted in a national election for the first time in 1920, and Sigmund Freud and Havelock Ellis were preaching sexual freedom. Flappers (so called because their unfastened galoshes flapped when the young women walked) were bobbing their hair and using cosmetics, and many were beginning to smoke cigarettes. But of even greater concern to parents, they were frank, opinionated, and extremely difficult to control.

☛ MARKETING

Curtiss Candy Company head Otto Schering promoted his Baby Ruth candy by parachuting free candy bars into the streets of Pittsburgh, Pennsylvania, from an airplane. This merchandising technique was so successful that it would be expanded to other large cities in forty states and included a new Curtiss bar, the Butterfinger.

Introduced in 1920, the Baby Ruth had a center of caramel filled with peanuts enrobed in chocolate. Baseball star Babe Ruth had sued Curtiss for royalties, believing that his name had been used without permission. Curtiss claimed that the bar had been named for Ruth Cleveland, the daughter of ex-President Grover Cleveland, who had become a national favorite when she was the first child born to a president in the White House. Curtiss won the case and was later influential in Ruth's being denied a patent when he tried to put Babe Ruth's Home Run Candy on the market.

Lemonade-mix salesman Frank Epperson accidentally left a glass of lemonade with a spoon in it on his windowsill overnight. The lemonade froze, giving Epperson the inspiration for a product he would soon patent—the Popsicle.

George Barnes Lambert sold his share of the Listerine business for $25 million to pursue his love for sailing on a full-time basis. Invented by Lambert's father as an all-purpose antiseptic, Listerine was promoted as the answer to "bad breath," an affliction that had never been addressed through advertising. In 1921, Lambert had created the condition "halitosis," from the Latin word for "breath," and preying upon the latent social consciousness of Americans, he had advertised aggressively. Consumers rapidly funded his retirement.

☛ MEDICINE

In 1922, Canadian Lord Atholstan had offered a $100,000 prize for a cure for cancer. A year later, 2,716 entries had been received from forty-one countries claiming the prize.

Cancer was reported to be the fourth largest killing disease in the United States, topped only by organic heart disease, pneumonia, and tuberculosis.

☛ WHERE WERE THEY THEN?

Louis Armstrong was playing the cornet with the King Oliver Creole Jazz Band in Chicago. At thirteen, he had been sent to reform school for firing a shot into a parade in New Orleans on New Year's Day. At the Colored Waifs' Home for Boys, Armstrong had taught himself how to play the cornet, first mastering the song "Home Sweet Home."

A son, James Earl, was born to the Carter family in rural Plains, Georgia. His parents did not know at the time that the birth was a historic first. Their child would be the first president to be born in a hospital. All previous chief executives had been born at home.

1923   Alexander Calder, twenty-five, was attending the Art Students League in New York City, supporting himself by working as an illustrator for one of the raciest magazines of the era, the *Police Gazette*. His sculpture would excite Parisian art lovers in 1926, and he would become particularly well known for inventing the mobile.

Alfred Charles Kinsey, twenty-nine, was teaching zoology at Indiana University, and by the end of the decade became the world's leading authority on the gall wasp, collecting over 2 million of them. He would later switch his field to human sexual behavior and shock Americans with his book *Sexual Behavior in the Human Male* published in 1948, pointing out that sexual acts heretofore considered perverted were comon place in many American homes.

1924

I'll give you a definite maybe.

A verbal contract isn't worth the paper it's written on.
                    —Movie mogul Samuel Goldwyn

☞ NATIONAL NEWS

At the Republican Convention in Cleveland, delegates took little time in selecting their party's presidential candidate, awarding the nomination to Calvin Coolidge on the first ballot.

The Democratic Convention was an entirely different story. Sweltering in a New York City heat wave, the party set records for the length of a convention (thirteen days) and the number of ballots cast for presidential candidates (103). Feelings ran high, and the police were summoned on numerous occasions to break up fistfights among the delegates; four days went by before the first ballot was cast. Two early highlights:

• A proposal to denounce the Ku Klux Klan in the party's platform fell one vote short of passage.

• A reference to President Harding in the party platform, "Our party stands uncovered at the bier of Warren Harding" was challenged because

21

1924 the word "bier" might ruffle the feathers of Prohibitionists. After debate, the word "grave" was substituted.

When the delegates got around to selecting a candidate, they wrangled for nine more days over the merits of New York's Catholic Governor Al Smith and California's William McAdoo, son-in-law of President Wilson. But neither could obtain the necessary votes for nomination, and the compromise winner on the 103rd ballot was John D. Davis, former solicitor general and ambassador to Great Britain. The delegates finally departed, and the country breathed a sigh of relief.

During the convention, the delegates had paused to send their condolences to President and Mrs. Coolidge upon the death of their son, Calvin, Jr. The sixteen-year-old Mercersburg Academy student had developed a blister on his toe while playing tennis on the White House courts, contracted blood poisoning, and the distraught family had watched helplessly as his condition worsened. He died just two weeks after the fateful tennis game, his last words reflecting his suffering. "I surrender," said the boy to his nurse, and five years later his father would write, "When he went, the power and glory of the Presidency went with him."

Political parties that labor too long in the vineyards selecting a candidate seldom produce a winner, and 1924 saw a repeat of 1920 for the Democrats. The voters reflected their contentment with the status quo, and Coolidge won in a landslide.

• "In a fat and happy world, Coolidge is the man of the hour." (William Allen White)

• "I don't expect anything very astonishing from it. I don't want anything astonishing." (Oliver Wendell Holmes, Jr.)

Thrill killers Nathan Leopold, eighteen, and Richard Loeb, seventeen, sons of wealthy parents and graduate students at the University of Chicago, murdered fourteen-year-old Bobbie Franks in an attempt to commit "the perfect crime." Although they had planned the murder for several months, they had not chosen a victim until they accidentally saw Franks when they drove by a private school he attended and offered him a ride. Franks admired the older boys and was flattered to be asked to join them.

Having gagged Franks, they bludgeoned him on the skull with a chisel and then calmly reconnoitered the area, seeking a place to dispose of the corpse. They dumped the boy's body into a culvert and poured acid over his face to prevent identification. The two then went to a restaurant for a snack before calling Franks's father to demand a $10,000 ransom, claiming that they had kidnapped his son.

Although they were brilliant (Loeb was the University of Michigan's

22

youngest graduate, Leopold the University of Chicago's youngest), they **1924** had left a trail of amateurish clues. The body was quickly discovered by two workmen, Loeb's glasses were found nearby, and Leopold's chauffeur disputed his alibi. The police soon had their confession, and the state's attorney declared, "I have a hanging case." The public enthusiastically agreed, and the death sentence appeared inevitable.

Enter Clarence Darrow, sixty-seven, the preeminent defense attorney in the country (see year 1925). In court, Darrow made no attempt to deny his clients' guilt. Instead, he focused on the mental condition of the young killers, describing Leopold as a paranoiac and manic depressive and Loeb as a schizophrenic. He delved deeply into Freud and the intricacies of psychoanalysis, and in an impassioned twelve-hour summation, argued that no purpose would be served by demanding the death sentence. "Do you think you can cure the hatred and maladjustments of the world by hanging them? You simply show your ignorance and your hate when you say it. You may heal and cure hatred with love and understanding, but you can only add fuel to the flames with cruelty and hating."

Leopold and Loeb were given life sentences, and Loeb was killed in prison in 1936 by fellow inmate, James Day. Day claimed that Loeb had assaulted him sexually in the prison showers and was acquitted. Leopold was paroled on the twenty-fifth anniversary of Darrow's death, in 1963.

Women had been voting in some states since 1869 (when the first legislature in the Territory of Wyoming gave women there that right) and throughout the United States since passage of the Nineteenth Amendment in 1920. Having campaigned aggressively for women's suffrage, they failed to turn out in large numbers for the presidential election in 1924.

Many nations had preceded the United States in granting women the right to vote, the first having been New Zealand (1893), followed by Australia (1902), and Finland (1906). Chauvinistic Frenchmen would not grant the vote to women until 1944.

An act of Congress made all American Indians citizens of the United States. Prior to this legislation, citizenship had been granted only to members of certain tribes under specific treaties. As citizens, Indians were required to pay both federal and state taxes, but were excused from land taxes on their reservations.

The American farmer was suffering through a depression that would last for almost two decades. Agricultural prices plummeted, as increased efficiency in farming methods, coupled with stiff competition from European nations, produced an oversupply of crops. Production dropped 6 percent, and prices fell 63 percent between 1920 and 1932.

1924 Americans were enjoying longer daylight hours during the summer, daylight savings time having been adopted by the United States during World War I as a means of conserving electricity. Benjamin Franklin had suggested this means of extending daylight hours over one hundred years before it was put into effect.

Congress reduced immigration quotas to 150,000 per year, and all Japanese except those with relatives in the United States were restricted from entry. Just under 10 percent of the 1924 quota had been processed in one day at Ellis Island in 1917.

A post-World War I song had asked, "How you gonna keep 'em down on the farm, after they've seen Paree?" Indeed, the country was turning from rural to urban, with over 50 percent of the population for the first time living in towns with over 2,500 inhabitants.

☛ FOREIGN NEWS

England
James Ramsay MacDonald became prime minister and headed the first Labour government in British history in January 1923. The Labour regime was short-lived, and the Conservatives took over in November under Stanley Baldwin. Baldwin's chancellor of the exchequer was Winston Churchill, fifty, who had recently changed his party allegiance from Liberal to Conservative.

By the end of his career, Churchill would have held nearly every major position in the British government. His posts would include two terms as prime minister, first lord of the admiralty and undersecretary to the colonies, and single terms as privy councillor, president of the board of trade, home secretary, minister of munitions, secretary of state for war and air, chancellor of the exchequer, chairman of the armed services committee, minister of defense, and first lord of the treasury. He was first appointed in 1906 and would end his government service forty-nine years later, in 1955.

France
The French Boxing Federation banned boxers from kissing one another at the conclusion of a bout.

Ireland
A crowd of approximately twenty people watched an exhibition baseball game between the New York Giants and the Chicago White Sox

24

in Dublin. Irish newspapers blamed the poor attendance on a conflicting event—church services.

Soviet Union

Soviet leader Nikolai Lenin, fifty-three, died in a Moscow suburb, having been in ill health for several years. One of his last acts was to write a letter to the Central Committee complaining about Joseph Stalin, who had studied for the priesthood before embracing Marxism, and whom Lenin had elevated within party ranks. Lenin wrote:

> Stalin is too coarse, and this fault, though tolerable in dealing among us Communists, becomes unbearable in a General Secretary. Therefore, I propose to the comrades to find some way of removing Stalin from his position and appointing somebody else who differs in all respects from Comrade Stalin in one characteristic—namely, someone more tolerant, more loyal, more polite and considerate to his comrades, less capricious, etc. This circumstance may seem to be a mere trifle, but I think that . . . it is a trifle which may acquire a decisive importance.

By the time of his death, Lenin's right side was paralyzed, he could barely speak, and he could write only with his left hand. He spent much time in his last months collecting mushrooms. When he finally died of convulsions, many suspected Stalin of having poisoned his mentor. Ironically, Lenin was buried in a mausoleum that he would have to share with Stalin from 1953 to 1961.

Nepal

British climbers attempted an ascent to the summit of Mount Everest. Discovered in 1852, the Himalayan peak on the border of Tibet and Nepal had been named for Sir George Everest, an early surveyor general of British India. In 1852, surveyors took its measurements in six places and found that the average height was exactly 29,000 feet. Because the number sounded like a random estimate, the surveyors submitted a height of 29,002 feet. A survey in 1954 showed that the mountain continues to grow. The 1954 height was 29,028 feet, and a recent measurement recorded 29,141 feet, assuring future successful climbers of a new record each time.

An Everest committee was formed by the British in 1920 to plot the conquest of the mountain, drawing from members of the British Alpine Club and the Royal Geographic Society. George Leigh-Mallory was a member of the first group to attempt the climb, but 100-mph winds made the ascent impossible. However, the British had no thoughts of giving up,

1924 and team member Geoffrey Bruce summed up their determination to return, saying, "Just you wait, old thing! We'll get you yet!"

George Leigh-Mallory was also a participant in the second attempt in 1922, which was aborted 1,800 feet from the summit. The entire party was caught in an avalanche, and seven porters died when they were swept over a cliff and fell 500 feet onto a glacier. The more fortunate members of the group had "breaststroked" sideways through the avalanche, coming to a stop at the edge of the precipice.

The British returned again in 1924, determined to succeed; once again George Leigh-Mallory was a member of the team. When reporters asked him his reason for so desperately wanting to conquer Everest, Leigh-Mallory said, "Because it is there." He added prophetically, "For better or for worse, we expect no mercy from Everest."

This time the group was divided into two-man assault teams, which made two unsuccessful tries, one from 26,800 feet. Leigh-Mallory and his twenty-three-year-old partner, A. C. Irvine, made the last attempt, realizing that seasonal snow monsoons would soon make further climbing impossible. The frustrated Leigh-Mallory vowed to stand on top of "my" mountain or be killed trying, and a team member would later recall him as "the living soul of the offensive; the thing had become a personal matter with him, and was ultimately somewhat different from what it was to the rest of us."

Leigh-Mallory and Irvine set out on June 6, accompanied by eight Sherpa porters. Four of the porters returned later that day, the remaining four the next morning, bringing an optimistic note from Leigh-Mallory, "Perfect weather for the job." Yet when geologist N. E. Odell searched the upper slope the next morning with his telescope, the top of the mountain was obscured by clouds. The clouds suddenly disappeared just after noon, and Odell saw "a tiny black spot silhouetted on a small snow crest beneath a rock-step in the ridge, and the black spot moved. Another black spot became apparent and moved up the snow to join the other on the crest. The first black spot then approached the great rock-step and shortly emerged at the top; the second did likewise. Then the whole fascinating vision vanished, enveloped in a cloud once more." A snow monsoon soon began, and Leigh-Mallory and Irvine would never be seen again; neither their bodies nor any portion of their equipment would ever be recovered.

• "I consider it very probable that they sheltered in some rock recess and fell asleep, and a painless death followed due to the excessive cold at those altitudes. . . . Considering all the circumstances and the position they had reached on the mountain, I am of the opinion that Mallory and Irvine must have made the summit." (N. E. Odell)

• "Since they were roped together, the best guess is that one of them

26

slipped, that they fell to their deaths together, that they lie in the eternal ice and snow in the Himalayas." (Lowell Thomas)

• Leigh-Mallory and his fellow climbers often repeated this maxim while climbing on Everest:

> No game was ever worth a rap
> For a rational man to play
> Into which no accident, no mishap
> Could possibly find a way.

• "Because it is there." (Sir Edmund Hillary, who repeated Leigh-Mallory's words when he was asked why he had attempted the ascent of Everest in 1953. Hillary and the Sherpa Tenzing Norkay made the first successful climb to the summit and, since then, scores of mountaineers have reached the top, including a thirty-five-year-old, ninety-two-pound Japanese housewife, who became the first female to scale the peak in 1971. There are now so many requests to climb Everest that the Nepalese government has a seven-year waiting list.)

☛ REGIONAL NEWS

Pennsylvania

Pep, a normally friendly male Labrador retriever, killed the much-loved cat of the wife of Pennsylvania's governor, Gifford Pinchot. The incensed Pinchot promptly tried Pep for murder and sentenced him to life imprisonment in the state penitentiary. Prisoner C2559 was popular with his fellow inmates and slept nightly in the cell of his choice. He answered work call each morning when his number was called and lived contentedly at the prison until he died of old age.

Illinois

Gangster "Nails" Norton was thrown from a horse in Chicago's Lincoln Park and died of his injuries. His fellow gang members kidnapped the horse from its stable and executed it at the spot where Norton had been unseated, employing a form of retribution that had been practiced in the Old West when a horse caused the death of a human.

Three men walked into Dion O'Banion's Chicago flower shop. Recognizing them, O'Banion stepped forward to greet them, and the caller in the middle of the three took his hand and held it securely while his two associates pulled out revolvers and killed him. An arch rival of gangster Al Capone, O'Banion had been suspected of twenty-five

27

unsolved murders but had never been convicted of homicide. Ironically, his flower shop profited heavily from his death, Capone alone buying an $8,000 floral piece.

A former choir boy, O'Banion was denied the last rites of the Catholic Church, but the Reverend Patrick Mulloy went to the cemetery in mufti to say Hail Marys and the Lord's Prayer over his grave. Mrs. O'Banion said, "Dion loved his home and spent most of his evenings in it, fooling with his radio, singing a song, listening to the player piano. He was not a man to run around nights with women. . . . I was his only sweetheart. . . . He never left home without telling me where he was going and kissing me good-bye." Despite his expensive floral piece, Al Capone was acknowledged to have engineered O'Banion's death, although it was never proved.

New York

Readers of the August 16, 1923, edition of the *New York Herald Tribune* were shocked by the front-page headline: "NEW YORKERS DRINK SUMPTUOUSLY ON 17,000-TON FLOATING CAFE AT ANCHOR 15 MILES OFF FIRE ISLAND." Reporter Sanford Jarrell's three-column story told a tale of rich men and young women dancing, drinking, and carousing at sea and of speedboats returning the comatose to Manhattan at dawn. Jarrell reported that the ship flew the British flag but carried no name on the bow; "Friedrich der Grosse" was monogrammed on the dinner napkins. But the coast guard and police searched in vain while *Tribune* readers clamored for more information, and Jarrell's next communication with his editors was his resignation. Prior to his big scoop, Jarrell had not filed a newsworthy story for several months, and he had fabricated the sensational sea story in hopes of keeping his job.

Texas

A black farm worker who had sworn at his white employer was whipped to death in Marshall, Texas.

☛ MEDICINE

Physician and scientist Albert Abrams died, having become a millionaire by inventing a machine known as the dynamizer, which diagnosed human ailments. The dynamizer was a heavily wired box that plugged into an electrical outlet. A wire from the box was then attached to the forehead of the patient; a drop of the patient's blood was then placed on a piece of paper that was fed into the machine. With the patient facing west, the machine was then activated and produced a diagnosis. Success led to the manufacture of the dynamizer, which Abrams began to lease for **1924** $250, plus an additional fee for instructing the lessee in how to operate it and interpret its findings. Users were instructed never to open the machine, which was elaborately sealed.

In 1922, a group of suspicious scientists opened one of Abrams's dynamizers and found a tangle of interconnected wires that functioned but appeared to serve no constructive purpose. Branded a charlatan, Abrams was defended by social reformer Upton Sinclair, who regarded the dynamizer as a tremendous advance in medical science. To test the reliability of the machine, the blood of roosters and guinea pigs were submitted for analysis. It was diagnosed as that of a female human suffering from venereal disease, diabetes, cancer, and malaria.

☛ ENTERTAINMENT

Film producer Samuel Goldwyn was in his first year as the head of Samuel Goldwyn, Inc. He had run away from his Warsaw home at thirteen and immigrated to the United States, where an Ellis Island official, unable to decipher his Polish name, had given him the name Goldfish, which he later changed to Goldwyn, a combination of his Americanized name and that of an earlier partner, Edgar Selwyn. While selling gloves in upstate New York, Goldwyn saw his first movie and was so excited by it that he paid a visit to the theater's manager. After a short briefing on the economics of the movie business, Goldwyn exclaimed: "You mean you give nothing away. The customer walks out with nothing. He pays to watch a film which you keep and show over and over to new customers. What a wonderful business!"

In partnership with three others in their own production company, Goldwyn went to Arizona in 1912 to find a location for their first film and wired home: "FLAGSTAFF NO GOOD FOR OUR PURPOSE. HAVE PROCEEDED TO CALIFORNIA. WANT AUTHORITY TO RENT BARN IN PLACE CALLED HOLLYWOOD FOR 75 DOLLARS A MONTH." Goldwyn became a legendary Hollywood mogul whose malapropisms and mixed metaphors amused those in the film business for many years. Some examples:
- "You've got to take the bull between your teeth."
- "In this business it's dog-eat-dog and nobody's going to eat me."
- "I don't care if it doesn't make a nickel, I just want every man, woman, and child to see it."
- "Our comedies are not to be laughed at."
- "Motion pictures in color? I won't believe it until I see it in black and white."
- "That's the trouble with directors. Always biting the hand that lays the golden egg."

29

1924
- "Anyone seeing a psychiatrist should have his head examined."
- "Include me out."
- "In two words, im--possible!"

An "All American Music Concert" took place at New York's Aeolian Hall. George Gershwin, twenty-five, introduced his jazz-symphonic composition *Rhapsody in Blue* to an audience that had already heard twenty-two offerings by other American composers. Paul Whiteman conducted a thirty-two-piece orchestra with Gershwin at the piano, totally captivating an audience that included Jascha Heifetz, Igor Stravinsky, Serge Rachmaninoff, Victor Herbert, and Walter Damrosch. Whiteman recalled: "Somewhere in the middle of the score, I began crying. When I came to myself, I was eleven pages along, and until this day I cannot tell you how I conducted that far."

Gershwin, born Jacob Gershvin, had published his first song at sixteen and had written *Rhapsody in Blue* in only three weeks. His songs included "Oh Lady be Good," "Fascinating Rhythm," "Someone to Watch Over Me," "Swanee," "Embraceable You," "S'Wonderful," "Liza," and "I've Got a Crush on You," and three of his songs contained the words "who could ask for anything more."

A popular song of 1924: "Does the Spearmint Lose Its Flavor on the Bedpost Overnight?"

☛ EDUCATION

James "Buck" Buchanan Duke had been born near Durham, North Carolina, in 1856. A childhood of poverty appeared inevitable when the family farm was destroyed by Union troops during the Civil War, and only one field of tobacco survived. But the crop was sold, and the family tobacco business was born. After attending the Eastman Business School in Poughkeepsie, New York, young Duke became a partner in W. Duke and Sons, a company that sold cigars, pipe tobacco, and snuff. The cigarette business soon followed when a machine was developed that could roll cigarettes, a task previously done by hand. Duke founded the American Tobacco Company in 1890 and went on to become one of the richest men in the United States.

In 1924, Duke approached North Carolina's Trinity College and promised a contribution of $40 million if it would satisfy two conditions: (1) Trinity must change its name to Duke, and (2) Duke must be buried on the campus upon his death. When Trinity hesitated, Duke sweetened the pot with an offer of an additional $9 million, and the college agreed to his terms just nine days before he died. He was laid to rest in the chapel there, and just outside stands a bronze statue of Duke holding a large cigar.

Duke had enough money left over to leave $40 million to his thirteen-year-old daughter, along with his private railroad car, "Doris," which he had named after her. Astute investments increased her fortune to $250 million in just ten years.

Stanford University acknowledged the increased interest in college football by offering a course in cheerleading. Topics for study included "bleacher psychology," "correct use of the voice," and "what the coach expects of the yell leader."

☛ PRODUCTS

Scientist Ernest Mahler developed a disposable handkerchief that was introduced as "Celluwipes" by Kimberly Clark. The name was later changed to Kleenex "Kerchiefs," and eventually shortened to "Kleenex."

Mahler had earlier developed a cotton substitute made of wood cellulose, which had been used to make bandages during World War I. Having learned that Red Cross nurses were using the bandages as sanitary napkins, Kimberly Clark had used the fiber to open up a totally new manufactured product category for women in 1921. The product was called Kotex.

Public relations man Ivy Lee created the slogan "Breakfast of Champions" for General Mills's Wheaties, and the new cereal was successfully introduced. Lee had already invented Betty Crocker in 1921 as the symbol for several General Mills products. Six different portraits of the fictitious Betty Crocker have been used since 1921, all depicting her from the waist up. She became so well known that she later finished second in a poll to determine the most famous woman in the United States. The winner was Eleanor Roosevelt.

☛ TRANSPORTATION

The use of traffic lights was spreading, having been introduced in 1920 by Detroit policeman William L. Potts. Potts chose the colors red, yellow, and green because they were already being used by the railroads to regulate traffic.

1924   ☞ COMICS

Cartoonist Harold Gray took an idea for a new strip called "Little Orphan Otto" to *Chicago Tribune* publisher Joseph Patterson. Patterson advised, "Put a skirt on the kid and call her Little Orphan Annie." Annie, who had "a heart of gold but a wicked left," would battle evil on many fronts, helped by her dog Sandy, who emitted an occasional "Arf," and by her guardian, Oliver "Daddy" Warbucks, a billionaire capitalist and defender of free enterprise, rugged individualism, the Puritan ethic, and the Gospel of Wealth. The strip was eventually syndicated in 400 newspapers and continued to be produced after Gray's death in 1968.

☞ RELIGION

The Lutheran Church altered the Apostles' Creed by replacing the word "Hell" with "Hades."

☞ BUSINESS

Clarence Birdseye's frozen fish business was in its first year in New York City. Birdseye had lived for several years in Labrador, where a lack of fresh vegetables for most of the year led to his experiments with freezing cabbages. He had placed several cabbages in the bottom of a barrel, covered them with water, and after they were frozen, repeated the process until the barrel was full. At mealtime, Birdseye simply chopped out an ice-covered cabbage, thawed it, and cooked it just like a fresh one.

When he returned to the United States, it took Birdseye several years to figure out how to freeze large quantities of food since it had to be frozen quickly at very low temperatures to maintain its flavor. He finally froze fish successfully by spraying them with a brine solution and freezing them at 40 degrees below zero. In 1929, General Foods acquired his business and called it Bird's Eye, reverting to the original two-word family name, deriving from an ancestor who was such a proficient bowsman that he had shot an arrow through the eye of a hawk.

Twenty-seven-year-old Howard Johnson owned a small variety store in Wollaston, Massachusetts, and was $40,000 in debt. Because of its high profitability, his accountant recommended that he concentrate on selling ice cream. Johnson did not like the smell of the artificial flavoring in the vanilla ice cream he sold, so he set out to make his own from scratch.

A postal inspector charged the University of Mississippi's postmaster with neglecting his duties, mistreatment of mail, and lack of interest in serving his customers. The postmaster spent most of his time writing, playing bridge with his friends, and reading his customers' magazines; large quantities of mail were found in the garbage can.

Postmaster William Cuthbert Falkner first published *The Marble Faun*, a book of poetry, in 1924, adding a "u" to his name on the title page. He subsequently switched to fiction, and many of his books concerned the mythical Snopes clan of Yoknapatawpha County. Faulkner's long sentences (his novel *Absalom! Absalom!* contained one sentence of 1,300 words) and elusive prose would confound many American students. Americans were slow to recognize his literary talents, although he achieved earlier recognition in Europe. He won the Nobel Prize for literature in 1949, and two Pulitzer prizes.

The 5 foot 5 inch, 140-pound Faulkner also wrote for Hollywood. An alcoholic, as was his wife, father, and grandfather, he employed a bodyguard on weekends to transport him and his bourbon and to assure his prompt arrival at the studio on Monday mornings. It was rumored that Faulkner's wife had tried to commit suicide on their honeymoon, but they remained together, although their marriage was not a happy one.

☛ SPORTS

The United States dominated the Paris Olympic games, although Finnish runner Paavo Nurmi won four gold medals.
• Johnny Weissmuller, twenty, was the first person to swim 100 meters in less than a minute, having lowered the world's record to 57.4, a time that would not be bettered for a decade. In a 1-2-3 American finish, Hawaiian brothers Duke and Sam Kahanamoku followed him over the line. Named after the first duke of Edinburgh, younger son of Queen Victoria, thirty-four-year-old Duke had won the event in the 1912 and 1920 games. Weissmuller won two other swimming gold medals, and the future Hollywood Tarzan also took a bronze medal in water polo.

The son of an Austrian immigrant, his status as an American citizen had been questioned before the games. His father assured the public that he had been born in Chicago, although there was no record of his birth.

In 1984, *Sports Illustrated* reported that Weissmuller had indeed been ineligible for the games. Investigation revealed that he had been born in Freidorf, Romania, a part of Hungary before World War I treaties

1924 changed the boundaries. He had been brought to the United States by his parents seven months later and had never obtained American citizenship.

• American DeHart Hubbard won the long jump, becoming the first black to win an individual medal in the Olympics.

• The much acclaimed movie *Chariots of Fire* had sprinter Harold Abrahams, the devout Scot Eric Liddell, and their well-born friend Lord Burghley competing in the 1924 Olympics, with Abrahams and Liddell winning gold medals. This actually did happen, but the film also credited Abrahams with running around the Great Court at Cambridge's Trinity College before the tower clock could finish tolling noon, a feat that had supposedly never been accomplished before. But Lord Burghley was the one who raced around the court, although he did not make the historic run until 1927. The seventy-six-year-old peer was so offended when he heard of the liberties that had been taken with the supposedly authentic plot that he refused to see the film.

David George Brownlow Cecil, Lord Burghley, was also not the first to master the court run, but there is little doubt that his time was the fastest. Sir Walter Borley Fletcher had done it in the 1890s, but the clock had taken five more seconds to strike the hour. A medal winner in the 1928 games, Lord Burghley was elected to Parliament in 1931 and later served as the governor of Bermuda.

• Benjamin McLane Spock, 6 feet 4 inches, won a gold medal in the Paris Olympics as a member of the Yale crew that represented the United States. In 1946, he wrote *The Common Sense Book of Baby and Child Care,* and eventually over 25 million copies of the book would be sold.

Harold "Red" Grange took the opening kickoff and returned it 95 yards for a touchdown against Michigan State. The University of Illinois halfback personally decimated the previously unbeaten Wolverines, scoring three more touchdowns in the first quarter, finishing the game with a total of five. Sportswriter Grantland Rice nicknamed the three-time All-American the Galloping Ghost.

1925

I don't believe in God because I don't believe in Mother Goose.

—Clarence Darrow

☞ NATIONAL NEWS

A brief phone call from Dayton, Tennessee, druggist Fred Robinson to the *Chattanooga News* precipitated one of the most famous trials in American history: "This is Fred Robinson. I'm chairman of the [school] board here. We've just arrested a man for teaching evolution."

Robinson's call brought about what would be known as the Monkey Trial. A young schoolteacher named John T. Scopes, twenty-four, had read this sentence from Hunter's *Civic Biology* to his Rhea High School science class: "We have now learned that animal forms may be arranged so as to begin with the simple one-celled forms and culminate with the group which includes man himself." By exposing his students to these seemingly innocuous words, Scopes had violated a new Tennessee law that had been passed to stop the teaching of evolution, making it a crime to "teach any theory [of Creation] that denies the story of man as taught in the Bible." Another Tennessee law required that at least ten verses of the Bible be read at the opening of each public school session.

Scopes's illegal act had been intentional. He had been convinced by George Rappelyea, a Dayton mining engineer, that the new law should be tested in the courts. Little did Scopes suspect that the trial would be front-page news in newspapers across the country in one of history's classic confrontations between science and religion.

It is doubtful if the trial would have caught the imagination of the American public had it not pitted two famous Americans against one another:

• William Jennings Bryan had been born in Illinois, where he practiced law before moving to Lincoln, Nebraska. He served two terms as a Democratic congressman, the last elected office he would hold. He then became editor of the *Omaha World Herald* and a champion of farmers in the South and West. As a delegate at the Democratic Convention in Chicago in 1896, Bryan achieved national prominence by delivering a speech on a subject that has had a somnolent effect on millions of students of American history—the free coinage of silver. Bryan said, "You shall not press down upon the brow of labor this crown of thorns. You shall not crucify mankind upon a cross of gold."

The next day, Bryan received his party's nomination for the presidency and would be so rewarded three times. He went on to become one of the great losers in American politics: Bryan was defeated by William McKinley in 1896 and 1900 and by William Howard Taft in 1908. Yet this series of losses failed to loosen his hold over the party, and he was influential in gaining the nomination for Woodrow Wilson in 1912, for which the great agrarian was rewarded with the unlikely post of secretary of state. In that office, he amused many Americans by inviting the Swiss navy to send a delegation to the opening of the Panama Canal. Bryan came to Dayton as a retired resident of Florida, where he had been influential in drafting a resolution banning the teaching of evolution in the public schools. He had volunteered his services to the prosecution as a witness in order to "protect the Word of God from the greatest atheist and agnostic in the United States," a title that most men would have regarded as libelous but which Darrow took as a compliment. Fresh from his success in the Leopold and Loeb trial, Darrow came to Dayton to represent the first and last client whom he defended free of charge. The trial was as much a crusade for Darrow as it was for Bryan because he wanted "to show up Fundamentalism to prevent bigots and ignoramuses from controlling education in the United States."

• Clarence Darrow had been born in Kinsman, Ohio, in 1857. After brief stays at Allegheny College and at the University of Michigan law school, he was admitted to the bar in 1878, shortly thereafter moving to Chicago. There he became a well-known labor lawyer, defending Socialist

Eugene Debs in the Pullman strike, West Coast labor leader William "Big Bill" Haywood, and a group charged with the bombing of the *Los Angeles Times*. As Darrow's reputation spread, his ability to use publicity to promote his liberal views on civil rights increased; his use of the Leopold and Loeb trial to attack capital punishment had displayed how he could sway both juries and public opinion. The Scopes trial offered another perfect forum to promote his views.

This was not the first airing of Bryan's fundamentalist views, nor was it Darrow's first public opposition to them. The cognoscenti had been vilifying Bryan's literal interpretation of the Bible for several years, and on July 4, 1923, Darrow entered the fray. On the front page of the *Chicago Tribune,* Darrow had addressed fifty-five questions to Bryan concerning the Bible. Bryan did not respond, but Darrow's efforts had not been wasted. He used much of the material he had gathered in his cross-examination of Bryan during the trial.

In a country fair atmosphere, visitors flocked to Dayton (population 1,800). Country people mingled with college professors and liberals of every stripe, and the *New York Post* wrote, "Greenwich Village is on its way to Rhea County." The *Chicago Tribune* prepared to broadcast the proceedings, the first trial beamed to American radio listeners; 100 reporters who came to town filed an estimated 2 million words of copy. The sentiments of local residents were expressed by the signs that dotted the downtown area: "GOD IS LOVE," "SWEETHEARTS COME TO JESUS," and "WHERE WILL YOU SPEND ETERNITY?" were just a few; vendors sold pins reading, "YOUR OLD MAN'S A MONKEY." When Bryan arrived in Dayton, he added fuel to the flames, saying, "The contest between evolution and Christianity is a duel to the death. If evolution wins in Dayton, Christianity goes—not suddenly, of course, but gradually—for the two cannot stand together."

The trial began on Friday, July 10, in the Eighteenth Circuit court. Eleven of the twelve jurors selected were regular churchgoers, including six Baptists, four Methodists, and one Disciple of Christ; a lone juror said he "didn't go to church as often as he should." There were ten farmers, a shipping clerk, and a part-time teacher. All but one juror had read the Bible, the exception being illiterate; none of the jurors had read a book on evolution. Reporter H. L. Mencken wired his paper that "it was obvious after a few rounds that the jury would be unanimously hot for Genesis."

The trial was presided over by Judge John T. Raulston, by his own definition "jest a reg'lar mountin'er jedge." A spittoon was placed near Raulston, and a sign was hung on the wall behind the bench facing the jury with the exhortation "READ YOUR BIBLE." When Judge Raulston opened the trial with a prayer, Darrow objected and was overruled. Then Darrow objected to the "READ YOUR BIBLE" sign, his objection was sustained, and the sign was taken down. The prosecution then produced ɪree students who verified that they had been present when Scopes had ɪad the offensive sentence to his class, and the prosecution rested its case.

The defense then called its first expert witness, hoping to prove the soundness of evolution and the broad acceptance of Darwin's theory to account for it. The prosecution objected, contending that scientific testimony was personal opinion. Judge Raulston considered the matter overnight and the next day ruled that scientific testimony would not be allowed.

The trial droned on, and the expected pyrotechnics failed to materialize. Many visitors left town, and a number of reporters departed for more promising assignments. Scopes was obviously guilty, and without expert testimony, there appeared to be no way to debate the merits of evolution versus the Bible as the true origin of man.

But on July 20, ten days into the trial, the long-awaited confrontation between Bryan and Darrow came to pass. When the defense called Bryan to the witness stand, the prosecution immediately objected, and it appeared that Judge Raulston would sustain the objection because of Bryan's standing as an expert witness. But before the judge could rule on the objection, Bryan took the stand, just as eager as Darrow was to argue the merits of his beliefs. What took place resulted in Bryan's total humiliation and, in the opinion of many, his death.

A heat wave had struck Dayton, and spectators and participants sweltered in the crowded courtroom. Judge Raulston moved the trial outdoors in the shade of a large tree, and there the two shirt-sleeved antagonists battled, with inquisitor Darrow questioning Bryan on his blanket acceptance of everything taught in the Bible. According to reporter Mark Sullivan:

> Darrow asked Bryan about Jonah and the whale, Joshua and the sun, where Cain got his wife, the date of the Flood, the signifi-cance of the Tower of Babel. Bryan affirmed his belief that the world was created in 4004 B.C., and the Flood occurred in or about 2348 B.C.; that Eve was literally made out of Adam's rib; that the Tower of Babel was responsible for the diversity of the languages in the world; and that a "big fish" had swallowed Jonah. When Darrow asked him if he had ever discovered where Cain got his wife, Bryan answered: "No sir; I leave the agnostics to hunt for her." When Darrow inquired, "Do you say you do not believe that there were any civilizations on this earth that reach back beyond five thousand years?" Bryan stout-ly replied, "I am not satisfied by any evidence I have seen."

The trial was ended abruptly by Judge Raulston the next day. Scopes was found guilty and fined $100. A subsequent appeal to the Tennessee

Supreme Court was turned down, and the law remained constitutional,
although Scopes was freed on a technicality.

Bryan was shocked by the quick termination of the trial. He knew
that he had won the battle but lost the war with Darrow, and he had
prepared an elaborate summation that he hoped would gain back the lost
ground. He died five days later in Dayton while taking a nap after a large
meal. Some people attributed his death to overeating because Bryan was
well known for his gluttony. But quite a few newspapers attributed his
death to Darrow's verbal assault, one observer declaring that "Darrow had
cross-examined the helpless William Jennings Bryan into the ground."
When Darrow was queried about Bryan's death, he said that Bryan "was a
man of strong convictions and always espoused his causes with ability and
courage. I differed with him on many questions, but always respected his
sincerity and devotion." After those kind words, one Darrow biographer
claimed that Darrow told his friends, "Now wasn't that man a Goddamned fool?" When it was suggested that Bryan had died of a broken
heart, another Darrow biographer insisted that Darrow had responded,
"Broken heart nothing. He died of a busted belly."

• "I laughed until my sides were sore." (Alan Sedgwick, British
geologist, in a letter to Charles Darwin after reading his theory of natural
selection in *Origin of Species* in 1856.)

• "In memory of William Jennings Bryan, the greatest Klansman of
our times, this cross is burned; he stood at Armageddon and battled for
the Lord." (Salute to Bryan by the Ku Klux Klan on the night he was
buried.)

• "The Bible states it. It must be so." (William Jennings Bryan)

• Judge to Darrow during an earlier trial: "Mr. Darrow, what you are
saying is going into one ear and out the other." Darrow's reply: "I'm not
surprised, Your Honor. Maybe it's because there's nothing to interfere
with the passage."

• During another trial, an opposing lawyer with a beard made
repeated reference to Darrow as "my beardless adversary." In his
summation, Darrow said, "My opponent seems to condemn me for not
having a beard. Let me reply with an anecdote: The King of Spain once
entrusted a youthful liege with an important message to the court of a
neighboring monarch. The neighboring monarch flew into a rage and
cried, 'Does the King of Spain lack men that he sends me a beardless
boy?' The young ambassador answered, 'Sire, had my king but known you
imputed wisdom to a beard, he would have sent you a goat!'" (Darrow
won the case.)

• In 1968, the State of Tennessee abolished the law preventing the
teaching of evolution.

Members of the Senate gave themselves and their confreres in the
House a raise from $7,500 to $10,000 a year. They also hiked the salaries

1925 of the vice president, speaker of the House, and members of the Cabinet from $12,000 to $15,000. Since the vote took place without a roll call, there was no official record of how individual members had voted.

"Uncle Shylock" replaced "Uncle Sam" in the foreign press when President Coolidge came out in opposition to canceling or reducing the British and French debts incurred during World War I, each country owing the United States over $4 billion. Coolidge's response: "They hired the money, didn't they?"

☛ FOREIGN NEWS

Italy

Keeping it in the family was Fascist dictator Benito Mussolini. A virtual one-man band, in 1925 he held five of Italy's top cabinet posts, including premier, minister of foreign affairs, minister of war, minister of air, and minister of marine. The hardworking Mussolini also functioned as minister of agriculture, a noncabinet post.

Sweden

Achievers in various fields were distressed by the brief announcement issued from Stockholm: "The Board of Directors of the Nobel Fund announces that, for the first time since the initial awards twenty-four years ago, all five of the annual Nobel Prizes will be withheld for the current year." In the judgment of the directors, no outstanding accomplishment had taken place in the fields of physics, chemistry, medicine, literature, and the promotion of peace.

Swedish-born Alfred Nobel had made his fortune in explosives and left $9 million to fund the prizes. After a nitroglycerine factory he built had blown up, killing his brother, Nobel had worked to develop safer explosives, inventing and patenting dynamite in 1897.

• Starting in 1969, an award would also be made in the field of economics.

• Judges in Sweden determine the prizewinners, except for the Peace Prize, which is awarded by a committee of five, elected by the Norwegian parliament.

• In 1976, the United States became the first country to win all the prizes in a single year.

Argentina

Britain's Prince of Wales visited Argentina, and the goodly number of formal events feting the potential successor to the throne brought joy to

40

the country's clothing industry. One store sold 200 dress suits and 500 morning coats in just one week.

England

Vivian Carter, secretary of the British Rotarians, commented on the group's recent trip to America: "We could not help observing the tremendous wealth of America. The American is mad over golf."

A former Scottish actor named Arthur Ferguson was making a handsome living from American tourists in London. Posing as a British agent, he confided to gullible American visitors that the government had to sell off some of its national monuments to pay off the country's war debts. The wily Ferguson "sold" Nelson's Column in Trafalgar Square for £6,000, Big Ben for £1,000, and received a £2,000 downpayment on Buckingham Palace. Ferguson then took his talents to the United States, where he "sold" several New York landmarks and managed to "rent" the White House for $10,000 a year, paid in advance.

France

Across the English Channel, one Victor Lustig was showing that Frenchmen could be bilked just as easily as Americans. Lustig checked into the Hotel de Crillon with an accomplice named "Dapper Dan" Collins. Noticing a news item on the possible destruction of the Eiffel Tower, Lustig had official-looking stationery produced and contacted the leading scrap iron dealers in France, summoning them to a meeting to discuss a government contract for tearing down the Eiffel Tower and removing the 7,000 tons of scrap metal, the proceeds of which were to go toward paying off France's war debt. The con men identified the most eager of the group, and "Dapper Dan" Collins, posing as Lustig's secretary, notified him that his bid would be accepted if he came forth with a bribe for the deputy (Lustig) to assure clearance through government channels. So Lustig and Collins received money for both the bribe and the "sale" of the Eiffel Tower, purported to be a hefty sum, although the exact amount was never known since the duped scrap metal dealer was too embarrassed to complain to the police. The resourceful Lustig would go on to "sell" the Eiffel Tower one more time before ending up in Alcatraz.

Frenchman Albert Wooly attempted a twenty-one-day fast in a glass case in full view of curious Parisians. After twelve days, 40,000 people were estimated to have passed by, often tempting him with various edibles and potables. On day 13, a woman took up a position directly in front of Wooly and proceeded to eat a chocolate eclair, slowly and tantalizingly consuming each morsel, after which she carefully licked each

41

1925 of her fingers. Suddenly, the famished Wooly became incensed, smashing open the glass case with a chair. Police escorted him to a nearby hospital.

Germany

The remains of World War I ace Baron Manfred von Richthofen were returned to Germany from France for reinterment. Thousands paid tribute to the man known as the Flying Siegfried, the Red Knight of Germany, and the Red Baron, who had been credited with downing eighty Allied planes before being shot down in 1917.

At the time of his death, the twenty-five-year-old von Richthofen was in command of a squadron credited with the destruction of 200 aircraft. He had taken off in his red Fokker triplane after posing for a photograph, violating a superstition among fighter pilots that having one's picture taken before a mission was bad luck. Over France, his squadron of twenty-four planes attacked fifteen RAF aircraft, von Richthofen's Fokker being sent to the earth in the ensuing dogfight, where it landed intact in a French field. The Red Baron was found dead in an upright position in the cockpit and was photographed by the Allies, who would later drop copies of the picture behind German lines in order to undermine the morale of the troops. Under his uniform, von Richthofen had been wearing dark red pajamas. He was buried by the French with full military honors.

☛ REGIONAL NEWS

Connecticut

The Connecticut legislature defeated a bill that would have taxed cat owners. Legislators were swayed by a compelling statistic: One pair of rats can accumulate 359 million descendants in three years if they are allowed to multiply at will.

Delaware

The Delaware legislature voted 31–1 not to abolish whipping as a means of punishing certain crimes. Sheriffs, deputies, and constables could continue to use the lash, and the penalty for individual violations was as follows:

CRIME	NUMBER OF LASHES
Attempt to poison	60
Lying in wait to maim	30

Assault to rape	30
Wife beating	30
Robbery (near highway or in house)	40
Robbery (elsewhere)	20
Breaking and entering	40
Perjury	40
Setting fire to courthouse	60
Setting fire to vessel, church, or school	20

☛ BUSINESS

As American females bobbed their hair, the number of hair-cutting parlors increased from 5,000 to 23,000 during the 1920s, and the barbershop was no longer exclusively male. Females would keep their hair short into the 1930s, and sales of a new aid to hair care would boom: the bobby pin.

Twin brothers Francis E. and Freeland O. Stanley closed down production of the Stanley Steamer, bringing an end to broad-scale sales of steam-powered automobiles. The first steam-powered vehicle had been produced in France in 1769. The Stanleys had gone into business in 1897 at a time when steam appeared to be a growing power source for automobiles. Electric engines needed frequent recharging, and hand-cranked internal combustion engines were difficult to start and complicated to run and maintain. The Steamer had no gearshift, transmission, or spark plugs, ran on any burnable fuel, and was simple to start: You just lighted the boiler, and when the water was hot, you were on your way. The cars were also extremely fast, having reached the unheard-of speed of 127.66 mph in 1906. But the Stanleys had no goals for expansion and were content to produce only 1,000 cars a year, which they sold for $2,000 each. They did not promote, nor did they make any attempt to improve, their models. The invention of the electric self-starter began to turn the tide for the internal combustion engine; Ford's assembly line efficiencies then dropped prices significantly, and steam-powered vehicles ceased to be a major factor in American auto sales.

"The Yellow Drive-It-Yourself System, Inc." began renting cars at rates of twelve to seventeen cents a mile, depending on the vehicle selected. The company was owned by taxicab mogul John Hertz.

1925 ☞ PRODUCTS

Heinz's "57 varieties" were prospering and numbered well in excess of fifty-seven. Henry John Heinz had been impressed by an advertisement for "21 styles of shoes," and would maintain the slogan long after his product line had grown into the hundreds.

The Kodak camera had already popularized do-it-yourself photography—"You press the button, we do the rest." George Eastman had chosen the name "Kodak," saying, "I know a trade name must be short, vigorous, incapable of being misspelled to an extent that will destroy its identity, and in order to satisfy the trademark laws it must mean nothing." The first Kodak hand camera had been introduced in 1888 with the film built into the camera. When the film was used up, the camera had to be sent back to Kodak for processing and was returned to the owner loaded with fresh film.

Aunt Jemima pancake mix was an American favorite, having been introduced in 1893 at the World's Columbian Exposition at Chicago by R. T. Davis. Davis had hired ex-slave Nancy Green to demonstrate the mix.

☞ RELIGION

The Episcopal Church dropped the word "obey" from the wedding liturgy as well as the phrase "with all my worldly goods I thee endow."

☞ ADVERTISING

A new form of advertising appeared along American roads. Burma-Shave used a series of small signs spaced at sufficient intervals so that people in passing automobiles could read them even at high speeds. Their lighthearted approach to advertising made them popular with amused motorists for forty-six years—until the last boards disappeared in the early 1960s. Some examples:

> A peach looks good
> with lots of fuzz
> but man's no peach
> and never was
> Burma-Shave

Henry the Eighth
Prince of Friskers
lost five wives
but kept his whiskers
Burma-Shave

Does your husband misbehave
grunt and grumble
rant and rave
shoot the brute some
Burma-Shave

☞ LANGUAGE

Prohibition had introduced a whole new vocabulary to describe the results of drinking too much. One could become blind, blotto, buried, cockeyed, embalmed, high, lit, oiled, ossified, paralyzed, pickled, pie-eyed, polluted, soused, squiffy, stewed, stiff, stinko, woozy, or zozzled, just to name a few.

☞ PROHIBITION

The U.S. Coast Guard had reconditioned twenty World War I navy destroyers, but efforts to keep illegal liquor from being smuggled into the United States were drastically inadequate. Mexico, Canada, Bermuda, the Bahamas, and the West Indies all increased their British imports to far above pre-Prohibition levels. Many Americans within striking distance of Canada traveled there to drink on weekends, an exodus that was put to music in the song, "Goodbye Broadway, Hello Montreal." Another popular song of the era: "Show Me the Way to Go Home."

Prohibition was a boon to the soft drink industry, whose products were used to hide the harsh taste of illegal alcohol. The sugar content of mixers was reduced and tart ingredients added, making drinks like the Tom Collins and the whiskey sour popular.

Government agents seized 696,933 stills between 1921 and 1925. General Lincoln C. Andres remarked to a congressional committee, "This means that a great many people are distilling."

1925

☞ EDUCATION

Always proper Vassar College changed its dress code, making it mandatory for dresses to cover the knees.

An equally prestigious female institution of higher learning also made a rule change. Bryn Mawr allowed students to smoke on campus, rescinding a twenty-eight-year ban.

☞ MEDICINE

Antitoxin arrived in Nome, Alaska, in time to prevent a diphtheria epidemic. In answer to an appeal telegraphed by a local physician, when an Eskimo came down with the disease, relays of dog teams were used to carry the serum. One team covered 655 miles in five and a half days in 80-mph winds, with temperatures as low as 50 degrees below zero. Musher Gunnar Kaasen arrived nearly blind, and his lead dog Balto, a malamute half-breed, became a national hero. A statue of Balto stands near the zoo in New York's Central Park.

Champions of birth control were elated to receive the support of the American Medical Association, the New York Academy of Medicine, and the New York Obstetrical Society; and the Rockefeller Foundation funded medical research into methods of contraception.

The term "birth control" had first been used by nurse Margaret Sanger in her publication *The Woman Rebel* in 1914. She had been sentenced to a month in jail for starting the first birth control clinic in 1916 and had been arrested for sending birth control data through the mail, regarded as obscene material under the Comstock Act.

☞ BOOKS

Pursuing the almighty dollar was considered a noble quest in 1925; ministers spoke from their pulpits in support of the dignity of business. A book was published in 1925 called *The Man Nobody Knows*, in which author Bruce Barton linked Christianity to business. Jesus, wrote Barton, was a superior executive who "had picked up twelve men from the bottom ranks of business and forged them into the organization that conquered the world." His parables were the "most powerful advertisements of all time." Barton went on, "It was not to preach that he came into the world nor to teach; nor to heal. These are all departments of his Father's business but the business itself is larger, more inclusive. Thus all business is his Father's business. All work is worship; all useful service prayer." Barton's book was the best-selling work of nonfiction in 1925 and 1926, and he would become a co-founder of Batten Barton Durstine and Osborne in 1928, an advertising agency that would be known to many as just BBD&O.

The Great Gatsby by Francis Scott Key Fitzgerald was published in 1925. Before settling on the final title, Fitzgerald had considered a number of alternates, including *Incident at West Egg, Among Ash Heaps and Millionaires, Trimalchio in West Egg, On the Road to West Egg, Gold-Hatted Gatsby,* and *The High-Bounding Lover.*

Also published during 1925 were Theodore Dreiser's *An American Tragedy,* John Dos Passos's *Manhattan Transfer,* and Sinclair Lewis's *Arrowsmith,* which, with *The Great Gatsby,* were appreciated by lovers of good literature, although none of the books were public favorites.

☞ ENTERTAINMENT

Grand Old Opry had its origins when radio station WSM in Nashville, Tennessee, started broadcasting the *WSM Barn Dance*. Early performers were Dave Macon, the Dixie Dew Drop, the Fruit Jar Drinkers, the Gully Jumpers, Possum Hunter, and twenty-two-year-old Roy Acuff, who would go on to stardom and be named the most popular singer of World War II, beating out a young crooner named Frank Sinatra for the honor. Acuff ran for governor of Tennessee in 1948. The show changed its name to the "Grand Old Opry" in 1927.

Ben Hur was released in 1925, the movie adapted from the book by General Lewis Wallace, former Civil War hero and governor of the New Mexico Territory. In order to assure a lively chariot race, studio stuntmen had been guaranteed a bonus of $150 for finishing first, $100 for second place, and $50 for third.

☞ SPORTS

Undefeated Dartmouth was the number one college football team in the nation. The squad included twenty-two members of Phi Beta Kappa and was probably the most intelligent team ever to do battle on the gridiron. Academic requirements for most football players outside of the

1925 Ivy League diminished as the popularity of college football increased, bringing tremendous revenues to the nation's pigskin powers.

Notre Dame defeated Stanford in the Rose Bowl, ending the college career of their talented backfield known as the Four Horsemen. During their three years at South Bend, the Fighting Irish had won twenty-seven games, lost two, and tied one.

They had been christened the Four Horsemen by sportswriter Grantland Rice in his coverage of the Notre Dame-Army game in 1924:

> Outlined against a blue-gray October sky, the Four Horsemen rode again. In dramatic lore they are known as Famine, Pestilence, Destruction and Death. These are only aliases. Their real names are Stuhldreher, Miller, Crowley and Layden. They formed the crest of the South Bend cyclone before which another fighting Army football team was swept over the precipice at the Polo Grounds yesterday afternoon as 55,000 spectators peered down on the bewildering panorama on the green plain below.

By today's standards, this talented quartet would be considered far too light to bash helmets with the behemoths who play modern college football. Halfbacks Don Miller and Jim Crowley weighted in at 164 and 166 pounds respectively, fullback Elmer Layden was a lean 163, and quarterback Harry Stuhldreher tipped the scales at 156.

On June 2, when starting New York Yankee first baseman Wally Pipp complained of a headache, manager Miller Huggins gave him the day off. Pipp went to the racetrack, little knowing that he would never reclaim his position. Henry Louis Gehrig, twenty-one, played the first of 2,130 consecutive games for the Yankees that day, a record that has never been seriously challenged.

The son of immigrant parents (his father worked as a janitor and his mother as a domestic servant), Gehrig had excelled at football, basketball, and baseball at the High School of Commerce in the Bronx, his talents on the gridiron gaining him a scholarship at Columbia University. But his ability to hit a baseball long distances convinced his coaches that he should not risk injury on the gridiron, and Gehrig looked as though he would terrorize Ivy League pitching until his graduation. However, it was discovered that Gehrig had been paid to play baseball during the summer following his graduation from high school, thus making him ineligible for college athletics. He left college to sign a contract with the Yankees, and after a brief stay with Hartford in the Eastern League, his powerful bat brought him back to New York.

48

• In one of the baseball games that Gehrig played at Columbia, he hit a ball from home plate, located at 114th Street and Amsterdam Avenue, to just short of 116th Street and Broadway, where it shattered a window in the Journalism Building. The ball had traveled over 600 feet in the air.

Red Grange made his professional debut with the Chicago Bears before a crowd of 35,000 at Chicago's Wrigley Field. The National Football League had not caught on during its first four years and could muster only tiny crowds. But Grange would put the NFL on the map, and a crowd of 73,000 came to see him play in New York later in the season.

ARMED FORCES

The court-martial of William "Billy" Mitchell was followed closely by a press and public divided over whether he should be found guilty of charges of insubordination. Mitchell's military career through World War I had established him as one of the rising stars in the U.S. Army. He had been the youngest second lieutenant at eighteen, the youngest captain, and had become a general at thirty-six. He had directed the army's Air Service in World War I, was the first American officer to be fired upon by the enemy, and the first to pilot his plane over enemy lines. He was also the first Yank to be awarded France's Legion of Honor and had also won the Croix de Guerre. Mitchell had taken England's Prince of Wales up for a spin and had been received by King George V.

Mitchell's belief that air power would be a significant factor in modern warfare had come in 1906, just three years after the Wright brothers' first flight and two years before the army would receive its first plane. In 1906, the twenty-six-year-old Mitchell had said, "Conflicts no doubt will be carried out in the future in the air, on the surface of the earth and water, and underwater."

On his return from World War I, Mitchell began a vigorous campaign for a separate and vastly expanded air force. He was ridiculed by the navy for claiming that battleships could be sunk by bombs dropped from the air. He then incurred that navy's enduring enmity by doing just that when a group of planes under his command bombed several captured battleships at anchor, sending them to Davy Jones's locker. Mitchell's persistent lobbying for improved air capability held back his army career, and he was passed over twice for promotion to head the army's Air Service. The fact that he was frequently quoted by an admiring press did not aid his cause in Washington, and his superiors ordered him to remain silent. But Mitchell was determined to alert the military hierarchy and the public to the country's vulnerability in the face of future attack, which he believed

1925 would come from Japan and be directed at the Hawaiian Islands. The last straw came when he accused the navy of incompetence in the loss of its dirigible *Shenandoah*. Mitchell was convicted of insubordination and busted to private with no pay and allowances for five years and resigned from the service in February 1926.

• "He has done more for aviation than any man in the nation's history except the Wright brothers." (*Aero Digest*)

• President Harry Truman awarded Mitchell a special medal in 1946 for contributions to American aviation, but his son's petition to overturn his conviction was turned down in 1957.

Airplanes roared over Honolulu, and tanks lumbered through the streets as the United States staged war exercises. After three days of "battle," military brass concluded that Pearl Harbor was safe from attack.

☛ MEDIA

The first edition of *The New Yorker* was published, edited by Harold Ross, former editor of *Stars and Stripes, American Legion Weekly,* and *Judge* magazine. The first edition had thirty-two pages and cost fifteen cents, and the cover carried the drawing of an elegant dandy observing a butterfly through a magnifying glass. Eustace Tilley, as they called him, would reappear on the cover annually on the anniversary of the magazine's first issue. Charter employees were Alexander Woollcott, George S. Kaufman, Marc Connelly, Dorothy Parker, and young cartoonists Helen Hokinson, twenty-six, and Curtis Arnoux Peters, twenty-one, who illustrated under the name "Peter Arno." Promotional materials stated that the magazine would be "sophisticated" and "will not be edited for the old lady in Dubuque," vows that Ross and his followers scrupulously adhered to. The editorial policy also excluded any materials that could even be vaguely construed as off-color. Ross's one exception: a cartoon entitled "News" that depicted a dog being sprayed by a fire hydrant.

The nation hung on every word regarding the fate of Floyd Collins, a spelunker who was trapped by a rock slide while exploring Sand Cave in Cave City, Kentucky. After Collins's cries had been heard by local residents, a twenty-one-year-old *Louisville Courier Journal* reporter named William Burke "Skeets" Miller raced to the scene. The diminutive Miller risked his life by crawling through a narrow tunnel that could barely accommodate his slight frame. When he reached Collins, he found him pinned by a huge boulder. Miller made repeated trips back to Collins's side while rescuers attempted various ways to free the trapped

50

man, the last of which was to drill down into the cave from above. But **1925** when the rescue team finally reached Collins after seventeen days, he was dead. The body could not be removed, and the cave was filled in to prevent further accidents.

☞ FUN AND GAMES

The *New York World* had started publishing crossword puzzles in 1912, and they had attracted a modest number of habitués. It was not until 1925 that two young men named Simon and Schuster precipitated a national addiction by publishing the first book of crossword puzzles in the United States.

Richard Simon and M. Lincoln "Max" Schuster paid a visit to Simon's aunt. In the course of the conversation, she asked if they knew of a crossword puzzle book because she wanted to give one to her niece. They told her that no such book was available and decided to publish one themselves. Not wanting to associate their names with a book devoid of literary merit, they brought out *The Crossword Puzzle Book* under the banner of the hastily formed Plaza Publishing Company. The book became an instant best-seller, and a new mania swept the country.

• A Chicago woman took her husband to court, claiming that her marriage was in jeopardy because her husband spent all his time at home working on crossword puzzles. The judge restricted the offender to three puzzles a day.

• A restaurant owner brought one of his patrons to court. The accused had been so engrossed in a crossword puzzle that he had refused to leave the premises at closing time despite repeated requests, resulting in a call to the police. The offender was sentenced to several days in jail, saying he was pleased to go there because it would give him a chance to work on his puzzles in peace.

• The Baltimore & Ohio Railroad placed dictionaries on all its trains.

• *The Bookman* magazine described the following discussion between two crossword puzzle afficionados:

MRS. W: What is it that you are working at, my dear?

MRS. B: I'm tatting Joe's initials on his moreen vest. Are you making that ebon garment for yourself?

MRS. W.: Yeah. Just a black dress for every day. Henry says I look rather naif in black.

MRS. F: Well, perhaps; but it's a bit too anile for me. Give me something in indigo or, say, ecru.

MRS. W: Quite right. There is really no neb in such solemn vestments.

MRS. F: Stet.

1925 Mrs. W: By the way, didn't I hear that your little Junior met with an accident?

Mrs. F: Yes, the little oaf fell from an apse and fractured his artus.

Mrs. W: Egad.

☛ PEOPLE

Ex-First Lady Florence Harding died. At her request, her favorite hymn was sung at her funeral: "The End of a Perfect Day."

1926

Valentino had silently acted out the fantasies of women all over the world. Valentino and his world were a dream. A whole generation of females wanted to ride off into a sandy paradise with him.
—Bette Davis

☞ NATIONAL NEWS

Americans were pursuing the almighty dollar with a vengeance, the stock market fell back but then surged ahead again, and few noticed, or cared, when someone named Joseph Stalin established a virtual dictatorship in Russia that would last for the next twenty-seven years. Isolationism was the mood of a war-weary nation, laissez-faire government the hallmark of the Coolidge administration. Since little news was coming out of Washington, the nation's newspapers dealt with more frivolous fare. And no news story received more attention in 1926 than the sudden death of one Rodolpho Alfonzo Raffaelo Pierre Filibert Guglielmi di Valentina d'Antonguolla, known to millions of movie fans around the world simply as Rudolph Valentino.

The son of a veterinarian, Valentino had come to New York from Italy in 1913. Details of his early years in the United States have not been precisely recorded, but Valentino appears to have held a variety of jobs,

53

1926 including stints as gardener, dishwasher, dancer, gigolo, movie extra, and actor in minor stage roles; unsavory rumors later surfaced hinting at homosexual encounters and blackmail.

Hollywood legend has it that Valentino got his big break when he was seen in a minor Broadway part and offered the role of Julio Desmoyers in the film version of *The Four Horsemen of the Apocalypse*. Although the part was not a large one, his Latin looks and torrid tango scored a hit. Increasingly larger parts resulted, his career reaching its apex in a Middle Eastern melodrama called *The Sheik*. His flashing eyes, quivering nostrils, and what author Ethan Mordden described as his "resourceful hand placement," totally captivated American womanhood. Little did it matter that many of their husbands and boyfriends thought Valentino effeminate. To women, he represented excitement, passion, adventure— the promise of an exotic world far from Main Street, U.S.A.

Such was the impact of *The Sheik* that the word immediately entered the lexicon of young America, predatory men becoming "sheiks," their women, "shebas," "The Sheik of Araby" became a hit song, and Tin Pan Alley revived "Hindustan"; Paramount geared up to produce a sequel, *The Son of the Sheik*, with Valentino playing the roles of both father and son.

While Valentino turned countless females into jelly, the Great Lover was far less successful in his private life. His first marriage had found the bloom off the rose before the nuptial day was out. Refusing the traditional lift across the threshold, actress Jean Acker beat Rudy to the door of their honeymoon retreat and promptly locked him out. She later sued him for desertion, and the marriage ended in divorce. But not before Rudy had married his next love, Natacha Rambova, the former Winifred Shaughnessy. Because the ceremony had taken place before Valentino's divorce from wife number one had become final, he was charged with bigamy. To satisfy the courts, the couple lived apart until the divorce was finally granted. But Valentino's marriage to Rambova, whom he called the Boss, was also short-lived, it too ending in divorce.

His unsuccessful marriages coupled with recurring rumors alleging his homosexuality resulted in an increasingly hostile press. "ALL MEN HATE VALENTINO," headlined one newspaper; another labeled him a "painted pansy." Nevertheless, Valentino had embarked upon a highly successful personal appearance tour, *The Son of the Sheik* was scheduled to open in the fall, and his hold on his fans appeared to be just as strong as ever when he arrived in New York City in August 1926.

Staying at the Ambassador Hotel, Valentino suddenly collapsed and was rushed to the Polyclinic Hospital, where doctors diagnosed his condition as an inflamed appendix and two perforated ulcers. Following an operation, he appeared to be on the mend. When his temperature shot

54

upward, pleurisy developed, and the screen idol died on August 23 **1926** shortly after noon, at the tender age of thirty-one.

Public relations men, Hollywood flacks, and the media wasted no time in moving into action:

• It was announced that Valentino's last words had been, "Let the tent be struck," considered to be an appropriate final exclamation for one whom tents had served so well as a locus for many of his cinematic seductions. When it was noted that these had been the last words of Gen. Robert E. Lee, it was subsequently revealed that a mistake had been made, Valentino's actual last words having been, "I want the sunlight to greet me—don't pull the shades!"

• A local tabloid carried a composite photograph depicting Valentino being greeted at the gates of heaven by Enrico Caruso, the famous opera singer.

• Tin Pan Alley quickly produced a song entitled, "There's a New Star in Heaven Tonight."

• Actress Pola Negri, the Polish Bombshell, fainted at a New York memorial service for Valentino, but recovered to reveal that she and the actor had been secret lovers. Negri reported that his final words to her had been, "I love you and will love you in eternity," adding that she was seriously considering entering a convent.

• Ex-wife Rambova reported that she had contacted Valentino in the hereafter and that he was "quite happy over there." Pressed for details, Rambova said that he was enjoying listening to Caruso sing, that he attended worthwhile lectures and the theater, and that he was thinking of acting on the stage. Movies were out because there was no film equipment there. When reporters asked Rambova if Valentino had told her whom he loved, she replied that it was her alone, being sure to add that he had made no mention of Miss Negri.

• Several women committed suicide, including two distraught young Japanese women, who were said to have jumped into a volcano hand in hand.

Fifteen days after his death, the Great Lover was finally laid to rest in California. Valentino had died in debt, and his agent later admitted that he had been responsible for most of the hoopla surrounding the actor's death in order to assure the success of his upcoming movie. Sure enough, *The Son of the Sheik* was a big hit, Valentino's estate ending up $700,000 in the black.

New York City mounted the biggest ticker tape parade in the city's history to honor Gertrude "Trudy" Ederle. Ederle had not only become the first woman to swim the English Channel, but her time had beaten the record of the fastest man by the incredible margin of nearly two hours.

1926   A British merchant captain named Matthew Webb had made the first successful Channel swim in 1875, breaststroking from Dover, England, to Cap Gris-Nez, France, in 21 hours and 45 minutes. Although the straight-line distance between the two towns was twenty-one miles, the Channel's powerful currents continually pushed Webb off course, and it was estimated that he had been forced to swim nearly forty miles before reaching the French coast.

Thirty-six years went by before another Englishman braved the cold water and treacherous currents to best the Channel in 1911. But it would not be until the 1920s that long-distance swimmers attempted the crossing in large numbers. Two Americans and an Argentine—all men— were successful in 1923. But by August 1926, no women had yet gone the distance, although Ederle and Jean Simon of France had both come tantalizingly close to their goal in 1925.

Clare Belle Barrett of Pelham Manor, New York, was the first woman to try in 1926. She was just two miles short of the British coast when she was overcome by exhaustion, having spent over twenty-one hours in the water, her trainer calculating that she had made 26,400 strokes in her futile attempt.

Gertrude Ederle was next, and her credentials were impressive. She had broken her first world's record at twelve, and between 1921 and 1925 had held twenty-nine different national and world records, having broken seven in one day in 1922; and she had won three medals at the 1924 Olympics. The daughter of a New York City butcher, Ederle kept up her strength by consuming large amounts of her father's rare roast beef.

On August 6, shortly after seven o'clock in the morning, she plunged into the water at Cap Gris-Nez, France, and headed for England, despite heavy seas and storm warnings posted on both coasts. On the same morning, the *London Daily News* published an editorial that would cause it considerable embarrassment. The *News* wrote, "Even the most uncompromising champion of the rights and capacities of women must admit that in contests of physical skill, speed and endurance, they must remain forever the weaker sex."

Ederle set out at a pace of 28 strokes per minute, and by six o'clock that evening she was in sight of land. But then the tide changed, and for the next three hours, it took all her strength just to hold her own, waiting desperately for a tide change that would allow her to make the final run to the beach. Finally, just before nine o'clock, the current shifted, and Ederle forged ahead again, wading ashore just before ten o'clock, nearly fifteen hours after leaving France. Ederle's triumph came in the nick of time. Just three weeks later, Mrs. Clemington Corson of New York also conquered the English Channel.

Such was Ederle's popularity that she embarked on a swimming tour at the queenly salary of $2,000 a week. But, ironically, the water in her ears began to affect her hearing, and she became increasingly deaf. She later suffered a nervous breakdown and incurred a back injury that forced her to wear a cast for more than four years. But Ederle recovered, and she devoted a considerable amount of her time in later years to teaching deaf children how to swim.

No newspaper story of the era would stay on the front pages as long as the events surrounding the disappearance of Sister Aimee Semple McPherson, self-billed as the "World's Most Pulchritudinous Evangelist," founder of the highly successful International Institute of Four-Square Evangelism in Los Angeles, California.

Sister Aimee had been born in Ontario, Canada, in 1890, and had heard the Lord's call as a teenager. She had married a minister named Robert Semple, joining him in missionary work in China. When her husband had been taken ill and died, she returned to Canada and married grocer Harold McPherson. Their marriage was a brief one, Aimee deciding to take to the road as a full-time evangelist, McPherson preferring to stay home and mind the store. Traveling through the United States, England, and Australia, Sister Aimee did not hit her full stride until she arrived in Southern California in 1918 to find a flock of sinners who responded to her preaching. Over the next eight years, Sister Aimee, aided by her mother's financial acumen, built her church into a highly successful venture headquartered in the Angelus Temple, built at a cost of $1.5 million. The building included a church where 5,000 of the faithful could worship at one time, a Miracle Room holding the braces and crutches of those whom the good sister had cured of various ailments, a children's chapel, a lonely hearts club, and a radio station that carried the message to thousands of homes. A community center had twenty-four separate departments, including a Bible school attended by a thousand students. Members of the Four-Square City Sisters passed out food to the needy and nursed the sick while men of the parish provided jobs for ex-convicts and the unemployed.

Clad in white satin robes, the high priestess had a statuesque figure, crowned with long red-blonde hair. Her sermons were well-shaped theatrical productions supported by the church's three bands, two orchestras, three choirs, and six quartets.

When Sister Aimee had traveled to England, crowds jammed Albert Hall in London to attend what one newspaper called one of the "merriest religious revivals the world has ever known." The media also noted the sister's "short skirts, her flesh-colored stockings, and elaborate coiffure." Aimee also wore Paris dresses, expensive shoes, imported lingerie, and lipstick and rouge, none of which were apparently contrary to her religious beliefs.

One sunny day in May, Sister Aimee and her secretary, Emma

1926 Schaffer, went to a beach near Los Angeles for a day of swimming and relaxation. They pitched a tent to serve as a changing area and resting place, and Sister Aimee donned a green bathing suit. She then sent her secretary on an errand to a nearby hotel, strolled down the beach, and plunged into the ocean. But when Schaffer returned a few minutes later, Sister Aimee was nowhere to be found.

Although her body was not recovered, it was assumed that Sister Aimee had drowned. "We know she is with Jesus," her mother told a large crowd of believers who had flocked to the temple upon news of McPherson's disappearance. Eleven thousand people grieved for the departed evangelist at a memorial service.

Just over a month after Sister Aimee's disappearance, the nation was shocked to learn that the good sister was alive, having escaped from kidnappers and made her way to Douglas, Arizona. According to Sister Aimee, she had been headed toward the water on that fateful day when she had been stopped by a distraught couple seeking help. When they told her that their child was very sick in a nearby car, McPherson followed them to their automobile to see if she could help. But when they reached the car, Sister Aimee had been shoved into the backseat, drugged, and spirited away to Mexico, where her kidnappers—two men called Steve and Jake, and a woman named Rose—confined her to a desert shack. Her abductors told Sister Aimee that if $500,000 in ransom money was not forthcoming, she would be sold to a Mexican named Felipe. Aimee also said that she had been tortured with a lighted cigar but had finally eluded her captors, hiking thirteen hours across the desert to Douglas.

Bedded down in the local hospital, Sister Aimee answered questions put to her by local law enforcement officers and members of the press. The more she talked, the more suspicious her interrogators became. For someone who had tramped the burning desert sands for thirteen hours, her shoes appeared little the worse for wear, and she had blisters that were only slightly developed; her dress also seemed to be in remarkably good shape. It was also considered extremely odd that Sister Aimee had emerged from her Gethsemane with no evidence of dehydration. In fact, she had not even asked for a single glass of water when she had arrived in Douglas.

As newspaper readers pondered Sister Aimee's strange tale, a new development suggested an entirely different motive for her disappearance. It was reported that Kenneth Ormistan, a married radio technician at the Angelus Temple, had also been missing, having spent several weeks traveling with a blonde companion matching Sister Aimee's description. The couple had used several aliases at different California resort hotels, including an inn in Carmel, where they had stayed for ten days.

Having returned to Los Angeles, Sister Aimee vehemently denied that she had traveled with Ormistan, asking him to come forward and

58

clear her name. Although Ormistan remained in seclusion, he did forward a statement to the Los Angeles police denying that he had been with Sister Aimee, claiming to have traveled with a woman whom he would identify only as Miss X. Ormistan's statement failed to convince the district attorney, who indicted Sister Aimee on charges of obstructing justice. McPherson countered with a newspaper series dramatically entitled, "Saint or Sinner—Did I Go from Pulpit to Paramour?" claiming that she was the innocent victim of a conspiracy by mobsters who wanted her discredited because she had shown so many prostitutes the way to a better life.

At the trial, the prosecution brought forth numerous witnesses who identified Sister Aimee as Ormistan's traveling companion, and Ormistan himself was finally located in Harrisburg, Pennsylvania. But just when the district attorney appeared to hold all the trumps, he suddenly called for Sister Aimee's acquittal for reasons that were never made clear.

Although her name had been cleared, things would never be quite the same for Sister Aimee Semple McPherson, but the Institute of Four-Square Evangelism continued to prosper. She made several more trips to Europe and Asia and took another husband, that marriage also ending in divorce. She died in Oakland, California, in 1944, from an overdose of sleeping pills.

☛ FOREIGN NEWS

France

The French government devalued the franc to one fifth of its prewar value, obliterating the savings of millions of Frenchmen. Many citizens would never trust their nation's currency again and would squirrel away vast quantities of gold as a hedge against inflation.

A "miracle" occurred at Lourdes that would enhance its reputation as a place where the seriously afflicted might find a cure for their ailments. A Frenchwoman named Augustine Augualt was carried to the shrine on a stretcher, seeking a cure for what physicians had agreed was a large fibroid tumor of the uterus. Following her visit, the tumor completely disappeared, with thirty physicians verifying the "cure."

Charles Wells, "The Man Who Broke the Bank at Monte Carlo," died penniless in Paris. The Englishman had arrived in Monte Carlo in 1887 with £200 that he had obtained by selling some worthless patents in his home country. Playing roulette, Wells quickly "broke the bank," exhausting the table's 100,000-franc reserve, which had to be replenished from the casino's vaults.

Having joined the tiny, elite corps who had "broken the bank" at

1926 Monte Carlo, Wells proceeded to repeat the feat twice more in 1887, and won nearly 100,000 francs in 1888 when he started with modest wagers and profited from a run on Number 5. Casino executives watched Wells like hawks in an attempt to explain his fantastic winnings. They checked and rechecked their roulette wheels, interrogated their croupiers, but came up with no plausible reason for his extraordinary success. Onlookers tried to duplicate Wells's play but lost heavily. Said Wells, "Anyone is free to watch me play and imitate me, but the general defect of the ordinary gambler is that he lacks courage. He will not risk sufficiently large stakes, and he is afraid of his losses."

Wells's gambling exploits were followed by newspapers around the globe, and he became known as "Monte Carlo" Wells; a song was written called "The Man Who Broke the Bank at Monte Carlo." And when he returned to Monte Carlo in 1892, it was by yacht, sporting a beautiful artists' model named Joan Burns. At the casino, Wells demonstrated that he had not lost his touch by breaking the bank six more times. But then the tables turned, and Wells began to lose as flamboyantly as he had won until he had exhausted his winnings and his original stake. He telegraphed friends in England for more cash; when it arrived, it also found its way into the casino's vaults.

The denouement? Wells was arrested and brought to trial in England for fleecing investors who had funded his "inventions," including a fuel-saving device for steamships. He was jailed, and when released assumed the name of Davenport, joining up with a bogus priest. He was soon back in jail, serving a three-year term for fraud. Free once more, he promoted an investment that promised investors 1 percent interest per day. After having bilked numerous Frenchmen in this lucrative scam, Wells was apprehended and jailed for another five years.

Before his death, Wells attributed his fantastic run at the tables to pure luck. The winner? The casinos, of course. The publicity surrounding Wells's success drew to Monte Carlo thousands who had been unfamiliar with the heady wine of games of chance until "Monte Carlo" Wells had shown them the way.

Greece

When General Theodore Pangalos took over the Greek government, restrictions were placed upon the press, the constitution was suspended, opposition leaders were exiled, and corrupt civil servants were executed—all in a day's work for a military dictator. But the conservative Pangalos added a new wrinkle, forbidding females over twelve to appear in public in dresses with hemlines more than fourteen inches above terra firma. Some of his detractors whispered that the reason for their leader's rigid dress code was a novel one: His wife was bowlegged.

Saudi Arabia
Ibn-Saud, 6 feet 4 inches, 240 pounds, became the first king of Arabia and guardian of the Holy Cities, including Mecca; in 1932, he added the family name to his country, which would become known as Saudi Arabia. A devout member of the Wehabis, a strict Muslim sect, he did not smoke, drink, or gamble, but his religion allowed him unlimited marital rights. He had 120 wives, although tradition required that he not be married to any more than four at one time.

☞ REGIONAL NEWS

Wisconsin
Halbert Louis Hoard, editor-publisher of the *Jefferson County Union,* circulated a petition in Fort Atkinson, Wisconsin, urging Congress to ban the brassiere. (In that era of the "boyish" look, a brassiere was employed to flatten and reduce the size of the breasts.) He secured the signatures of twenty-seven of the town's most prominent citizens and printed this petition in his newspaper:

> The undersigned note with alarm the increase in divorce since the Nineteenth Amendment—the woman suffrage law. We note that many more women wear breeches than ever before. We can stand that, but this new fad, slab-sided dresses in front—showing women in the fashion pictures as flat-chested as man, we regard with jealous eyes as an infringement. . . . We ask that the Congress of the United States do its utmost to break down these brassieres as an evil that menaces the future well-being of society.

Hoard and the signers of the petition were besieged with protests from the women of the county. Coming to their support, however, was Dr. J. J. Seelman of the State Board of Health, who claimed that the wearing of brassieres caused rickets in babies. Nevertheless, the signers of the petition were feeling the heat from members of the fair sex and many recanted their endorsement, claiming that they had not read the petition before signing it, believing it to be just another one of the publisher's "good causes."

Florida
In 1919, a forty-two-year-old one-time forger named Carlos Ponzi, with assets of just over $100, had dreamed up a get-rich scheme that had

1926 taken Boston by storm. The $20-a-week clerk had opened the Old Colony Foreign Exchange Company, dealing in international money orders, promising investors a 150 percent return on their money in ninety days. Few plungers came forward, but those who did were duly paid the promised handsome quarterly interest. Reporters learned of Ponzi's dealings, and aided by a flood of publicity, he was soon receiving $1 million a week from eager investors. Ponzi purchased a large house with servants, took over his former employers, fired his old boss, and toured Boston streets in a chauffeur-driven town car, besieged by admiring crowds. But one reporter became suspicious and dug into Ponzi's affairs, finding that the total number of foreign money orders sold in the entire country during 1919 had totaled only $58,560, a tiny portion of the funds that Ponzi had taken in. To add to the bad news, it was reported that Ponzi had served prison terms in both Atlanta and Montreal. Despite increasingly unfavorable publicity, the dollars kept rolling in, and Ponzi continued to honor the ninety-day notes. But on August 16, 1920, Ponzi's company finally went under, declaring liabilities of $2 million, and Ponzi went off to jail. But it is hard to keep a good man down, and Ponzi's dealings were far from over. By 1926, one of the biggest real estate booms seen anywhere in the nation was raging in Florida, ready-made for an inventive salesman like Ponzi.

The town of Miami had been a tiny crossroads in 1896, with a population of only sixty. By 1924, there were 60,000 residents, and it was growing faster than any area in the country, with plans for an eventual population of 300,000 by the end of the 1930s. Most of the credit for the town's incredible growth fell to one Carl G. Fisher, who had filled in a mangrove swamp where malaria had been common and created Miami Beach—an island resort separated from Miami proper by Biscayne Bay. Fisher posed bathing beauties on the beach in the middle of winter and sent the pictures to the New York newspapers, accompanied by descriptions of a palm-tree-dotted fairyland where the sun never failed to shine. He and his partners cut away the jungle foliage, erected a seawall, and built a causeway, the first of an eventual three connections between Miami Beach and the mainland. Lots that had been valueless were soon fetching thousands, and the boom spread like wildfire around the state. By 1925 ocean-front land in Palm Beach (an earlier resort, promoted in the 1890s by Henry M. Flagler) was selling for over $3,000 a foot. Investors could get in with only a 10 percent down payment, lots were sold in fetid swamps right off the blueprints, and some people bought property, sight unseen, that turned out to be under water. But buy they did, by the thousands, because everyone wanted to get in on the big Florida land boom.

It is not surprising that Charles Ponzi came directly to Florida after **1926** having paid back his latest debt to society. He established the Charpon Land Syndicate, which he claimed dealt in land "near Jacksonville," but actually involved property as far as sixty-five miles away from the city itself. Once again, Ponzi offered creative financing, selling "unit certificates of indebtedness" for $310 each, guaranteeing a Ponzi-like return of 200 percent within three months.

Author Geoffrey Perrett writes of a newspaperwoman who traveled to Florida to write a scathing article about the craziness of it all but who soon became a willing participant in the wild speculation. For $2,000 down, she put a binder on 34.5 acres. Before the month was out, she sold the binder, clearing a $13,000 profit. And so it went. The *Miami Herald* was so chock-full of ads for property that it carried more advertising than any other newspaper in the world.

And then one night in September 1926, Mother Nature stepped in and brought an end to the boom. The barometer plummeted to 27.75 in Miami, the lowest pressure ever recorded in the United States, with winds reaching 130 mph. Over 100 people drowned, some 40,000 were estimated to be homeless, and property damage in southern Florida was put at $300 million. Property value fell to a fraction of its original cost; rents dropped 75 percent. Although Florida would rise again, the pace would never match the frenzy that existed there in the first five and a half years of the 1920s.

☞ PROHIBITION

A poll was taken by the Newspapers Enterprise Association to determine people's attitudes toward Prohibition. Through 326 newspapers in forty-seven states, nearly 2 million people participated. The results of the poll: 18.9 percent were content with existing legislation, 49.8 percent felt that there should be modification to existing laws, and 31.3 percent opted for outright repeal.

Testifying before a Senate committee, Carnegie Institute of Technology president Dr. Samuel Harden stated that spirits were "one of the greatest blessings that God has given to men out of the teeming bosom of Mother Earth," declaring that hip flasks were de rigueur among his students.

Restricted from producing beer, the Coors brewery began turning out large quantities of malted milk.

1926 ☞ BOOKS

Editor Charles Hanson Towne, in the *International Book Review,* wrote of the extreme vigilance that magazine editors must exercise to avoid publishing plagiarized material. While serving as the editor of a magazine called *Smart Set,* Towne had unwittingly published a piece that had made its debut in the *Atlantic Monthly* three years before. But the most flagrant misrepresentation was a poem that had been submitted to Towne, which he immediately recognized.

He had written it himself.

Both the Book of the Month Club and the Literary Guild made their debuts in 1926, and by the late 1940s, book club sales accounted for 30 percent of all books sold. The BOMC's first selection was *Lolly Willowes, or the Loving Huntsman,* by Sylvia Townsend Warner.

☞ LANGUAGE

Attractive girls were beauts, the cat's pajamas, the cat's whiskers, or the cat's meow; their male counterparts were lounge lizards, jelly beans, cake-eaters, or jazbos. Girls lacking in intelligence were dumb Doras or dumbbells, while tough guys were hard-boiled eggs. When the party really got going, dancers were exhorted to "Get hot! Get hot!"

☞ BUSINESS

The first slide fastener had been demonstrated at the Chicago World's Fair in 1893 and was called the "Clasp Locker or Unlocker for Shoes." Metal teeth had been added in 1913, but this ingenious invention languished until British novelist Gilbert Frankau exclaimed at a demonstration in 1926, "Zip! It's open. Zip! It's closed." Zipper sales would really take off in 1931 when designer Elsa Schiaparelli became the first couturier to include the new fastener in her designs.

☞ ARMED FORCES

The navy rescinded its fifteen-year ban on chewing gum.

Dr. Charles Henry Tyler Townsend, an eminent entomologist, claimed that a certain species of deer botfly of the genus *Cephenomyia* was the fastest creature on earth. Although the botfly was no larger than the head of a pin, Townsend claimed that it could reach a speed of 818 mph. However, said Townsend, only the male could fly that fast, explaining that "the males are faster than the females because they must overtake the latter for coition." Scientists debunked Townsend's claim, pointing out that at 818 mph the botfly would be moving against air pressure of 8 pounds per square inch, more than enough to crush it; further, that it would have to consume 1.5 times its own weight in food every second to attain such a high speed. They concluded that the botfly would be lucky to clock 25 mph, aided by a strong following wind. Townsend reduced his estimate to 700 mph but died two years later without having convinced the scientific community of the legitimacy of his claim.

Physicist Robert H. Goddard launched the first rocket propelled by liquid fuel on a 2.5-second flight from a field near Worcester, Massachusetts. The rocket covered a distance of 184 feet, reaching a height of 41 feet and attaining a speed of 60 mph. The *New York Times* ridiculed Goddard, saying that he lacked the "knowledge ladled out daily in our high schools," debunking his theory that a rocket could function in a vacuum.

When captured German rocketeers were brought to the United States after World War II, they were questioned about the development of German rocketry and were incredulous that Americans had not already learned the answers from Goddard. But Goddard finally received his due, albeit posthumously, when the *New York Times* published an apology to the scientist forty-nine years after his first rocket launch, on the day Apollo 11 headed to the moon. In 1975, the *Times* wrote: "It is now definitely established that the rocket can function in a vacuum. The *Times* regrets the error."

SPORTS

Brown defeated Yale in football, using their starting eleven during the entire game.

1926   New York Yankee slugger Babe Ruth continued to make headlines:
• An Essex Fells, New Jersey, boy developed a case of blood poisoning and was given only a short time to live. Ruth sent a message of encouragement to the boy and then went out and broke a record by hitting three home runs in the World Series. Shortly thereafter, the boy's fever broke, and he made a complete recovery.
• Ruth gathered in what was probably the highest fly ball in history. The ball was dropped 250 feet from an airplane over Mitchell Field, Long Island.

☛ PEOPLE

A well-built young lad named Ronald Reagan, fifteen, was working as a summer lifeguard at a resort near Dixon, Illinois, a job he would hold for the next seven years, and the number 7 would prove to be important in his life. During his seven-year stint as a lifeguard, he saved seventy-seven people from drowning; he acted in his first film in 1937; he was inaugurated as governor of California in 1967 and won a second term in 1970; he accepted his party's presidential nomination in 1980 on 7/17 and celebrated his seventieth birthday just seventeen days after his inauguration; he was shot on his seventieth day in office, the bullet being deflected by his seventh rib. If President Reagan completes his second term, he will be seventy-seven when he leaves the White House.

Robert Todd Lincoln, the son of President Abraham Lincoln, died. A Harvard graduate, Lincoln had served as a captain on General Ulysses S. Grant's staff during the Civil War and had been present when General Robert E. Lee surrendered. He then had pursued a successful career in both business and government service.
The dictates of fate had put Lincoln at the scene of three tragic events in our nation's history—the death of his father by assassination, as well as those of President Garfield and President McKinley. Lincoln had been at his father's bedside when he died; he had served in President Garfield's cabinet and had been at the railroad station in Washington seeing him off on a trip when the chief executive was shot; he had been standing close to McKinley at the Buffalo Exposition when the president received the gunshot wound that resulted in his death. After the McKinley shooting in 1901, Lincoln turned down all invitations to attend events that would include the president, "because there seems to be a certain fatality about presidential functions when I am present."
Lincoln's father and a later president, John Fitzgerald Kennedy, also shared some startling coincidences:
• Lincoln and Kennedy were both shot on a Friday.

- Each man was wounded in the head by a bullet fired from behind him.
- John Wilkes Booth shot Lincoln in a theater and fled to a warehouse; Lee Harvey Oswald shot Kennedy from a warehouse and fled to a theater.
- Lincoln and Kennedy were both followed by presidents named Johnson. Andrew Johnson was born in 1808, Lyndon Johnson in 1908; both were Southerners and Democrats.
- John Wilkes Booth had been born in 1839, Lee Harvey Oswald in 1939.
- Lincoln's secretary, named Kennedy, advised him not to attend the theater the night he was shot; Kennedy's secretary, named Lincoln, tried to discourage JFK from going to Dallas.
- Each of the victim's last names contain seven letters; the full names of the assassins number fifteen letters.
- Both assassins were shot to death before they could stand trial.
- The wives of both presidents spoke French, both were pregnant four times and lost two children, and each miscarried once while living in the White House; neither would return to the White House after her husband's death.
- After Lincoln was buried, his son moved to 3014 N Street in Georgetown. Kennedy's son would move to the same address after his father's burial.
- The car Kennedy was driving in when he was shot was a Lincoln.
- Lincoln was elected to Congress in 1846, Kennedy in 1946.
- Lincoln became president in 1860, Kennedy in 1960.

Seventy-eight-year-old Bobby Leach died in Christchurch, New Zealand. Leach had performed a number of courageous feats in his younger days, including having gone over Niagara Falls twice. As fate would have it, the former daredevil slipped on an orange peel while walking down the street, breaking his leg so badly that it had to be amputated. He died of complications following the operation.

Harry Houdini, the escape artist, died suddenly in 1926. No magician—before or since—has so dazzled the world. Born in Budapest, Hungary, in 1874, Ehrich Weiss had emigrated several weeks later to the United States with his parents, the family settling in Appleton, Wisconsin. Houdini took up magic as a child, and by the age of twenty had become an accomplished illusionist, particularly skilled at removing himself from seemingly escape-proof situations. He had moved his family to New York and taken the name of Houdini because of his admiration for a French magician named Jean Eugène Robert Houdin.

In 1900, Houdini traveled to England and performed a feat that

67

1926 brought him instant worldwide fame, accepting an invitation to attempt an escape from that shrine of law and order, Scotland Yard. Superintendent Melville, the Yard's senior officer, handcuffed him to a pillar in the inner recesses of the prison. But before Melville had left the building, Houdini had freed himself and caught up with the official. Houdini's reputation was made, and a subsequent European tour proved that his escape from Scotland Yard had not been a fluke. He escaped from prisons in Moscow, Amsterdam, Liverpool, and The Hague, and later added the jail of virtually every major city in the United States to his list. But these jailbreaks paled in comparison to some of his other feats:

• He would ask a policeman to put him into a straitjacket of a type reserved for the most violent criminals and mental cases. He then instructed the law officer to secure him with ropes and shackles, turn him upside down, and by means of a rope and pulley, elevate him to a stationary position approximately 75 feet off the ground. He would then quickly free himself in full view of numerous onlookers.

• He once jumped off a bridge into San Francisco Bay with his hands tightly secured behind his back and an iron ball chained to his body, quickly surfacing without his bonds.

• He was tossed into New York City's East River, handcuffed inside a box that was then loaded down with 200 pounds of iron. In under two minutes, he freed himself and was removed from the river unharmed.

How could the great magician manage one apparently impossible escape after another? Many people thought he was blessed with supernatural powers, but Houdini vehemently denied this. After his death, his notebooks supplied some insight into how he managed a number of his tricks, but a review of the material made it quite clear that Houdini's feats could not have been performed without a number of skills and abilities that were unique to him alone.

Houdini may have been one of the finest athletes who ever lived. He could control his body so completely that he could flex each individual muscle and contract it as well. His physical dexterity once enabled him to leap from the wing of one airplane to another while handcuffed. No lock existed that he could not open with ease, an ability that he demonstrated to a group of Europe's leading locksmiths by conquering each one of their supposedly unopenable creations, aided by a tactile sense that was almost superhuman. "His fingers had the strength of pliers and his teeth could be used like a can opener." He also had the capacity to breathe when confined in small spaces, while consuming a minimum of air. Finally, he was blessed with incredible courage, composure under pressure, and a willingness to risk life, limb, and reputation on his seemingly effortless feats of derring-do.

Perhaps Houdini's greatest escape was successfully executed just months before his death. He took his place in a coffin that was carefully

68

sealed before it was dropped into a swimming pool, viewed by a cadre of doctors and nurses who waited patiently for an hour and a half before Houdini freed himself and emerged, submitting to an extensive medical examination that showed no trace of any physical irregularities.

On October 22, Houdini was entertaining several guests after a performance. A student friend named J. Gordon Whitehead asked the illusionist if it were true that he could absorb a blow to the midsection without discomfort. Houdini replied in the affirmative, and Whitehead quickly delivered four tremendous blows to his stomach before Houdini could brace himself for the attack. Houdini soon began to experience tremendous pain and was hospitalized several days later with acute appendicitis. Peritonitis set in, and he died on October 31 at forty-three.

• Producers Charles Dillingham and Florenz Ziegfeld were pallbearers at Houdini's funeral. As they were carrying the casket from the church, Dillingham whispered to Ziegfeld, "Ziggy, I'll bet you a hundred bucks he ain't in here."

1927

Lindbergh flew like a poem into the heart of America.
—Springfield Republican

☞ NATIONAL NEWS

In 1919, A French-born New York hotel owner named Raymond Orteig had offered a prize of $25,000 for the first successful nonstop flight between New York and Paris in either direction. But by the spring of 1927, the prize had not been won because no airplane had sufficient range to cover the more than 3,500 miles that separated the two cities. The nonstop record, established in 1923, was only 2,500 miles, set on a flight from San Diego to New York. But aero technology was expanding rapidly, and a number of top-notch American and European pilots were preparing for the flight, convinced that the prize would be won before 1927 came to an end.

The rules governing the competition placed no limitation on either the size of the aircraft or the crew, and work was underway on both two- and three-engine aircraft, to be manned by crews of from two to four. But there was one exception: a young, lanky, sandy-haired airmail pilot named

70

Charles Lindbergh, twenty-five, who had made a startling decision. Lindbergh would attempt to make the over-the-water trip in a plane with only one engine. And he would make the flight alone.

Lindbergh's decision to go it alone was not the bravado of one who was long on courage but short on brains. The less weight allotted to crew, engines, and gear, reasoned Lindbergh, the more gasoline he could carry; and fuel capacity was critical because the winner would have to travel a thousand miles farther than anyone had ever flown before without refueling. Lindbergh's plane was being made to his specifications by Ryan Airlines in San Diego at a cost of $10,580, part contributed by Lindbergh, the rest underwritten by a group of St. Louis businessmen, and was named *The Spirit of St. Louis* in their honor. Lindbergh's seat in the cockpit was behind the fuel tank, and he would dispense with much of the normal cabin equipment to keep the weight of the aircraft down. No radio, no special instruments for night flying, no gauges for the gas tanks, no sextant—Lindbergh would not even take a parachute because it added twenty pounds. He was offered $1,000 by a stamp collector to carry a pound of mail with him to Paris but declined to add that mere 16 ounces of extra weight as well.

In March 1927, the newspapers were full of news about the preparations of the leading challengers. Anthony Fokker and Igor Sikorsky were building planes for Commander Richard Byrd and René Fonck; the American Legion was funding Commander Noel Davis; and Captain Charles Nungesser and Lieutenant François Coli were going to attempt to win the prize by flying from France against prevailing winds in a biplane with a 450-horsepower engine.

The Spirit of St. Louis was finished on April 28, and Lindbergh was pleased with the results. But on May 8, Nungesser and Coli took off from Le Bourget Field outside Paris. Lindbergh was so convinced of their success that he began to check his charts for a possible flight across the Pacific. Their plane, *White Bird*, was reported sighted several times en route, including over Boston. But whether these sightings were accurate was never known since no trace of Nungesser, Coli, or the plane was ever found.

Hard luck began to plague the other competitors as well. Byrd's Fokker crashed during a test flight; Davis and his copilot, Stanton H. Wooster, were killed when their plane went down in Virginia. Reporters turned their attention to Lindbergh, whom the tabloids dubbed the Flyin' Fool and the Flyin' Kid. He had flown *The Spirit of St. Louis* to Long Island, but a period of poor weather had delayed his departure.

On May 19, Lindbergh and a group of friends were in New York City for dinner and the theater on a dismal rainy evening. But a chance call to the weather bureau brought a prediction of clearing skies over the Atlantic, and they raced back to Long Island, picking up at a local

1927 drugstore five sandwiches, which Lindbergh would take with him on the flight. After an unsuccessful attempt to snatch a few hours' sleep, Lindbergh drove to Curtiss Field, where the weather was still poor but showing signs of improvement. The plane was towed to nearby Roosevelt Field, the gas tanks filled, and Lindbergh climbed into the cockpit. At 7:52 A.M., *The Spirit of St. Louis* lumbered down the runway and climbed with agonizing slowness, clearing the telephone wires at the end of the runway by a scant 20 feet. Lindbergh was on his way to Paris at last.

Lindbergh crossed Long Island Sound and flew over Connecticut at an altitude of 600 feet, flying at an air speed of 102 mph. As he passed over Massachusetts and started the two-hour over-water flight to Nova Scotia, Lindbergh began to feel tired, since he had not slept for over twenty-four hours. But he pressed on. Over Nova Scotia, he ran into fog, heavy rain, and jarring turbulence; when he climbed in search of smoother air, ice began to form on his wings. But soon the air started to warm up as he flew over the Gulf Stream, and although the fog persisted, the terrible threat of ice buildup disappeared as he headed for his next landfall over Ireland.

Seventeen hours into his flight, Lindbergh tried frantically to hold his eyes open with his fingers, but they kept closing; he slapped his face hard but didn't feel a thing. He began to have hallucinations: His childhood raced before him, and he saw dragons and strange shapes in the sea. Realizing that he was fighting for his life, he threw open the cockpit window and sucked in huge breaths of air but still could not shake his drowsiness. And then, as if by magic, and for no logical reason, his head began to clear, and his feeling of fatigue totally disappeared. But had he wandered off course, wasting precious fuel, stretching the flight to Paris even farther? He would just have to wait and see.

Finally, twenty-six hours after leaving Long Island, he saw a seabird, a harbinger of land; shortly thereafter, he spied some fishing boats. He flew down to within a few feet of the water and yelled to a trawler, "Which way to Ireland?" but got no response. Within an hour, he did see land of a beautiful deep green, which he knew had to be Ireland. And miracle of miracles, he was only three miles off his original course and two hours ahead of schedule, meaning that the wind at his back had been stronger than he had thought. He flew over a small village and saw people in the streets waving to him.

Lindbergh pressed on, pushing his air speed to 110 mph. It was nearly dark when he saw the coast of France on the horizon, and he reckoned that he was only a little more than an hour from Paris. He suddenly remembered that he had no visa, and the only clothes he had were on his back. Then Lindbergh realized that he had flown 3,500 miles and had set a new record for nonstop flight in an airplane. To celebrate, he ate a sandwich and drank a little water, the first nourishment he had taken since he had left Long Island.

72

Soon the lights of Paris were ahead, and the jubilant Lindbergh **1927** could not resist circling the Eiffel Tower before heading for Le Bourget Field. As he approached Le Bourget, he wondered why there were so many floodlights but no landing lights to be seen; he also saw what looked like hundreds of automobiles on the road heading to the airport. And then he finally brought the plane into the wind and touched down at 10:22 P.M., thirty-three and a half hours after he had urged *The Spirit of St. Louis* down the runway at Roosevelt Field and headed east.

Just fourteen hours into his flight, a crowd of 40,000 at New York's Yankee Stadium attending the Maloney-Sharkey prizefight had observed a moment of prayer for Lindbergh. But for the first thirty hours of his trip across the Atlantic, there were no reports on his progress; America could only hold its breath and pray that he was making his way safely. When news of his being sighted over Ireland reached the United States, followed by another sighting over the French coast, emotions began to work toward a fever pitch that would culminate in the greatest outpouring of admiration and affection for one man that any individual accomplishment had produced in the history of the United States. Lindbergh had not been the first man to cross the Atlantic by air; in fact, he was the sixty-seventh! But what captivated the world was the fact that he was the first person to do it alone, with only a few of the most rudimentary navigational aids to help him.

The traffic jam that Lindbergh had noticed as he approached Le Bourget was part of a crowd estimated at 100,000 that had come to greet him. They surged past a regiment of soldiers with fixed bayonets and flooded the runway; only Lindbergh's quick thinking, immediately cutting his engine, avoided serious injuries. Before he could alight from the cockpit, his plane was surrounded; he could hear parts of the aircraft cracking and fabric being ripped away from the fuselage by souvenir hunters. "Are there any mechanics here?" he shouted. No response. "Does anyone here speak English?" Again, no response. He was then lifted upon the shoulders of the crowd, his flying helmet ripped from his head.

Somehow he was rescued by two French pilots named Detroyar and Delage, who diverted the crowd and shoved him into their small car, spiriting him away to a nearby hangar. The bona fide reception committee, which included the American ambassador, was a mile away at another part of the field, and Lindbergh never reached them. The two pilots drove Lindbergh to Paris by back roads to avoid traffic and then took him to the Tomb of the Unknown Soldier for a brief ceremonial visit before dropping him off at the U.S. Embassy. It was not until 2:00 A.M. that Ambassador Myron Herrick arrived to greet him; by that time Lindbergh had been given a room, a pair of the ambassador's pajamas, a sandwich, and a glass of milk. When he met with reporters, he told them that

73

1927 he had arrived with a surplus gasoline supply of 85 gallons and judged that he could have flown 500 to 1,000 miles farther. Finally, the reporters dispersed, and at 4:15 A.M., sixty-three hours after his last sleep, Lindbergh went to bed.

It was now left to Lindbergh to deal with the adulation that would roll over him like a giant wave, leaving him with an aversion to publicity and instilling in him a fierce, lifelong determination to maintain his privacy. It was months before Lindbergh was off the front pages of the nation's newspapers; so much recognition came his way that it is impossible to mention it all, but a few highlights are worth noting:

It was estimated that American newspapers upped their consumption of newsprint by 25,000 tons in telling the Lindbergh story. On the day after he arrived in Paris, the *New York Evening World* alone printed 114,000 extra copies, and the *New York Times* devoted its entire front page and five interior pages to the flight.

Excerpts from some of the newspaper editorials are as follows:

• "The greatest feat of a solitary man in the records of the human race." (*New York Evening World*)

• "Lindbergh personifies America . . . every parent sees him as an ideal son." (*Philadelphia Inquirer*)

• The *Washington Post* compared Lindbergh's pioneering spirit and determination to the Pilgrims, George Washington, John Paul Jones, David Farragut, and George Dewey.

• ". . . [Lindbergh] has done more to arouse a common spirit of hero worship than any man of modern times." (*New York Sun*)

• "The last man of his type that Europe knows anything about was George Washington." (*St. Louis Star*)

• "Romance lived again in him." (*New York Post*)

Lindbergh received 3.5 million letters during the twenty-seven day period from May 21 through June 17. Seventy-five percent of the mail came from females, and many of the letters enclosed personal photographs.

The following requests were made of President Coolidge:

• That he forbid Lindbergh to return to the United States by air. (The president sent a naval vessel to pick him up.)

• That May 21 be declared Lindbergh Day, a legal holiday, to commemorate the anniversary of the flight.

• That the gallant flyer be henceforth exempt from paying federal income taxes.

• That a new cabinet post be created for Lindbergh—secretary of aviation.

• That a star be named "Lindbergh."

• That Lindbergh's face join George Washington's on the three-cent stamp used on regular letters in 1927.

74

• That Lindbergh be appointed ambassador-at-large to undertake goodwill missions for the government.

It is estimated that 5,000 poems were written in the pilot's honor and that 250 songs were composed about him between 1927 and 1935, the most popular of which were "When Lindbergh Came Home," by George M. Cohan, and "Lucky Lindy." A dance was created called the "Lindbergh Hop," and a cantata commemorating the flight was written by Paul Hindemith and Kurt Weill.

Named after Lindbergh were hundreds of children, streets, public schools, a Pullman car, and a mountain in Colorado; eleven laundries in New York attempted to use the Lindbergh name.

• Odd things began to happen to the hero: Shirts and handkerchiefs did not come back from the laundry, having been kept as souvenirs; when Lindbergh left a St. Louis picnic, several women battled over custody of the corncobs left on his plate; while he was dining at a hotel one evening, a woman tried to peer into his mouth to identify what he was eating.

• Fifty-five thousand telegrams were sent to Lindbergh, including one with 17,500 signatures; 100,000 San Francisco schoolchildren signed a petition requesting that Lindbergh pay them a visit.

• More than $5 million in offers were received by Lindbergh for films, records, books, personal endorsements, vaudeville tours, newspaper articles, and business partnerships.

• Fifteen thousand gifts were sent from sixty-nine different countries, valued at over $2 million, including an airplane carved from a single diamond and a copy of the Koran.

• The *Boy Scout Handbook* was revamped to show an exemplary young Boy Scout walking shoulder to shoulder with Abraham Lincoln, Theodore Roosevelt, Daniel Boone, and Charles Lindbergh.

• Lindbergh received the Congressional Medal of Honor from President Coolidge, the Langley Medal from the Smithsonian Institution, the Wright Brothers Memorial Trophy, plus fifteen medals and commendations from thirty countries and hundreds of American cities.

• Four million people flooded the streets of New York for a ticker tape parade that still holds the record for the amount of paper rained down from the windows of office buildings.

Charles Lindbergh	(1927)	1,750 tons
Iranian hostages	(1981)	1,260 tons
New York Mets World Series Team	(1969)	1,254 tons

• In 1928, schoolboys in Belleville, New Jersey, were polled to determine whom they would most like to emulate. The results:

1927

Two admitted anarchists, Nicola Sacco and Bartolomeo Vanzetti, were executed in 1927 for robbery and murder of two factory payroll employees in South Braintree, Massachusetts, terminating one of the most controversial legal proceedings in the nation's history and causing demonstrations in cities all over the world.

Since their conviction six years earlier, considerable new evidence had been brought forth indicating that the verdict might well have been a gross miscarriage of justice. But repeated motions for a new trial were denied by Judge Webster Thayer, who was overheard in private referring to the convicted men as "sons of bitches" and "dagos," and who had boasted to a friend, "Did you see what I did to those anarchist bastards?" Said a veteran court reporter of Thayer, "His whole manner, his whole attitude, seemed to be that the jurors were there to convict the men." But while Thayer's objectivity was widely questioned, he alone could order a new trial, and none was forthcoming, and by April 9, 1927, all legal moves by the defense had been exhausted.

Judge Thayer scheduled the executions for the week of July 10, but Governor Alvan Fuller ordered a stay of execution until August 10 so that a special committee could review the case one more time. As committee members, Fuller chose Abbott Lawrence Lowell, president of Harvard, Dr. Samuel W. Stratton, president of MIT, and Robert A. Grant, a former judge.

The Lowell commission did not shirk its duty, hearing all the testimony, including one witness who stated that the foreman of the jury had declared before the trial, "Damn them, they ought to hang anyway." Although the commission members deplored Judge Thayer's "grave breach of official decorum" in making his out-of-courtroom pronouncements, they supported his decision.

There were riots from Warsaw to Japan, from Buenos Aires to Paris, Communists happily fanning the flames. Albert Einstein protested the sentence, as did George Bernard Shaw, H. G. Wells, John Dos Passos, H. L. Mencken, Arthur Schlesinger, Samuel Eliot Morison, Felix Frankfurter, Dorothy Parker, Robert Benchley, and a Frenchman who had been tried in another trial witnessed by the world, Alfred Dreyfus. But to no

avail. Sacco and Vanzetti died on August 23, 1927, in the electric chair. **1927**
Whether they were guilty or not is still debated today. Respected historian Francis Russell wrote a book in 1961 called *Tragedy in Dedham,* in which he concluded, after modern spectographic tests, that Sacco's pistol was indeed the murder weapon. Plays were written about the case, evidence examined and reexamined, and thousands were left with the belief that Sacco and Vanzetti had died for crimes they had not committed.

President Coolidge left Washington in an eight-car special train for a summer vacation in rural South Dakota. On August 2, newsmen were summoned to a local schoolhouse for a press conference. Once assembled, reporters were asked to file past the chief executive, who handed each one a piece of paper containing but eight words, "I do not choose to run in 1928." When asked if he had additional words to add to his statement, Coolidge replied, "None."

News of Coolidge's decision not to seek four more years in the White House shocked the country, since he was considered a shoo-in for another term.

• Rapid City, South Dakota, police found an automobile that had seen far better days. Written on the windshield were the words, "I do not choose to run in 1928."

Yet another Model T Ford came off the assembly line, the last of 15,077,033 produced, all black, and auto buffs could hardly wait for its successor, the Model A, an event described by one author as "one of the great events of the year 1927; not so thrilling as Lindbergh's flight, but rivaling the execution of Sacco and Vanzetti." The *New York Herald Tribune* estimated that 1 million New Yorkers lined up for a look at the new Ford when it was introduced on December 2, beginning at 3:00 A.M. Mounted police were called out to control huge crowds in Cleveland. In Kansas City, platforms had to be built to raise the automobile high enough so that everyone who had flocked to Convention Hall could see it. Ford salesmen took orders by the thousands in colors such as Arabian Sand and Niagara Blue. A Ford spokesman said:

> Good-looking as that car is, its performance is better than its appearance. We don't brag about it, but it has done seventy-one miles an hour. It will ride along a railroad track without bouncing, and you can drive across the rails, if you can find a place to do it, without pitching. It's the smoothest thing you ever rode in.

☞ FOREIGN NEWS

Italy

Vacationing in Rome, British Chancellor of the Exchequer Winston Churchill lauded the Fascist movement and its leader, Benito Mussolini: "I must say that your movement has rendered a service to the world." Discussing Mussolini, Churchill remarked, "I could not help being charmed by his gentle simple bearing and his calm, detached poise."

Little Bruno Mussolini, nine, underwent an oral grammar examination concerning the use of the imperative mood in the first, second, and third persons.

> EXAMINER: Now, Bruno, tell me, in what person one commands?
>
> BRUNO: There are two persons one cannot command—the King and my father.

Canada

Ontario liquor authorities tried to put a damper on Americans who crossed the border for a quick visit to slake their thirst for alcoholic beverages, declaring that "excursionists" and "American visitors" would not be served, although legitimate "tourists" staying for longer periods were permitted to imbibe. However, bartenders and innkeepers found it difficult to differentiate between weekend drinkers and legitimate vacationers, and both groups had no trouble tippling to their hearts' content.

☞ REGIONAL NEWS

California

Kern County, California, officials were up in arms. Attracted by local corn and barley crops, mice had invaded the area and multiplied rapidly until they were estimated to have reached a total population of 100 million. Houses and barns were teeming with the little rodents, and although thousands were exterminated each day, thousands more took their place. Cries for help were finally answered by the aptly named Samuel E. Piper of the U.S. Biological Survey. No, Piper did not lead the mice out of Kern County by enticing them with his flute music. But he did solve the problem aided by forty tons of alfalfa mixed with strychnine, and Kern County farmers were no longer under a state of siege.

North Carolina

The North Carolina supreme court ruled that it was permissible to flog convicts for various offenses.

Pennsylvania and New York

A team of stallions became the last fire horses retired from the Philadelphia Fire Department. In Rochester, New York, a tribute was paid to the animals that had served their fire department so well, and a parade was held in their honor. A commemorative brass tablet read, "Our fire horses, glorious in beauty and in service. Faithful friends, we cannot call them dumb because they spoke in deed every hour of danger. Perpetual remembrance enshrines their loyalty and courage."

☛ TRENDS

Americans were abandoning their forefathers' credo that one only purchased items by paying cash and that incurring debt was the work of the devil. Six billion dollars in installment-plan sales were recorded in 1927, approximately 15 percent of total purchases.

Housewives were being tempted by a variety of electrical appliances that promised a reduction in the time and energy that went into housework, including vacuum cleaners, irons, toasters, and fans to provide a welcome breeze on hot summer days. The electrification of America was spreading from the rich to the average family, and between 1913 and 1927, the number of homes with electricity increased by nearly 500 percent.

☛ TRANSPORTATION

The Aeronautical Chamber of Commerce reported that only 7,651 airline tickets had been purchased in 1926. While three times faster than train travel, flying was also three times as expensive. Nevertheless, the industry was betting on the future, and the number of airlines would increase rapidly. Eight passenger lines were operating in 1927, and the following figures compare train travel to air travel in cost and time between selected cities:

	AIR TRAVEL		TRAIN TRAVEL	
ROUTE	TIME	FARE	TIME	FARE
Chicago to San Francisco	22 hr 40 min	$200.00	68 hr	$79.84
New York to Boston	3 hr 5 min	30.00	5 hr 30 min	8.24
Portland to Los Angeles	11 hr 15 min	113.50	39 hr 30 min	40.88
Salt Lake City to Los Angeles	7 hr 15 min	60.00	30 hr	28.05
Chicago to Minneapolis	5 hr 50 min	40.00	12 hr	14.66
Cheyenne to Pueblo	3 hr	25.00	8 hr	8.16
Detroit to Grand Rapids	1 hr 45 min	18.00	4 hr	5.49
San Diego to Los Angeles	1 hr 10 min	17.50	3 hr 30 min	4.55

☞ LANGUAGE

Ohio State Professor George A. Knight was shocked by the unflattering terms used by his male English students to describe an unpopular female, citing the following examples: mess, flat tire, nutcracker face, crumb, oil can, rag, gloom, drag, chunk of lead, tomato, priss, dead one, lemon, pickle, and pill. For the popular ones, Knight's charges used descriptors like flesh-and-blood, angel, thrill, pretty Genevieve, snappy piece of work, sweetness, choice bit of calico, sweet patootie, star, pippin, baby vamp, whiz, live one, belle, bird, and peach.

Time added some of its own:

Unpopular Girl	*Popular Girl*
pig's coattail	tidy unit
washout	warm baby
sad Sadie	knockout
hard-boiled virgin	panic
dizzy egg	riot
teaser	red-hot witch
gripe	
bug-eyed Betty	

Princeton students were infuriated by a university decision no longer allowing undergraduates to keep motor vehicles at the college. They retaliated by harassing Dean Christian Gauss with a variety of pranks, including buzzing his office in airplanes flown at extremely low altitudes, since planes had not been included in the motor vehicle ban. But Dean Gauss remained cool and firm, stating: "We have so many machines on the ground, that we do not bother particularly about those up in the air, as a fleet of pursuit planes would be needed for effective control. Anyone may fly over Princeton—but if he lands here, and runs along the ground, we shall class his plane as a motor vehicle and return him and it to his parents."

🖝 ENTERTAINMENT

Singer-comedian Joe E. Lewis was performing at the Green Mill, a Chicago watering spot, where he was being paid $650 a week. Enticed by an offer of $1,000 a week, he moved to the New Rendezvous Café, despite threats from "Machine Gun" Jack McGurn, who had been offered part ownership in the Green Mill if he could persuade the popular entertainer to remain there. Infuriated by his departure from the Green Mill, McGurn sent three thugs to even his score with Lewis; they fractured his skull and sliced his jaw, tongue, and vocal cords with a knife. Although a six-hour operation saved his life, it would be nearly a year before he would speak, read, or write again; ten years would pass before he worked his way back to the top of his profession, performing only as a comic because he could no longer sing.

Lewis later received $10,000 from McGurn's boss, who may have regretted the severity of the reprisal. The man with the apparently guilty conscience was a gangster named Al Capone.

Hollywood actress Norma Talmadge tripped while walking outside Hollywood's Grauman's Chinese Theater, stepping into the wet cement of a newly laid section of sidewalk. Press agents capitalized on the chance event by making it a mandatory ritual of stardom to leave one's hand- or footprint in fresh cement outside Grauman's.

Al Jolson, forty-two, starred in the movie *The Jazz Singer*, often referred to as the first "talkie" made in the United States. The movie *Don Juan* had appeared in 1926 with no dialogue but accompanied by the recorded music of the New York Philharmonic Orchestra. *The Jazz Singer*

1927 contained some singing, musical accompaniment, and dialogue but did not have sound throughout. The first full-length movie that was a "talkie" from start to finish was *Lights of New York*, a Warner's Vitaphone production that would premiere in 1928.

The first Academy Awards presentation was held at Hollywood's Roosevelt Hotel on May 16, 1927, with the gold statuettes being awarded by the Academy of Motion Picture Arts and Sciences, recently founded by Louis B. Mayer. *Wings* was named the best picture, while Emil Jannings and twenty-one-year-old Janet Gaynor were chosen best actor and best actress, based on the quality of their acting in all the films that they had made during the previous year, although the awards would later be given for individual film performances. A crowd of 250 attended the first awards ceremony.

The coveted statuettes, known as "Oscars," were made by the Dodge Trophy Company, as they are today. They are 92.5 percent tin with a coating of gold, stand 13 inches high, and weigh 8 pounds, depicting a strong man brandishing a crusader's sword, perched upon a roll of film.

The origin of the name "Oscar" is much debated and is credited both to movie columnist Sidney Skolsky and to actress Bette Davis, whose reaction upon seeing the statuette for the first time was said to have been that it looked like her Uncle Oscar.

☞ MEDIA

On January 1, 1927, the first two national radio broadcasts took place: the Rose Bowl football game, followed by a concert featuring the New York Symphony Orchestra.

Robert L. Ripley's syndicated newspaper column, "Believe It or Not," featured a man who would capture the imagination of millions of readers—a one-armed paperhanger.

☞ PEOPLE

When California patron of the arts Henry F. Huntington was close to death, he summoned esteemed art dealer Joseph Duveen and purveyor of rare books A. S. N. Rosenback to his bedside. The two men had sold the Southern Pacific Railroad mogul a good portion of his art and rare book collections, to be valued upon his death of $30 million. When asked why Duveen and Rosenback had been asked to visit him when he was in

such poor health, Huntington explained that he wanted to die like Christ, **1927**
between two thieves.

Lizzie Borden died at sixty-six, having enjoyed considerable notorie-
ty in 1892 when she was found not guilty of the murder of her father and
stepmother in Fall River, Massachusetts. When Lizzie was a small child,
her mother had died, and shortly afterward her father had remarried.
Lizzie and her older sister were not fond of their stepmother, and time
only increased their dislike. On the morning of August 4, 1892, Lizzie
found the mutilated body of her father, apparently the victim of blows
from an axe; a short time afterward, her stepmother's body was discovered
in the family home, similarly disfigured. Police would later determine
that her father had been killed with ten blows from a hatchet, her
stepmother with nineteen, and an examination of the bodies indicated
that Mrs. Borden had predeceased her husband by approximately one
hour. Shortly thereafter, Lizzie was discovered attempting to burn a dress
in the kitchen stove and was placed under arrest for both crimes.
Although the prosecution produced considerable evidence against her, it
was mostly ambiguous, and she was acquitted. Lizzie remained in Fall
River for the rest of her life, but many of the townsfolk refused to talk to
her, feelings against her having been inflamed by considerable newspaper
publicity and this bit of inaccurate rhyme that was on everyone's lips:

> Lizzie Borden took an axe
> And gave her mother forty whacks,
> And when she saw what she had done
> She gave her father forty-one.

☛ FOOD AND DRINK

Peter Paul Halagian had started the Peter Paul Company in 1919,
later to be famous for two of America's favorite candy bars, Mounds and
Almond Joy. He and five fellow Armenian immigrants sold homemade
candy and ice cream in Torrington, Connecticut, and one of their early
attempts at advertising was a handbill that read as follows:

> Peter Paul has very good food
> You don't throw any down the chute
> His delicious ice cream your dreams will haunt
> The more you eat, the more you want
> Ice cream soda the year around

1927

No better soda was ever found
His homemade candy will make you fat
To Peter Paul take off your hat.

☞ SPORTS

No previous era in American history produced more sports heroes than the 1920s—Jack Dempsey, Gene Tunney, Johnny Weismuller, Gertrude Ederle, Bobby Jones, Walter Hagen, Red Grange, Ty Cobb, and the incomparable Bill Tilden, to name just a few in the galaxy of stars. But no athlete so awed the public as did George Herman Ruth, the mighty Babe, also referred to by the press as the Big Bambino, the Mauling Mastodon, the Behemoth of Bust, the Mammoth of Maul, the Colossus of Clout, the Sultan of Swat, a modern Beowulf, the Prince of Powders, the Mauling Monarch, the Blunderbuss, the Rajah of Rap, and the Wazir of Wham.

At eight, Ruth was no stranger to alcohol, chewing tobacco, and petty crime. His incarceration in St. Mary's Industrial School, his learning to play baseball there, and his signing a baseball contract with the Baltimore Orioles while still in his teens—all are part of a legend well known to every baseball fan. By twenty-four, Ruth was the best left-handed pitcher in baseball, but his pitching days were numbered, for he could hit a baseball harder, higher, and farther than anyone playing the game. In 1919, during spring training, Ruth had hit a ball over the wall of a stadium in Tampa. When it had gone over the railroad tracks and had finally come to rest, the ball was just 3 feet short of 600 feet away from home plate.

Until Ruth took charge, baseball had been a game of singles—of batters protecting the plate, just trying to make contact with the ball. If they managed a one-bagger, they hoped to be advanced to second and then sent home with another single, and low-scoring games were the norm. Home runs were few and far between, and "Home Run" Baker came by his lofty nickname after leading the league with a grand total of twelve.

Ruth had come to Boston to play for the Red Sox when the Orioles had experienced financial difficulties and had put their stars on the block for cash. Ruth had come to the Yankees for the same reason, commanding a price of $100,000 plus a $300,000 loan, then an astronomical sum for a player. After he had hit twenty-nine home runs in 1919, crowds flocked to see him work his wonders with a bat.

In 1920, Ruth had virtually doubled his home-run output—hitting fifty-four, just twice as many as Edward Williamson had managed with the Chicago Colts in 1884 when he had established a record that Ruth had

84

broken the year before. To illustrate just how prodigious a task Ruth had performed, it is worth noting that the 1920 American League runner-up to the Babe had managed nineteen, while the National League leader had hit but fifteen.

The Babe's off-the-field exploits equaled his actions at the plate. He drove his cream-colored convertible like Toad of Toad Hall, leaving pedestrians scattered in his wake; Ruth consumed huge meals and drank the night away, often in the company of one or more young ladies of dubious virtue. One sportswriter remembers Ruth as, "a large man in a camel's hair coat and camel's hair cap, standing in front of a hotel, his broad nostrils sniffing at the promise of the night." And when Ruth traveled with the team, his responsibilities as a player did little to diminish his carousing. When Ruth's on-the-road roommate was asked to describe what it was like to have shared quarters with the slugger, he replied, "I didn't room with Ruth, I roomed with his suitcase." Wild living was not only Ruth's style, but it was highly necessary to his on-field productivity. When restricted to quarters, he would invariably fall into a slump. But when left to roam at will, the Babe could stay out on the town all night, show up at the ballpark sleepless and hung over, and then proceed to smash out a batch of hits.

In 1927, Ruth was on another home-run tear and hoped to exceed his record of fifty-nine. And opposing pitchers could not afford to walk him because he was followed in the batting order by Lou Gehrig, who finished the year with a .373 batting average and hit forty-seven homers of his own. The rest of the supporting cast included Earl Coombs, who batted, .356, Bob Meusel .337, and Tony Lazzeri .309—aptly named Murderers' Row. The 1927 Yankees won 110 games and are the selection of most sportswriters as the best team in the history of the game.

Early in August, Ruth had hit only thirty-five home runs, well below a record-setting pace. But then the Babe shifted into high gear, hitting fifteen in the next month. But with nine games left in the season, Ruth still needed seven homers to break his record, a giant task even for the Babe. He was so concerned that his bat might be stolen during the stretch drive that he carried it with him while circling the bases after home run number fifty-six. With three games to go, Ruth needed three more homers and added two that day. He hit number 60 on the next-to-last day of the season off a pitcher named Tom Zachary. In his first three times at bat, the Babe had hit two singles and walked; on his final trip to the plate, he knew that he could not expect a decent pitch from Zachary. Sure enough, a curve ball was thrown in the general vicinity of the Babe's head. Of course, Ruth hit the unhittable pitch down the right field foul line and into the stands. Ruth said, "That's sixty home runs, count 'em. Sixty. Let's see some other SOB hit sixty home runs." Years later, when the impact of

1927 Ruth's achievement had settled in, Zachary commented, "If I'da known it was gonna be a famous record, I'da stuck it in his ear."

• "Born? Hell, Babe Ruth wasn't born. The sonofabitch fell from a tree?" (Joe Dugan)

• "It was part of our national history that all boys dream of being Babe Ruth before they are anyone else." (Jimmy Cannon)

• "You know, I saw it all happen, from beginning to end. But sometimes I still can't believe what I saw: This nineteen-year-old kid, crude, poorly educated, only lightly brushed by the social veneer we call civilization, gradually transformed into the idol of American youth and the symbol of baseball the world over—a man loved by more people and with more intensity of feeling than perhaps has ever been equaled before or since." (Harry Hooper)

• Sportswriter Grantland Rice asked Ruth to join him on his weekly radio show. To ensure a smooth performance, Rice supplied Ruth in advance with the answers to the questions he would be asked. In response to one question, Ruth replied: "Well, you know, Granny, Duke Ellington said the Battle of Waterloo was won on the playing fields of Elkton." After the show, Rice confronted the Babe. "Babe, the Ellington for the Duke of Wellington I understand. But how did you ever read Eton, Elkton? That's in Maryland, isn't it?" Responded Ruth, "I married my first wife there, and I always hated the goddam place."

On September 22, 1927, Gene Tunney defended his heavyweight title against Jack Dempsey in Chicago. As an underdog, Tunney had beaten Dempsey a year earlier in Philadelphia, and the rematch attracted a crowd of 140,000 to Soldiers' Field. Twenty-four special trains brought boxing fans from all over the country, the Twentieth Century Limited arriving from New York in seven sections, each carrying eleven Pullman cars; twelve hundred reporters were on hand, as well as six governors and a smattering of royalty, and the gate was a record-high $2,658,000. Graham McNamee brought the fight to a radio audience estimated at 60 million. Among the listeners were the inmates of Sing Sing Prison, who had been allowed to stay up beyond their normal bed hour to listen to the bout.

Jack Dempsey had been born in a small Montana mining town called Manassa, which had contributed to his nickname, the "Manassa Mauler." One of eleven children, Dempsey had left home at sixteen, moving about the country from job to job while training to be a boxer. Fighting first as Kid Blackie, Dempsey won most of his bouts, but failed to attract much attention until he caught the eye of promoter-manager Jack Kearns, who took him under his wing. Although he fought as a heavyweight at weights in the 180s and low 190s, Dempsey was so tough and mean that he defeated many much heavier opponents.

Dempsey held the title for seven years until he had been upset by **1927** Tunney in 1926. He had been an extremely unpopular champion whom the public did not take to until his bouts with Tunney, a boxer whom the fans liked even less than Dempsey. Two false rumors haunted Dempsey: that he had dodged the draft in World War I and that he fought with his hands encased in plaster of paris. He was also notorious, and rightfully so, for punching his opponents in the testicles, when the opportunity presented itself, as a means of testing their resolve.

Gene Tunney had been born in New York City in 1898 and had dropped out of school to go to work. He had fought in amateur bouts, turning pro at the beginning of World War I. Enlisting in the Marine Corps, he had won many fights as a light heavyweight while in the service and had taken the title in that division in 1922, advancing to the heavyweight class in 1924. The fact that Tunney held the boxing profession in low regard alienated fight fans, as did his relationship with a Greenwich, Connecticut, socialite, whom he would later marry. He just was not one of the boys, announcing after the first Dempsey fight that he was retiring to his hotel for a good cup of tea. Then Tunney had committed a public relations gaffe of major proportions, downplaying Lindbergh's heroism with the statement, "He had a wonderful motor." But if Tunney's relations with the fans were poor, they sank to rock bottom in 1928 when he lectured on Shakespeare at Yale.

The fight was extremely close for the first six rounds, scorers giving Tunney a slight edge. But in the seventh round, Dempsey sent Tunney to the canvas. The referee delayed the start of his count because the Manassa Mauler remained standing over the prostrate Tunney instead of moving to a neutral corner as the rules required. Dempsey later explained this by saying, "I couldn't move. I just couldn't. I wanted him to get up. I wanted to kill the son of a bitch." When the referee finally shoved Dempsey into a neutral corner and began to count, Tunney had gained considerable time to collect himself, rose at the count of eight, and went on to retain his title with a fifteen-round decision in a fight that would be known thereafter as the fight with the "long count."

1928

O hush thee, my babe, granny's bought some more shares.
Daddy's gone to play with the bulls and the bears.
Mother's buying on tips and she simply can't lose.
And baby shall have some expensive new shoes.

—Anonymous

☞ NATIONAL NEWS

The years of Calvin Coolidge's presidency had been placid ones, devoid of major foreign entanglements and domestic problems, a period of economic prosperity in the United States. Republican politicos were reluctant to rock a boat that sailed upon a sea of such tranquility and lobbied the president to reconsider his decision not to seek another term. But Coolidge's resolve remained firm, keeping him from a presidential campaign that became one of the most bitter in our nation's history. Protestants were pitted against Catholics, rural folk against big-city dwellers, Prohibition supporters against "wets," with the Ku Klux Klan fanning flames of hatred with a fusillade of inflammatory rhetoric.

The standard-bearer of the Democratic Party was Alfred Emanuel Smith, fifty-five, four-time governor of New York, the first Catholic to run for the presidency. Born in New York City, the diminutive Smith stood but 5 feet 7 inches tall and dressed in expensive suits and a brown derby, which had become his trademark. An affable man, he was a proficient joke teller and raconteur, who was seldom without a cigar and could be persuaded to take a drink now and again, despite the prevailing law of the land.

Smith had left school at an early age to work at the Fulton Fish Market and to run errands for Tammany Hall, the city's controlling political force. In 1903, Tammany had backed his candidacy for the state legislature, where he spent the next twelve years, the last two as speaker. He then served as sheriff of New York County, a political plum rumored to be worth $50,000 a year to the lucky officeholder, followed by two years as head of the city's board of aldermen. Smith was elected governor in 1918, only to be swept from office by the Republican landslide of 1920 that elevated Warren Harding to the White House. (New York governors were then elected every two years.) Undaunted, he was returned to Albany in 1922 with the largest plurality in the state's history and was reelected in both 1924 and 1926.

Despite his Tammany roots, Al Smith had been an honest, efficient, and humanitarian governor who pioneered social reforms such as rent control, minimum wage, low-cost housing, equal pay for women, and restricted hours for child workers. Labeling him the Happy Warrior, Franklin Roosevelt had put his name into nomination at the 1924 Democratic Convention, where Smith and William McAdoo were deadlocked until the 103rd ballot and John Davis was selected as a compromise candidate. Four years later, Smith was an easy victor on the first ballot.

Opposing Smith was Herbert Clark Hoover, fifty-four, who had won world renown as administrator of food supplies during World War I, followed by eight highly successful years as secretary of commerce under both Harding and Coolidge. Born in West Branch, Iowa, of Quaker parents, he became both the first president born west of the Mississippi and the first Quaker to occupy the White House. His father had died when he was six, his mother when he was eight, and he was sent to Oregon to be brought up by his maternal uncle. His proficiency in mathematics won him a place in what became Stanford University's first graduating class, despite English scores that were below standard. At Stanford, he held several jobs to finance his education, leaving him with time to earn only average grades. But he was a class leader, writing a campus constitution that has been little changed to this day; he was also elected treasurer of his class, the last elective office he held before winning the presidency of the United States.

At Stanford, Hoover had developed an interest in geology and mining, and the department head arranged summer jobs for him with geological surveys. But when he graduated in 1895, the only job he could find was working as a laborer in a Nevada silver mine on the ten-hour

1928 night shift, working seven days a week, for $2 a day. He then went to work for an eminent engineer in San Francisco, who was so impressed with Hoover that he recommended him for a job running a gold mine in Australia at a salary of $600 a week, although the specifications for the position required a man about thirty-five with considerable mining experience. The twenty-three-year-old Hoover grew a beard en route to his new post to suggest maturity beyond his meager years.

Over the next sixteen years, Hoover lived in Australia, China, Japan, New Zealand, India, Rhodesia, Egypt, Burma, Ceylon, Italy, Russia, Korea, Germany, and France, becoming a superb and much-sought-after mining engineer. He was also a talented executive with awesome administrative skills. By the age of forty, he had firmly established his company as a leader in world mining, with offices in San Francisco, New York, London, Melbourne, and Shanghai, and Hoover had become a multimillionaire. Just under six feet tall and stocky in build, he was shy, serious in demeanor, and deeply religious; his life centered around family, work, and church. His wife Lou, also a Stanford graduate, and their children often joined him in his travels; their firstborn son had circled the globe several times before his third birthday. Even in his hobbies, Hoover stayed close to his profession, he and his wife translating *De re metallica* into English, a sixteenth-century mining treatise written in Latin, whose technical terms had baffled many leading scholars. It took the couple fifteen years to master the work, visiting many of the ancient mines and duplicating numerous experiments described in the text. Hoover also found time to write *Principles of Mining*, published in 1909, which endured for decades as a college textbook.

With his stature in his profession and personal wealth assured, Hoover was eager to abide by the tenets of his religion and to give back something to the world in which he had prospered. So he embarked upon a career of public service that would last for over forty years, refusing any remuneration for his work. When he became involved in government jobs with set salaries, he always endorsed his checks to some deserving charity.

In 1914, his first challenge was the evacuation of 200,000 Americans stranded in Europe at the outset of World War I, many without funds. Hoover then headed up the Committee for Relief in Belgium, which literally saved that nation from starvation. His next post was directing the U.S. Food Administration, a massive undertaking that controlled the output and consumption of food in the United States as well as its distribution to our armed forces in Europe and to our allies. By the end of the war, he was known by such titles as the "Great Humanitarian" and the "Food Czar," and in the United States a new word entered into the language—to "hooverize," meaning to economize. A few quotes suggest
90

how extensively the shy Quaker was lionized both at home and abroad at
the end of World War I:

• "Never was a nobler work of disinterested goodwill carried through with more tenacity and sincerity and skill and with less thanks ever asked." (Economist John Maynard Keynes)

• "The biggest man who has emerged on the Allied side during the war." (*London Nation*)

• "Mr. Hoover is the food regulator of the world." (General John Pershing)

In 1919, a *New York Times* poll to determine the ten most important living Americans found Hoover among the top vote getters. A future Democratic Party protagonist named Franklin Delano Roosevelt penned a note to a colleague saying, "Herbert Hoover is certainly a winner, and I wish we could make him President of the United States."

But Hoover had been a registered Republican since he reached his majority and was offered his choice between the Interior and Commerce departments when Warren Harding was doling out cabinet posts. While Hoover was considering these assignments, his determination to pursue a career of public service was tested by what may at the time have been the most lucrative job offer in the history of American business. The Guggenheim family, one of the wealthiest families in the world, asked Hoover to administer its gigantic mining assets, offering him a full partnership in the family business at a minimum annual salary of $500,000. Although he must have undergone at least a few moments of temptation, he accepted the Department of Commerce appointment, a job that he carried out with his usual energy, skill, and imagination, instigating significant reforms. But one goal of Hoover's was not accomplished, because President Coolidge refused to act. This was Hoover's desire to curb the inflation of credit that was feeding Wall Street speculation. Coolidge's dedication to letting business alone could not be swayed, and his unwillingness to dampen speculation would contribute significantly to the financial catastrophe that lay ahead. Hoover won the Republican presidential nomination easily, but it was not at the behest of the scions of Wall Street; they feared he would institute credit restrictions that would end the halcyon days of the bull market.

The 1928 campaign was the first in which radio played a significant role, and the use of the medium by the presidential candidates portrayed two vastly different styles. The shy, withdrawn, and professorial Hoover contrasted to the down-to-earth, extrovertish Smith, who was at ease with the working man, speaking in a New York accent that many heartland Americans had never heard before, with words like "foist," "poisonally," "raddeo," and "horspital"—not to mention "dese, dem, and dose"—wafting across the airwaves. On the issues, there was very little to differentiate the candidates. Will Rogers commented:

1928 I have been studying the parties and here is the difference. Hoover wants all the drys and as many wets as possible. Smith wants all the wets and as many drys as possible. Hoover says he will relieve the farmer even if he has to call Congress. Smith says he will relieve the farmer even if he has to appoint a commission. Hoover says the tariff will be kept up. Smith says the tariff will not be lowered. Hoover is in favor of prosperity. Smith says he highly endorses prosperity. Hoover wants no votes merely on account of religion. Smith wants no votes solely on religious grounds. Both would accept Muhammed votes if offered. . . . If a man could tell the difference between the two parties, he could make a sucker out of Solomon.

But if substantive issues failed to set the candidates apart, emotional issues did, and the two presidential aspirants did not profit or suffer equally. Hoover emerged relatively unscathed, while Smith was snowed under by a blizzard of abuse. His Tammany Hall roots, his religion, and his supposed intention to end Prohibition brought about reactions like these:

• When Smith's campaign reached Billings, Montana, the Ku Klux Klan welcomed him with a giant burning cross set on a prominently visible hillside. Leaflets were distributed claiming that if Smith were elected, "bootleggers and harlots would dance on the White House lawn."

• Anti-Catholic forces distributed copies of *The Awful Disclosures of Maria Monk,* a book about the sexual escapades of priests and nuns.

• Another leaflet warned:

> When the Catholics rule the United States
> And the Jew grows a Christian nose on his face
> When Pope Pius is head of the Ku Klux Klan
> In the land of Uncle Sam
> Then Al Smith will be our president
> And the country not worth a damn.

• "It is not that Governor Smith is a Catholic and a wet which makes himself an offense to the village and town dwellers, but because his record shows the kind of President he would make—a Tammany President. . . . Tammany is Tammany, and Smith is its prophet." (William Allen White, *Emporia* [Kansas] *Gazette*)

But even without this incredible albatross of ill feeling, it is doubtful if Smith could have overcome what to many was the central issue of the campaign, the last four years of prosperity under a Republican president. Will Rogers wrote about Al Smith during the campaign, "Some have suggested that he would be elected if he changed his religion and turned Protestant. I think it would do more good if he kept his religion and turned Republican." People wanted to believe what Hoover had said in his speech accepting the Republican nomination: "We in America today are nearer to the final triumph over poverty than ever before in the history of the land. The poorhouse is vanishing from among us."

On November 6, Hoover won 58 percent of the popular vote and carried forty states, among them Al Smith's native New York, as he garnered 444 electoral votes to Smith's 87. After the election, a joke made the rounds that Al Smith had sent the following one-word telegram to the Pope: "UNPACK." Hoover's postelection statement probably summed it up best: "Prosperity was on my side."

Unfortunately, it would not stay on his side for long. In an editorial summing up 1928, the *New York Times* described the year as "a twelvemonth of unprecedented advance, of wonderful prosperity." Surely this euphoric view of America in 1928 was supported by the stock market, which continued to soar to new heights. Americans were traveling to Europe in droves, the Department of Commerce reporting that 437,000 people had left the United States by steamer for foreign climes, where they spent an estimated $650 million. But though no one paid much attention at the time, there were some signs that all was not totally well in the supposed land of milk and honey, signs that Monday morning quarterbacks later cited as precursors of bad economic times to come:

• Factory employment was down for the first time in a century, the AFL reporting that 18 percent of its members had been laid off.

• Thirty percent of the coal miners were without jobs, and many textile mills and shoe factories were closing down in New England; a canvass of Baltimore homes by local police found 43 percent of the work force unemployed.

Americans were learning that they did not have to have cash to buy the things they wanted. The percentage of goods purchased on credit moved steadily ahead in 1928: furniture (85 percent), phonographs (80 percent), washing machines (75 percent), and refrigerators (70 percent). But installment buying was not the only way to avoid paying hard cash. The charge account was gaining in popularity, and if you could not charge, you just went around the corner to Beneficial, Household, or one of the other finance companies that were growing at the rate of 30 percent a year. Better to get some extra cash there than face the steely eye of your conservative banker, who was likely to be sticky about annoying things like collateral for your loan or too much debt outstanding. So Americans were buying with money they did not have, a skill that they would develop even further in the future with the advent of credit cards.

☞ FOREIGN NEWS

Spain
The Spanish government enacted a bullfighting law to protect picadors and their horses from the bulls. Picadors were required to cover their legs with steel plating and their horses with protective padding.

Portugal
Portugal also passed some bullfighting legislation, banning the killing of bulls. Corridas would continue, but participating bulls were to be returned to their pastures after their afternoon's work.

England
England lowered the voting age for females from thirty to twenty-one, the same age as for males.

Soviet Union
Stalin inaugurated the first of a series of Five Year Plans in an attempt to increase productivity, incurring the wrath of Russian farmers by establishing collective farms, often by ruthless means. Many farmers protested by setting fire to their crops, destroying their livestock, and stashing their grain in hidden bins to evade collection by the government.

☞ REGIONAL NEWS

Nebraska
A summer storm sent a giant hailstone to the ground at Potter, Nebraska, which weighed in at 1.5 pounds.

Texas
An office building in San Antonio, Texas, was built to include central air-conditioning, an American first.

West Virginia
While tilling the soil of his farm, farmer William Hones came upon a shiny stone that appeared to be covered with grease. Hones put the stone away and would not find out until fifteen years later that he was the proud possessor of a 32-carat diamond. Though the bulk of the world's diamonds are mined in South Africa, large gems have been found in the American

interior, the largest of which was a 40-carat diamond unearthed in **1928** Murfreesboro, Arkansas.

☞ FOLKWAYS AND MORES

Professor Paul H. Nystrom had been keeping tabs on the length that American women were wearing their skirts by taking periodic measurements and plotting them on a graph. In 1919, Nystrom's average distance from earth to hem had been between 6 and 7 inches. By 1928, the graph showed that shirts had risen to knee length, where they would remain until late 1929.

The divorce rate showed a steady increase, having risen from 8.8 divorces per hundred marriages in 1910 to 13.4 in 1920, and 16.5 in 1928, almost double the 1910 figure. Author Frederick Lewis Allen wrote:

> There was a corresponding decline in the amount of disgrace accompanying divorce. In the urban communities, men and women who had been divorced were now socially accepted without question; indeed, there was often about the divorced person just enough of a touch of scarlet to be considered rather dashing and desirable. Many young women probably felt as did the New York girl who said, toward the end of the decade, that she was thinking of marrying Henry, although she didn't care very much for him, because even if they didn't get along, she could get a divorce and "it would be much more exciting to be a divorcee than to be an old maid."

☞ PROHIBITION

Chicago police estimated the number of stills in one area of the city at 100 per block.

City officials in North Tarrytown, New York, asked residents not to dispose of the residue from their stills through the town's sewer system, which had become clogged with grain, potato peelings, and all manner of material from base products used to make alcoholic beverages, including prune pits.

A San Francisco jury was indicted for destroying evidence in a Prohibition case, having imbibed the prosecution's key exhibit.

1928   Henry Ford commented, "The speed at which we run our motor cars, operate our machinery, and generally live, would be impossible with liquor."

☞ MEDICINE

A London bacteriologist had left some bacteria in a dish while he went away for his summer holiday. When he returned to his laboratory at St. Mary's Hospital, he noticed that a mold had formed on the bacterium *Staphylococcus aureus*, preventing any new germ formation. Dr. Alexander Fleming later commented on observing the mold formation, "I had no clue to the most powerful therapeutic substance yet to defeat bacterial infections in the human body."

Fleming's chance finding would lead to the development of penicillin, which would become the first antibiotic. But it would take over a decade and the help of others to develop the drug and produce it in sufficient quantity to make it broadly available, just in time to save thousands of lives at the end of World War II.

After Fleming's chance discovery, he would conduct further experimentation, finding that the mold was effective against some bacteria, ineffective against others. He would also find that it took huge amounts of the mold to provide an effective dose for a human. When his reports to the medical community failed to generate interest, development of the drug languished.

After the beginning of World War II, Dr. Howard Florey, seeking a more effective drug to treat the wounds of servicemen, recalled Fleming's mold. He assigned twenty scientists to the task of isolating the effective ingredients in the mold, and eventually they produced a penicillin salt. But the huge task of manufacturing the drug in sufficient quantities to make it broadly available was still to be mastered.

Penicillin was tested on a human for the first time in 1940. When a policeman with blood poisoning received frequent injections for several days, his condition markedly improved, but then he died because the supply of penicillin ran out.

Teams of British doctors, brought to the United States to continue their research under the auspices of the Rockefeller Institute, finally learned how to produce penicillin in quantity, resulting in Nobel prizes for Fleming and Florey, and a lifesaving drug for the world.

🖝 AIR TRAVEL

The Wright brothers were miffed when a Congressman introduced a bill calling for an investigation to determine whether they or a Dr. Samuel Langley had invented the first flying machine heavier than air. They shipped their aircraft to London's South Kensington Museum, where, said Orville Wright, "the plane will have its proper place and credit."

🖝 SPORTS

Seventy-five thousand football fans gathered in New York's Yankee Stadium on November 12, 1928, to watch the unbeaten Army team battle Notre Dame. Led by their star halfback, Chris Kagle, the Cadets were overwhelming favorites, since the Irish had been soundly defeated by both George Tech and Wisconsin.

Just before game time, Notre Dame coach Knute Rockne called his squad together for their last-minute instructions. Rockne said:

> You've all heard of George Gipp. You all know that I was at his bedside the day he died. And you may or may not have heard that just before he died he said to me, "Rock, some day when things are real tough for Notre Dame, ask the boys to go out there and win one for the Gipper." Well, I've never used Gipp's request until now. This is the time. It's up to you.

Inspired by Rockne's charge, the Fighting Irish upset Army 12–6, their victory to be later reenacted in a film called *Knute Rockne, All American*, starring Pat O'Brien as Rockne and Ronald Reagan as Gipp.

Promoter C. C. Pyle organized a unique long-distance running race to start from the Ascot Speedway in Los Angeles and finish at New York's Madison Square Garden. Offering $48,500 in prize money, Pyle had more than a sporting interest in the event, hoping to make a tidy sum from the $100 entry fees, program sales, promotional fees from the cities along the route, and product endorsements by the victor. But the public took little interest in what the press called the Bunion Derby, causing promotional support to be withdrawn. Seventy-six of the 199 starters dropped out of the race in the first sixteen miles.

The winner of the $25,000 first prize was a part-Cherokee Indian from Claremore, Oklahoma, named Andrew Pyne, who covered the distance in twenty-four days, not counting overnight rest periods. Pyle lost $15,000 on the event but did not shrink from his belief that there was money to be made from the cross-country event. He scheduled another coast-to-coast run in 1929, which would leave him $100,000 in the red, terminating the Bunion Derby once and for all.

The New York Rangers and Montreal Maroons reached the final round of the National Hockey League's Stanley Cup playoffs. Early in the second game, the Ranger's only goaltender was hit in the face by a shot and was forced to retire. Pressed into the fray was forty-five-year-old Ranger coach Lester Patrick, who had not played hockey in seven years and had never performed professionally as a goalie. Although the Maroons peppered the aging Patrick with numerous shots, he gave up only one goal, and the teams finished the regulation period tied 1–1. Seven minutes into sudden-death overtime, the Rangers scored the winning goal and assisted their exhausted coach to the locker room, going on to become the first team south of the Canadian border to win the coveted Stanley Cup.

☞ ENTERTAINMENT

Strolling past a warehouse at Hollywood's Twentieth Century-Fox studio, director Raoul Walsh observed a studio employee loading a truck. Impressed with his good looks and rugged frame, Walsh had ex-USC football player Marion Morrison signed to a contract and had his name changed to John Wayne.

In addition to cowboy parts, Wayne was also cast in the hero's role in a variety of World War II action films. However, he would not be able to serve in the armed forces, having been declared exempt from duty because he represented the sole means of support for his widowed mother.

Two 1928 song hits:
• "I Faw Down an' Go Boom"
• "I Love to Dunk a Hunk a Sponge Cake"

The film *Die Frau im Mond,* or *Woman of the Moon* (also known as *Rocket to the Moon*), originated the jargon for rocket launches, director Fritz Lang inventing the countdown, "five, four, three, two, one, lift-off."

Disney Studios gave birth to a cartoon character whom Walt Disney nearly called Mortimer Mouse, settling finally on Mickey Mouse, who made his cartoon debut in a film called *Steamboat Willie*. Disney did not draw the animated figures himself, but did supply the voice. **1928**

☞ FEATS OF DARING

Jean Lussier celebrated Independence Day by going over Niagara Falls in a 750-pound rubber ball, custom-made for Lussier at a cost of $1,485. The ball bobbed to the surface downstream, Lussier emerging from his rubber vehicle none the worse for wear.

Many brave souls had attempted the trip, with mixed results. The first person to survive the Niagara Falls descent had been a woman, a widowed schoolteacher named Anna Edison Taylor. In 1901, Taylor had climbed into a barrel equipped with shoulder straps and a blacksmith's anvil for ballast. She went over the Canadian side of the Falls, dropping 158 feet to the rapids below, the barrel not surfacing in the churning waters for over a minute. When a group of men dragged the barrel to shore and opened it, Taylor was found alive but unconscious and bleeding profusely from a severe facial cut. The battered schoolmarm took little joy in being the first to conquer the Falls, lamenting the "foolish thing I have done."

No daredevil defied death as often as "Professor" Ivy Baldwin. Baldwin had been a circus performer as a teenager, moving on to ballooning and the high wire. In 1907, he had negotiated a 635-foot cable stretched across a canyon at Eldorado Springs, Colorado, 500 feet above the river below. He had enjoyed the experience so much that he had repeated it eighty-six times.

In 1928, Baldwin retired from his aerial walks at sixty-two but sorely missed his trips on the wire. Twenty years later, in 1948, he took to the wire again at the same location on his eighty-second birthday, making so successful a crossing that the elated Baldwin repeated it the next day.

1929

Finance is the art of passing currency from hand to hand until it finally disappears.

—Robert W. Sarnoff

Downtown [the Stock Exchange], there are two emotions: fear and greed. The rest is bullshit.

—A New York stockbroker

☞ NATIONAL NEWS

Even the most casual student of American history can tell you that the most significant happening in the United States in 1929 was the stock market crash, bringing to an end the great bull market of the 1920s. And yet, when the year came to an end, the *New York Times* did not select this event as the biggest news story of 1929, choosing instead Admiral Richard Byrd's journey to the South Pole.

At first blush, the *Time*'s choice seems totally incomprehensible. But upon a review of events preceding and following the crash, it appears more logical. For when it happened, the Wall Street fiasco did not seem as earthshaking as it does today; it would be some time before history would escalate its importance.

For more than a century, America had suffered periodic economic downturns that struck the nation approximately every twenty years. The years 1829, 1837, 1857, 1873, and 1893 were ones that saw the beginning

100

of major recessions, and another hit twenty-one years later, in 1913. **1929**
Fortunately, the beginning of World War I brought about a need for
goods, which quickly revived the flagging economy. If one gives credence
to the old cliché "History repeats itself," then the 1929 stock market crash
and subsequent Depression were right on schedule.

Many have been left with the impression that the stock market crash
of October 1929 both brought the market to its nadir and triggered the
Depression. Although these were history-making days on Wall Street, the
market did not bottom out until November, followed by a year-end rally
that would see stock prices recover substantially; by the following spring,
more than half the losses from the crash had been recovered. When 1929
came to an end, most economists predicted that 1930 would be a good
year. And while the roots of the Depression were taking hold, it was nine
months after the market crash before it was broadly acknowledged that
the Great Depression was under way.

The year 1928 had seen security values increase by over $11 billion,
but it had not been a year without trauma in financial markets. There had
been sharp sell-offs in both June and December, the *New York Times*
commenting on the June downturn as follows: "Wall Street's bull market
collapsed with a detonation heard round the world." So investors had
become used to periodic price breaks and took them in stride, confident
that the overall trend of the market was in only one direction—up—
although one might have to take a few lumps along the way.

In January 1929, the market broke smartly from the starting gate,
with security values up a heady 7 percent for the month. In his State of
the Union address, President Coolidge painted a rosy picture: "No
Congress ever assembled has met with a more pleasing prospect than that
which appears at the present time. In the domestic field there is
tranquility and contentment . . . and the highest record years of
prosperity."

February and March, however, produced a few discordant notes:

• The Senate passed a resolution asking the Federal Reserve to work
up some guidelines for possible legislation to inhibit speculation.

• The House Banking and Currency Committee began preparations
for an investigation of the stock market.

• The Federal Reserve Board on February 2 sent a confidential
memorandum to its member banks across the land, requesting that they
refuse to lend money for the purpose of stock market speculation. Five
days later, the board warned of "the excessive amount of the country's
credit absorbed in speculative loans."

The Federal Reserve Bank lent money to its member banks, who in
turn lent it to stockbrokers, who lent it to their customers. Stocks could
be purchased on margin, with the investor coming up with only a portion
of the purchase price. When the Federal Reserve's member banks

1929 tightened their purse strings, interest rates on call money soared, to 10, to 15, and, finally, on March 26, to 20 percent. The market responded by going into a tailspin. But it appeared to have a mind of its own, stubborn in the extreme, for every time bad news sent it southward, some rationale was proposed, or some financial leader voiced confidence, and the market got back on its upward track. This time it was Charles Mitchell who stepped into the breach. As chairman of the National City Bank, he was, in the heady days of the bull market, a hero on Wall Street, although he would later be jailed for tax evasion. Mitchell announced that his bank would lend money to brokers at more favorable rates, totally undercutting the efforts of the Federal Reserve Bank to return the credit markets to some degree of sanity. Call money rates retreated, the stock market jumped forward again, and it was business as usual, with borrowed money used to fuel the furnaces of speculation.

There was another market break in May, but once again the market righted itself. Downs were regarded as "corrections" or "buying opportunities," and another came in July, but a record earnings report from U.S. Steel sent the market on its merry way upward again. In August, three luxury liners to Europe offered brokerage offices on board so that vacationing Americans would not miss a beat in their stock market dabbling while on the high seas. A seat on the New York Stock Exchange sold for a record $615,000, and GM executive John J. Raskob's article in the *Ladies' Home Journal*, entitled "Everybody Ought to Be Rich," advised that $15 put into the market monthly should produce a nest egg of $80,000 in just twenty years! A *Time* article published in the spring had said, "Most of the investors are new, small, ignorant. They speculate to double their capital rather than invest to get a steady increase. They are motivated by faith." And investors literally flocked to Wall Street in the summer of 1929 to see where the action was and, in some cases, to do some on-the-spot trading. NBC interviewed a visiting schoolteacher, who said that he had come to New York to speculate in the market and that he would be departing when he had made $50,000.

On August 20, the *Wall Street Journal*, which remained steadfastly bullish throughout the crash, commented that the recent rally "establishes the major upward trend," and that "the outlook for the fall is the brightest in years." On September 2, Evangeline Adams, an astrologer who had a large following, predicted that "the Dow Jones should climb to heaven." Whether it reached heaven or not must be left to higher powers, but the next day it reached what proved to be the high watermark of the great bull market, 381.17 on the Dow.

Just three days into September, economist Roger Babson stated that "Sooner or later a crash is coming," and the Dow plunged, to be righted by some consoling words from Professor Irving Fisher of Yale University, another well-regarded source of financial prophecy, who would remain

102

optimistic until virtually every hope had been removed. On September 11, although it was not public knowledge, Chase Bank chairman Alfred Wiggin began selling his bank's stock short, a bit of foresight that would net $4 million. Later in the month, a scandal shook London's financial markets when one Clarence Hatry was jailed for a swindle of hefty proportions, leaving a goodly number of the city's financial institutions considerably poorer. Many Englishmen liquidated their positions in the American stock market to obtain needed funds, and a good deal more money came back to the British Isles from America when higher interest rates became available than could be obtained in New York.

October did not begin auspiciously for Wall Street. In a statement on October 1, the American Bankers Association voiced its concern over the large amounts of loans to small borrowers. The market broke on October 5, only to rebound as if by reflex. Yale's Professor Fisher predicted on October 15 that he expected to see "the stock market a good deal higher than it is today within a few months." The next day, a committee of the Investment Bankers Association said that speculation "has reached the danger point and many stocks are selling above their values," a statement that sent security prices down once more, but values rebounded over the next three trading days. On October 22, President Hoover received a report from J. P. Morgan executive Thomas Lamont, declaring that "there is nothing in the present situation to suggest that the normal economic forces, working to correct excesses and to restore the proper balance, are still not operative and adequate."

Two days later, on October 24, often referred to as Black Thursday, there occurred what the *New York Times* described as "the most disastrous decline in the biggest and broadest market of history." By noon, security values had eroded by $6 billion, and the board of governors met to consider whether or not to close down the exchange. They decided not to, and a group of leading financiers decided to prop up the market, pooling $240 million for that purpose. Their broker, Richard Whitney, vice president of the New York Stock Exchange, later to be jailed for misappropriating the funds of some of his customers, marched dramatically on to the floor of the exchange and began to buy selected blue chip stocks, to the cheers of onlookers. Thomas Lamont told the press that there had been a "little distress selling," and that some funds had been marshaled "to fill the air pockets." The market recovered somewhat, but bankers called their broker customers for more collateral for their loans, and brokers in turn dunned their on-margin customers for additional collateral for theirs. If it was not directly forthcoming, brokers sold them out. A guard at the New York Stock Exchange described the scene on the floor of that august institution: "They roared like a lot of lions and tigers. They hollered and screamed, they clawed at one another's collars. It was like a bunch of crazy men. Every once in a while, when

1929 Radio or Steel or Auburn would take another tumble, you'd see some poor devil collapse on the floor." That night, astrologer Adams consoled her customers by predicting that the market would recover. She then called her broker and instructed him to sell all of her securities.

Despite statements of confidence by President Hoover and the leaders of Bethlehem Steel, Standard Oil, and General Motors, the stock market took another record-breaking plunge on Monday, October 28, setting the stage for October 29, when the loss in the value of stocks on the New York Stock Exchange alone would be twice the value of all the currency in circulation in the United States at the time. Men working at the exchange wept openly, and Trinity Church was jammed with worshipers. The director of the exchange's medical staff was well prepared for many of the cases he treated that day, having dealt with shell-shocked victims during World War I. Some comments the next day follow:

• "Stock prices virtually collapsed yesterday, swept downwind with gigantic losses in the most disastrous trading day in stock market history." (*New York Times*)

• "There is nothing in the business situation to warrant the destruction of values that has taken place in the past week, and my son and I have for some days been purchasing sound common stocks." (John D. Rockefeller, Sr.)

• "Sure he's buying. Who else has any money?" (Comedian Eddie Cantor)

• "WALL STREET LAYS AN EGG" (*Variety* headline)

During the next two trading days, stocks steadied somewhat. U.S. Steel declared an extra dividend, and the president announced plans to cut taxes. But then the market moved still lower, reaching its bottom in mid-November. The *London Times* reported that "hysteria has now disappeared from Wall Street," and Bernard Baruch wired his British friend Winston Churchill: "FINANCIAL STORM DEFINITELY PASSED." For the last six weeks of the year, the stock market was on the rise: U.S. Steel went from a low of 150 to 171, GE from 168 to 243, and AT&T from 193 to 243. Christmas shopping sales topped those of 1928, and the Department of Labor predicted "a splendid employment year" coming up in 1930. The *New York Times*, following the last trading day on the New York Stock Exchange, wrote, "A general price rise ends stock trading with Wall Street moderately bullish for 1930."

• "October. This is one of the peculiarly dangerous months to speculate in stocks. The others are July, January, September, April, November, May, March, December, June, August and February." (Mark Twain, *Pudd'nhead Wilson*)

To the White House came Herbert Clark Hoover, and the public was confident that it was in good hands with a man who had proved himself

104

such an able administrator. Anne O'Hare McCormick recalls her thoughts when Hoover was inaugurated on March 4, 1929: "We were in the mood for magic. We had summoned a great engineer to solve our problems for us; now we sat comfortably and confidently to watch the problems be solved." Hoover sensed the tremendous confidence that people had in him, and it left him concerned, fearing "the exaggerated idea the people have conceived of me. They have a conviction that I am a sort of superman, that no problem is beyond my capacity. If some unprecedented calamity should come upon the nation, I would be sacrificed to the unreasoning disappointment of a people who expected too much."

At 10:20 A.M. on February 14, four policemen—two in uniform, two in plain clothes—emerged from a blue car and walked into a garage belonging to the SMC Carting Company on Chicago's North Clark Street, a building that served as a depot for receiving and distributing bootlegged beer and liquor for the Moran gang. Six gang members were waiting for a pot of coffee to brew while a seventh was fixing a beer vat on one of the mob's trucks. Brandishing shotguns and submachine guns, the officers lined up the seven men along a wall of the garage and searched them for weapons. When all seven members of the gang had been frisked, the officers stepped back, and one gave the order, "Give it to 'em," and over 100 bullets blasted from the four guns, leaving six men dead. One miraculously was alive, with twenty bullets in his body, but would die shortly. Hearing the noise, a housewife looked out her window and saw the two uniformed police officers leading away at gunpoint the two men in plain clothes, their hands above their heads, and she assumed that the police were apprehending another couple of Chicago hoodlums.

What had disturbed the tranquility of that sunny Chicago morning would come to be known as the St. Valentine's Day Massacre. The four "policemen" had been members of the Capone gang, settling a dispute with rival mob leader George "Bugs" Moran, who had the good fortune that morning to be doing a little business in Detroit. His brother-in-law and coleader of the gang had not been so lucky.

Alphonse Capone had come to Chicago in 1920 from Brooklyn's Five Points Gang, a particularly vicious group of thugs, whose members included sobriquets such as "Lefty Louie" and "Gyp the Blood." Gang leader Johnny Torrio had imported the bullet-headed, scarfaced Capone, then twenty-one years old, to add some much needed muscle to his expanding bootlegging operations. Just three years later, Capone had risen to become the dominant person in Chicago rackets, with just about every Windy City politician in his pocket, as well as the mayor of nearby Cicero. Capone was the leader of a gang of 700 men, whose annual income was estimated at $100 million.

The publicity and public outcry precipitated by the St. Valentine's

1929 Day Massacre, as well as fears of retribution, convinced Capone that it might be prudent to go underground for a bit. He decided on jail as his safest haven and engineered his own arrest in Philadelphia in May on weapons charges. His arrest, trial, sentencing, and incarceration were accomplished in just sixteen hours and thirty-five minutes:

Arrest	8:15 P.M.
Lineup	9:30 A.M.
Indictment	10:25 A.M.
Trial	11:15 A.M.
Guilty plea	12:15 P.M.
Began sentence	12:50 P.M.

During Capone's year in jail, he had all the comforts of home. His cell had a rug, pictures on the wall, a desk, a bookcase, and a floor-model radio to keep him entertained. He was allowed unlimited visitors, and the warden let him use his phone when he felt the need to communicate with the outside world.

Until the St. Valentine's Day Massacre, Capone had not been held in severe public disfavor, perhaps because one of his main sources of revenue—supplying liquor—was not considered to be a very serious crime in a city where Prohibition was both unpopular and broadly flouted. But the savageness of the February slaughter brought about a hail of protests that reached all the way to the White House via a Chicago newspaper publisher, Frank Knox, causing President Hoover to pass down the word that Capone was to be put behind bars—for good. So when Al Capone emerged from jail in 1930, he found that federal agents were investigating his affairs and those of his associates. The government's key area of emphasis would be possible tax evasion, gangsters not being well known for the comprehensiveness and clarity of their tax returns. Ralph "Bottles" Capone, Al's brother, was followed to jail by Frank the "Enforcer" Nitti and Jake "Greasy Thumb" Guzik. Seeing the handwriting on the wall, Capone volunteered to pay up any back taxes that he might have inadvertently overlooked, hinting that he would make up to $4 million available for that purpose. But by then, the scent of blood was too strong, and government prosecutors refused to settle out of court.

Although the prosecution recommended a jail term of only two and one-half years, the judge sentenced Capone to eleven. He was sent to federal penal facilities in Atlanta but was later transferred to Alcatraz. When he was released in January 1939, he was a shadow of his former self, a past bout with syphilis having developed into paresis. He lived in Miami Beach until 1947, but he no longer was capable of defending his turf, and his empire fell to a new breed of ostensibly nonviolent racket czars, typified by Frank Costello.

106

Capone died at forty-eight, probably the best known criminal the country has ever produced. And one of the reasons he was so well known is that he had a flair for public relations, speaking to newspaper reporters freely and frequently. He poured out his problems with a certain simple logic and sincerity, making this killer a strangely sympathetic character to the man in the street. Some of his quotes:

• "All I ever did was to supply a demand that was pretty popular. Why the very guys that make my trade good are the ones that yell the loudest about me not being legitimate. Why, lady, nobody's on the legit when it comes down to cases; you know that."

• "The parasites will trail you begging for money and favors, and you can never get away from them no matter where you go. I have a wife and a boy who is eleven—a lad I idolize—and a beautiful home in Florida. If I could go there and forget it all, I would be the happiest man in the world. I want peace and I will live and let live."

• "I've been accused of every death except the casualty list of the World War."

• "Public service is my motto."

• "I haven't had any peace of mind. It's a tough life."

☛ REGIONAL NEWS

Texas
Bill Williams of Hondo, Texas, was the kind of betting man who was not averse to going to some lengths to win a wager. To win a $500 bet, he pushed a peanut up Colorado's Pikes Peak with his nose, a twenty two mile trip taking him thirty days.

Another Texan by the same last name left Galveston on foot, using a bamboo cane to advance an iron hoop 12 inches in diameter. H. P. Williams propelled the hoop for six months and 2,300 miles until man and hoop simultaneously reached the island of Manhattan.

Massachusetts
The Boston Braves baseball team was granted permission to play home games in Boston on Sundays.

Kentucky
Endurance contests were popular in 1929, and a Louisville radio station offered a $200 prize to the person who could listen to the radio for the longest period of time without sleep. Mother-of-two Mildred Daniel was the winner, keeping her ear to her set for 106 hours before being hospitalized for delirium and exhaustion.

1929

Illinois

Another mother of two, Clara Wagner, spent nineteen days rocking back and forth in a rocking chair with but ten minutes of respite per hour plus a two-hour nap break at dawn each day. She finally succumbed to exhaustion and was hospitalized.

Mississippi

A crowd of 2,000 looked on while an accused black rapist was burned alive. A coroner's jury later ruled that death had been due to "unknown causes."

☞ FOREIGN NEWS

Africa

Serengeti National Park had its beginning as a 900-square-mile animal sanctuary. It was created when professional hunters complained that tourists were driving Model T Fords out on the plains to slaughter lions.

Italy

The Lateran Treaty was worked out by Pope Pius XI and Italian dictator Benito Mussolini, creating the world's smallest state. The 108.7 acres of land in Rome would henceforth be ruled by the pope.

France

Two-time French premier Georges Clemenceau died at the age of eighty-eight. Intensely devoted to his native land, he was known to fellow Frenchmen as the Tiger.

Clemenceau had an unusual habit that might have provided grounds for a lesser man's institutionalization in a mental hospital. He went to bed each night impeccably garbed in a full dress suit—trousers, vest, coat, and gloves—totally ready for the boulevards except that he wore bedroom slippers instead of shoes and replaced his stiff shirt with a softer model.

Soviet Union

In late 1929, the U.S.S.R. initiated a calendar made up of five-day weeks, days of the week being differentiated by color rather than name and consisting of yellow, orange, red, purple, and green. Each worker was assigned one of the five colors that indicated his weekly day off. In an attempt to do away with the weekend and its religious significance, the Soviet government made several efforts to vary the standard week, moving to a six-day week from 1932 to 1940 before finally returning to the seven-day week.

Police burst into the chapel of a Massachusetts funeral parlor to find a speakeasy busily dispensing alcoholic beverages.

Canada's annual per capita liquor consumption had grown from 9 to 102 gallons during the 1920s, but no one was gullible enough to believe that our neighbors to the north had taken to the bottle with such a vengeance. Millions of dollars' worth of spirits were being smuggled over the border into the United States.

Wisconsin became the fifth state to refuse to enforce Prohibition, joining Maryland, Montana, Nevada, and New York.

The oft-quoted Henry Ford commented again on Prohibition: "Prohibition is here to stay. Absolute enforcement must come. Nobody wants to fly with a drunken aviator."

☛ PEOPLE

Long-distance walker Edward Payson Weston died at the ripe old age of ninety. In 1860, Weston had made an unusual wager on the outcome of the Lincoln-Douglas presidential election, the loser to travel on foot from Boston to Washington for the inauguration, a distance of 478 miles. Weston lost the bet and set out on February 22, 1861, from the State House in Boston, braving snow, rain, muddy roads, and curious dogs, to arrive in Washington and shake Lincoln's hand at the inaugural ball.

Weston's journey had whetted his appetite for further long-distance walks, and he took to the road again, betting $10,000 that he could walk from Portland, Maine, to Chicago in twenty-six days, a distance of 1,326 miles. Decked out in a red velvet tunic and derby hat, Weston's pace was so swift that he was soon comfortably ahead of schedule, allowing him to pause from time to time to attend church services and lecture to interested bystanders on the evils of drink. Weston won the bet easily, and the press lauded his journey as the Giant Pedestrian Feat. But Weston was just warming up for even more impressive hikes to come:

• In 1879, he journeyed to England to win the Astley Belt, the so-called world championship of walking. Weston outpaced the host country's best, one "Blower" Brown, walking 550 miles in six days. In addition to winning the prize, Weston won a $2,500 side bet with Sir John Astley, originator and sponsor of the event.

1929
• In 1909, Weston performed his pièce de résistance at the age of seventy, walking from New York to San Francisco and back in 187 days, a record that has yet to be bested.

Weston's walking was brought to an end in 1927 when he was hit by a taxi while walking down a Brooklyn, New York, street. He was paralyzed by the accident, a highly unfitting end to the career of such an accomplished pedestrian.

John Davidson Rockefeller III graduated from Princeton and was awarded two titles by fellow class members: "Most Likely to Succeed" and "Third Most Pious."

Future president Richard Milhous Nixon worked at a summer job in Prescott, Arizona, earning $1 an hour as a barker for a wheel-of-chance game at the Slippery Gulch Rodeo.

☞ SPORTS

The University of California and Georgia Tech were battling on even terms in the 1929 Rose Bowl football game when a Cal lineman scooped up a Tech fumble and took off for the goal line. Unfortunately, it was his own goal line that he was racing toward, and his teammates took off in hot pursuit, finally bringing him down on Cal's 2-yard line. Roy Riegel's wrong way dash proved to be costly when on the next play a Tech lineman burst into Cal's backfield to down their punter for a two-point safety. Georgia Tech won the game by just one point, 8–7.

Thirty-five years later, in 1964, Jim Marshall of the Minnesota Vikings would also come up with a loose ball, lose his bearings, and sprint into his own end zone; he hurled the ball skyward to celebrate his touchdown. It was not until he was embraced by members of the opposition San Francisco 49ers that Marshall realized his mistake. Fortunately for Marshall, the Vikings went on to win the game by a score of 27–22.

Danny London, a deaf-mute boxer, took a hard blow to the head during a bout in Brooklyn, New York, a blow that had a surprisingly therapeutic effect on him. After recovering from the punch, London found that he could both hear and speak.

Former Stanford star Ernie Nevers set a National Football League record that has never been eclipsed, scoring forty points for the Chicago Cardinals against the Chicago Bears, six touchdowns and four extra points, supplying all his team's scoring for the day in a 40–0 rout. In the previous game, Nevers had produced all nineteen of his team's points.
110

In 1929, most track meets included an event now relegated to church and school fairs—the sack race. Such races were usually conducted over a distance of 100 yards, competitors taking their places at the starting line, neck deep in a burlap sack. The ultimate sack racer was a Brooklyn, New York, Irish-American named Johnny Finn, who on May 1, 1929, negotiated the distance in the astounding time of 14.4 seconds, a world's record, and just two seconds more than the winning time in the 100-yard dash.

Trainer Clyde Van Dusen had prepared his horse for the Kentucky Derby with special care, and the colt won. The name of the winner: Clyde Van Dusen!

The New York Yankees became the first major league baseball team to put numbers on their players' uniforms; by 1933 all major league teams joined the Yanks in so identifying their personnel. The first man in the Yankee batting order got 1, the second 2, and so on through their starting lineup, resulting in Babe Ruth receiving 3 and cleanup hitter Lou Gehrig 4.

☞ ENTERTAINMENT

A young actor named Gary Cooper spoke a line to Walter Huston in the film *The Virginian*, a line that quickly entered the vernacular. Responding to an insult, Cooper said, "If you want to call me that, smile." Cooper's words were later changed by many to, "Smile when you say that, pardner."

Talking movies were the rage and were shown in theaters all over the world in dozens of languages. One was even made in Esperanto.

1930

If all the economists were laid end to end, they would not reach a conclusion.
—George Bernard Shaw

☛ NATIONAL NEWS

Pondering the arrival of a new decade, author Frederick Lewis Allen wrote, "What was to come in the nineteen-thirties? Only one thing could one be sure of. It would not be repetition. The stream of time often doubles on its course, but always it makes for itself a new channel."

How right he was. The year 1930 wasted only a few months on the status quo before taking a new direction. Until the late spring, life in the United States looked pretty much as it had in the 1920s. The president, certain cabinet members, and various business leaders made optimistic statements about the health of the economy and would continue to do so well into 1931. And there appeared to be some justification for their rosy view of the future as the first quarter of 1930 saw an upturn in business activity, reduced unemployment, increased capital spending, and record corporate profits for 1929. The frosting on the cake was May's booming

112

auto sales, reminding Detroit of some of the best days of the last decade.
But then the engine that drove America's economy sputtered, its
carburetor gasped for fuel, and it ran out of gas. Consumer demand for
goods turned down drastically, creating huge inventories and massive
production cutbacks, swelling the ranks of the unemployed. Commodity
prices fell like a stone, the stock market retreated, and the country
plunged into a depression, to be joined by most of the nations of the
industrialized world.

As if the nation's economic woes were not a large enough cross to
bear, a drought scorched the crops of mid-America, and cases of infantile
paralysis began to increase sharply. But perhaps the worst indignity of
1930 was that many Americans could not use their hard-earned savings to
tide them over until better days came. Over 1,000 banks closed their
doors that year, including the prestigious and loftily named Bank of the
United States, headquartered in New York City, which had fifty-nine
branches and 400,000 depositors. The bank went under because its
president, Bernard K. Marcus, had been using his depositors' money to
play the stock market and to support a life-style that each year found him
summering in Europe, where he deported himself like a maharajah.
When the crash came, he had surreptitiously removed $8 million of the
bank's funds to meet his margin calls. The inevitable came to pass, and on
December 11, 1930, the bank declared insolvency.

One of the bank's customers was a man named George Gelies, who
had worked as a janitor for forty years, depositing the few coins and
occasional dollars that he had managed to save from his meager salary,
until his balance finally reached $1,000. When he was turned away from
the bank and told that his savings had been lost, he went home and
hanged himself from a basement steam pipe.

The International Apple Shippers Association had a marketing idea
that it hoped would reduce its surplus fruit while supplying jobs for the
unemployed. It decided to sell apples on credit, and soon city sidewalks
across America were jammed with vendors. By November 1930, there
were 6,000 apple vendors in New York City alone, but in 1931 they would
be declared a public nuisance and removed from the streets, adding more
would-be workers to the legions of the jobless.

☞ FOREIGN NEWS

England

The first international bridge match took place in London in
September 1930, and the competition would do much to generate
interest in the game in the United States. Led by Ely Culbertson, the

1930 United States team defeated the British, winning the 200-deal match by 4,845 points, and sales of playing cards in America would see a sharp rise.

Soviet Union

The worldwide Depression found the Soviet government short of cash. The authorities decided to sell twenty-one paintings from Leningrad's Hermitage Museum to American multimillionaire Andrew Mellon, who appeared not to be suffering from the international financial crunch, anteing up $7 million in cash to the Russians.

France

The French government released some statistics that did not bode well for the tourist business in one city on the sunny Mediterranean. A tabulation of crimes committed in France since 1900 showed that 75 percent of them had been the work of either current or former residents of Marseilles.

Ireland

The Irish Sweepstakes was created to benefit several of the country's hospitals. Americans would help make it one of the most successful lotteries in the world, producing 214 of the 2,404 winners in 1933.

Turkey

Turks along the strait of Bosporus were getting used to calling their city by its new official name, "Istanbul." After fifteen hundred years of being known as Constantinople—Qostantiniyeh in Turkish, Stamboul to most Europeans—some residents had begun calling it Istanbul in the nineteenth century. Now the name had been formally adopted.

☞ PROHIBITION

The American Bar Association brought joy to anti-Prohibitionists when it voted 2–1 for the scuttling of the Eighteenth Amendment.

Jack Kriendler and his accountant cousin, Charlie Berns, moved their speakeasy to 21 West Fifty-second Street in New York City, caching their illegal booze behind hidden walls to avoid the gimlet eyes of Prohibition enforcers. Another ruse to foil the law was particularly ingenious. At the first sign of a visit from the constabulary, the bartender pushed a button that tilted the bar's shelves, sending all the whiskey bottles down a chute to the basement, where they smashed to smithereens on the concrete floor below, leaving no evidence for Prohibition agents to use in prosecuting the owners.

114

This speakeasy survived Repeal to become "21," a high-priced and
glamorous restaurant, which is still prospering today.

☛ AIR TRAVEL

Nurse and student pilot Ellen Church petitioned United Airlines
with the suggestion that it would be wise to add women to its all-male
crews. Church reasoned, "Don't you think it would be good psychology to
have women up in the air? How is a man going to say he is afraid to fly
when a woman is working on the plane?"

United concurred with Church's logic, making her chief stewardess
and authorizing her to hire seven additional female attendants. Specifications were prepared requiring that they be single, registered nurses, not
over 115 pounds or 5 feet 4 inches, and not older than twenty-five.
Starting pay was $125 a month for 100 hours of flying time.

The first four women took to the skies on May 15, 1930, on a flight
from Oakland to Cheyenne, decked out in green woolen uniforms with
capes and caps; they were replaced in Cheyenne by the four other flight
attendants for the final leg of the flight to Chicago. En route they served a
meal of fruit cocktail, fried chicken, and coffee or tea, but the nourishment of the passengers was not their sole function. They were required to
help the crew push the plane out of the hangar, clean and fuel the aircraft,
and carry the passengers' luggage.

☛ METEOROLOGY

A Baltimore, Maryland, cat named Napoleon developed quite a
reputation for predicting the weather during a severe drought that kept
the city sweltering in the summer of 1930. When weather forecasters
continued to predict dry weather after weeks without rain, Francis
Shields called local newspapers to disagree with their prognoses, assuring
them that rain would come to the area within twenty-four hours. When
asked for the basis for her optimistic prediction, Shields said that she had
observed her cat, Napoleon, reposing with his front paw extended and his
head on the floor, a position that he assumed only just prior to rain.
Although she was dismissed as a quack by the press, her prophecy came
true when a rainstorm broke the drought the following day. Impressed by
Napoleon's meteorological skills, the newspapers took to publishing the
cat's forecasts on a regular basis, their accuracy comparing favorably with
those of the professionals.

1930 ☛ ART

A new style of realistic American art was initiated by Grant Wood with his work *American Gothic,* which depicted a somber rural couple standing in front of their Indiana farmhouse. Wood's sister, Nan Wood Graham, had been the model for the female, while a dentist friend, Dr. Byron McKeeby, had posed as the male. Wood would later find out that the "farmhouse" had once served as a bordello.

☛ TRENDS

Cigarette sales were growing by leaps and bounds, the habit having taken hold during World War I when American doughboys found it more convenient to carry cigarettes than cigars or pipes.

In the late 1920s, the tobacco industry began to realize that female smokers represented a large sales potential, although it was still taboo in many areas for women to smoke in public. At first, ladies were shown not smoking in ads, a Chesterfield ad picturing a woman exhorting her man to "Blow It My Way."

Cigarette advertisers were not encumbered by government restrictions on the claims that they could make for their brands and were not reticent to take a few liberties in their advertising:

• "For years this has been no secret to those who keep fit and trim. They know that Luckies steady the nerves and do not hurt their physical condition. They know that Lucky Strikes are the favorite cigarette of many prominent athletes who must keep in good shape. They respect the opinions of 20,679 physicians who maintain that Luckies are less irritating to the throat than other cigarettes."

• "Light a Lucky and you'll never miss sweets that make you fat."

The tuxedo dinner jacket had taken over from the tailcoat as accepted dress at all but the most formal occasions. It had first been introduced by Griswold Lorillard at the Autumn Ball of the Tuxedo Park Country Club in fashionable Tuxedo, New York, before the turn of the century. Eyebrows had been raised to dangerously high levels when Lorillard had appeared in this new form of formal dress fashioned after the British smoking jacket.

116

For twenty years, H. L. (Haroldson Lafayette) Hunt had had his ups and downs in cotton and oil and was saved from going broke on several occasions by his proficiency at the poker table, which had gained him the nickname "Arkansas Slim." But after 1930, Hunt would no longer have to worry about where his next meal was coming from. With a $30,000 loan, Hunt bought control of an oil field in East Texas's Rusk County, paying wildcatter Columbus Joiner some cash, promissory notes, and a guarantee of a share of future profits. Never was a better deal struck, for two years later there would be 900 active wells on the property, and the field would produce nearly 4 billion barrels of oil. Profits from the "black gold" would form the cornerstone of a financial empire that would be estimated at $4 billion at the time of Hunt's death in 1974.

MEDICINE

The legendary "Typhoid Mary" Mallon had spent the last fifteen years in quarantine in a New York City hospital and would remain in seclusion for the rest of her life.

In 1906, ten days after they had been guests at an Oyster Bay, Long Island, dinner party, several people came down with typhoid fever. When health officials went to the house where the party had been given, they found that the cook had left. Her former employers identified her as one Mary Mallon.

Sanitation engineer George Soper took up the investigation. He learned that Mallon had worked as a cook for many years, changing jobs frequently. Soper also determined that at least one case of typhoid fever had been diagnosed in every place where she had presided over the stove. Mallon was finally tracked down by Soper, once again employed in her usual profession. She was told that she was probably a typhoid carrier and asked to submit to a physical examination. She promptly took a nearby rolling pin in hand and saw Soper to the door.

With the aid of police, Soper finally had Mallon removed to a hospital, where tests confirmed that she was indeed a typhoid carrier; her freedom could not be granted unless she agreed never to prepare or handle food again, and to submit to quarterly checkups at the health department. Mallon agreed, but she did neither. Instead, she changed her name, disappeared, and took to the skillet again. So when a typhoid

1930 epidemic was reported at New York's Sloane Hospital for Women not long after Mallon's disappearance, health officials were not surprised to find that she had been employed in the hospital's kitchen. She was found in a suburban New York home, contentedly cooking away and was placed in permanent quarantine. Fifty-one cases of typhoid fever and three deaths were attributed to Typhoid Mary.

☛ BOOKS

World War I combat veteran Robert E. Burns had survived the war only to become a casualty of civilian life. He had returned home to find his girlfriend married and his job as an accountant given to another man. After suffering a nervous breakdown, he had taken to the road, moving from job to job until, in 1922, he was caught holding up an Atlanta store with two other men, the robbery netting $5.80. He was sentenced to from six to ten years on a chain gang, escaped, was apprehended, and made his escape again in 1930. A sympathetic governor resisted his extradition, and Burns wrote *I Am a Fugitive from a Georgia Chain Gang*, describing the horrors of his experiences on the chain gang, laboring from five in the morning until dusk while shackled at each ankle. Prisoners were routinely flogged without cause, poorly fed, and even chained together while they slept. Burns's book and a movie adaptation would be instrumental in rallying public support for the elimination of chain gangs and bringing about significant prison reforms.

☛ FOOD AND DRINK

The Continental Baking Company introduced Americans to Wonder Bread, the first bread to be packaged already sliced. This new convenience food would give birth to an expression still in use today: "The greatest thing since sliced bread."

The Depression had its effect even on the Popsicle, which began to appear in two individual sherbet-covered sticks joined together instead of one large one, so that two youngsters could share the five-cent treat.

A new soft drink was in its first year on the market, its name hardly designed for easy consumer recall. It was called Bib-Label Lithiated Lemon-Lime Soda and had a slogan directed at the hangover market: "Take the ouch out of grouch." And it may well have delivered its promise, since it contained lithium carbonate, an ingredient whose
118

soporific effects would not be discovered until 1949, when an Australian psychiatrist would inject some guinea pigs with the drug, causing them to fall on their backs in a stupor. Bib-Label Lithiated Lemon-Lime Soda would later switch to a simpler monicker, 7-Up. Lithium would be listed on the label until the mid-1940s, but the drug can now be obtained only with a prescription and is often used for the treatment of manic depressives.

• Medical authorities have conjectured that the reason for the low incidence of mental health disorders in El Paso, Texas, derives from the natural presence of lithium in the city's water supply.

☞ ENTERTAINMENT

Swedish beauty Greta Garbo appeared in *Anna Christie,* her first talking movie. Her first line: "Gif me a viskey—ginger ale on the side—and don't be stingy, baby."

Actor Edward G. Robinson tackled a Hollywood role that would begin a lucrative career as a cinema gangster, playing the part of Caesar Enrico Bandello in the film, *Little Caesar.* Robinson was gunned down at the end of the movie and would meet a similar fate in *Silver Dollar* (1932), *I Loved a Woman* (1933), *Barbary Coast* (1935), *Bullets or Ballots* (1936), and *Kid Galahad* (1937). In an about-face from his on-screen image, Robinson became a serious art collector.

Also considered for Robinson's part in *Little Caesar* was an actor named Clark Gable. But when studio boss Jack Warner looked at his screen test, he pronounced Gable too ugly for even a mobster's role. Warner said, "What can you do with a guy with ears like that?"

The Lone Ranger made its radio debut on Detroit's WXYZ. With music from Rossini's *William Tell* overture in the background, the announcer intoned, "Out of the West comes a fiery horse with the speed of light, a cloud of dust, and a hearty 'Hi-yo Silver'—the Lone Ranger rides again." Millions of listeners would enjoy the saga of the masked defender of law and order and his faithful Indian companion Tonto, who called the masked man "Kemo Sabe," which supposedly means "trusting brave." Writer James E. Jewell had actually taken the words "Kemo Sabe" from the name of his future father-in-law's Michigan summer camp.

The Lone Ranger would thrill the youngsters of America for two decades and be joined by a host of other shows directed at the youth audience. The plot lines of several of the more popular programs follow:

119

• *The Shadow* was the continuing saga of "wealthy young man about town," Lamont Cranston, who in the Orient had learned "the hypnotic power to cloud men's minds." With "his friend and companion, the lovely Margot Lane," the Shadow carried out "the hard and relentless fight of one man against the forces of evil. Who knows what evil lurks in the hearts of men? The Shadow knows." (Orson Welles and Agnes Moorehead would spend several years in the lead roles.)

• *The Green Hornet* was the creation of Fran Striker and George W. Trendle, originators of *The Long Ranger*, and chronicled the adventures of "Britt Reid, daring young publisher," who "with the aid of his faithful valet, Kato, matches wits with the underworld, risking his life that criminals and racketeers . . . may feel the sting of the Green Hornet." Kato pilots Reid's automobile, the "superpowered Black Beauty," and the show's background music was the "Flight of the Bumble Bee" by Nicolai Rimsky-Korsakov.

• *Jack Armstrong, the All-American Boy* was introduced by the words, "Wheaties, the breakfast of champions, presents Jack Armstrong, the All-American Boy. [SINGING] Wave the flag for Hudson High, boys. Show them how we stand. Ever shall our team be champions, known throughout the land!"

☛ SPORTS

One of the greatest accomplishments in sports took place in 1930 when amateur Robert Tyre Jones, Jr., of Atlanta, Georgia, won all four major golf titles—the amateur and open championships of both Great Britain and the United States—overcoming odds of 50–1 offered by Lloyds of London against any individual accomplishing the Grand Slam.

Jones had been a golf prodigy. His parents' house was close to a course, and by the time Bobby was five he was knocking a ball around with a set of cut-down clubs; at twelve, he had shot a round of 70 on a full-length course. But although Jones could master the most difficult shots, he had a foul temper, which played havoc with his self-control. In the 1921 British Open, he had committed one of the cardinal sins of golf. Playing poorly, the nineteen-year-old had stalked off the course in the middle of a round, a serious breach of good sportsmanship, for which he had been roundly roasted in the British press.

After that unfortunate incident, Jones had gotten his temper under control but still could not manage to win a major tournament. In 1923, he was beginning to lose his love for competitive golf and was considering abandoning the links to pursue the study of law. But he decided to take one more crack at a major title at the U.S. Open, and fortune seemed to

smile on the good-looking Georgian when he stepped to the tee of the
72nd and last hole, needing only a bogey to win. But Jones had taken a
horrendous double bogey, finishing in a tie with Bobby Cruickshank, who
was favored to beat the erratic Jones in an eighteen-hole play-off the next
day. Playing the last hole of the play-off round all-even, Jones had driven
into the rough but recovered with a magnificent iron shot that traveled
190 yards, landing just five feet from the pin, to take the championship.

From then on, it was onward and upward for Emperor Jones,
performing before adoring crowds on both sides of the Atlantic. By 1930,
he had won the U.S. Open three times, the U.S. Amateur four times, and
the British Open twice, a total of nine major championships.

The year in which he "stormed the impregnable quadrilateral of
golf," he started with the British Amateur at St. Andrews in Scotland. He
was forced to squeeze out three narrow one-up victories in the early
rounds, including one match in which he was two holes down with five to
play, but won the final handily, as he did the British Open at Royal Liverpool three weeks later. These two victories were considered sufficient
accomplishment to earn him a ticker tape parade up New York City's
Broadway when he returned to the United States.

But more was to come. Jones won the U.S. Open in Minneapolis, a
stroke play championship, by two shots. Now all that remained to take the
elusive Grand Slam was the U.S. Amateur at Merion, outside of
Philadelphia, and it would have made a better story if Jones had won a
narrow victory. But Jones's closest calls were behind him, and he was
striking the ball perfectly. He was never behind in any of his matches,
winning the 36-hole final from Eugene Homans on the twenty-ninth hole
by a score of 8 and 7.

Jones retired from competitive golf after winning the Grand Slam,
and with degrees from Harvard and Emory Law School, he practiced law
in Atlanta, playing golf only socially. In 1936, he traveled to Europe for
the Berlin Olympics and some sightseeing, which brought him to
Scotland once more. On a whim, he decided to take one more crack at St.
Andrews, telephoning the course professional from an inn nearby, telling
him that he would be over the next morning and imploring him not to tell
anyone that he was coming to play. The pro would not tell a soul, or so he
claimed, but somehow word got out, and Jones arrived to find 5,000
spectators on hand. By the time he strolled up the fairway to the
eighteenth green, the crowd had swelled to 10,000. Sportswriter
Grantland Rice wrote, "One bewhiskered, venerable Scot, smoking a
large pipe, said to Mrs. Jones—not knowing who she was—'Isn't it
graund . . . isn't it graund . . . Bobby's back.' Tears were coursing
through his beard."

Oh, yes, Bobby Jones shot a 70 on the Old Course that day, not too shoddy for a weekend golfer. And in 1958, he was made an honorary freeman of the Borough of St. Andrews. The last American to have been so honored was Benjamin Franklin.

🖝 PEOPLE

Prohibition spawned a New York City institution named Texas Guinan, a Waco, Texas–born woman who had arrived in New York from Hollywood, where she had been known as the female Bill Hart, riding horses and twirling a lariat in a variety of westerns. In Manhattan, she had become a gifted mistress of ceremonies. Saloon owner Larry Fay paid her as much as $4,000 a week to keep the thirsty flocking to his establishments, which were frequently padlocked for Prohibition violations, forcing him to reopen in a new location. Texas kept up a running exchange with her patrons and introduced the acts, exhorting customers to "give the little girls a great big hand" when the chorus line finished their number. She greeted strangers with the words, "Hello, sucker," coined the expression "Never give a sucker an even break," and originated a descriptive phrase for well-to-do men of commerce by labeling a dairy tycoon a "big butter-and-egg man."

Henry Louis Mencken had passed the last decade as the darling of intellectuals and liberals, directing the power of his prose at anything that smacked of pretentiousness, bigotry, censorship, bad taste, restriction of personal freedom, and a host of other ills that he perceived in society. Mencken had started as a newspaper reporter at eighteen and became the best-read columnist of his era. He would spend most of his career with the *Baltimore Sun* as both writer and editor; he wrote several books, including *The American Language*, a definitive treatise on English usage in the United States. But he was perhaps best known as the editor of *American Mercury*, a magazine he had founded in 1924 with fellow critic George Jean Nathan, which quickly became one of the most influential publications in America. The two parted company in 1930, leaving Mencken in sole charge of the editorial content of the magazine.

Mencken charged into every intellectual battle of the day. He despised the materialistic gaucheness of the Babbitts of middle America—on whom he laid the label "Boobus Americanus"—railed at the religious fundamentalists during the Scopes trial, and took up the cudgel against Prohibitionists and the Ku Klux Klan, just to name a few who aroused his ire. Mencken's attacks were delivered in impeccable prose, with the logic of a skilled debater and the strong conviction of the rightness of his cause.

In 1925, Mencken had launched a furious attack on the Ku Klux Klan, bringing him a slap on the wrist from the Baltimore Chamber of Commerce for what it judged to be excessive vituperation. It also brought a resolution from the Klan's Arkansas branch, supplying an example of the depth of emotion that Mencken's prose could provoke:

> RESOLVED, By the Knights of the Ku Klux Klan of Arkansas, a state the said Mencken has in times past slandered as "a land of morons," that we condemn in the strongest possible language the vile mouthings of this prince of blackguards among the writers of America, to whom virtue, patriotism and democracy are only a subject upon which to expend the venom of a poison pen; that we further condemn the *Baltimore Sun* for heaping insults upon the good men and women of America, and that we commend the course of the Baltimore Chamber of Commerce in protesting against a calumny too degrading and false to come from the heart of one who is not himself a moral pervert.

Alvin A, "Shipwreck" Kelly was the nation's leading flagpole sitter, a spectator sport for big-city Americans that was common in the late 1920s and early 1930s. By the end of his career, Kelly claimed to have spent 20,613 hours in high places, including 47 in snow, 1,400 in rain or sleet, and 210 in below-freezing conditions.

Shipwreck Kelly had come by his nickname because he claimed to have survived without injury five sea disasters, three auto accidents, and a train wreck; he had developed a tolerance for heights while doing construction work on skyscrapers. Kelly's flagpole sitting had started modestly in 1924 with a stint of thirteen hours and thirteen minutes atop the flagpole of a Los Angeles hotel. His talents reached their zenith in 1930 when he spent 1,077 hours, or just over forty-nine days, above the Steel Pier in Atlantic City.

His location was usually a flagpole on the roof of a major hotel, where he perched on a 13-inch-wide wooden seat attached to the ball at the top of the pole. The seat had holes on each side in which he placed his thumbs when he wanted to sleep so that any change in his position resulted in sharp pain that alerted him at once. Spectators watched from the streets below, and those who were willing to pay fifty cents were allowed to view him from the hotel roof. Shipwreck took occasional nourishment, but only in liquid form—soup, coffee, or milk being hoisted up to him in a bucket.

One day, a man observing Kelly from the street below remarked to no one in particular that "He's nothing but a damn fool." A young woman nearby took offense, saying, "He is not. He knows exactly what he's

123

1930 doing," and slapped the man's face. Word of the incident reached Kelly, who asked to meet the woman. She was brought to the roof for a conversation, and shortly thereafter, the flagpole sitter and his female admirer became husband and wife.

1931

Ten men in our country could buy the whole world and ten million can't buy enough to eat.

—Will Rogers

☛ NATIONAL NEWS

As the Depression deepened in 1931, an increasingly desperate nation began to vent its anger and frustration upon the country's chief executive, Herbert Hoover, who, in the words of author Dixon Wechter, was "blamed for a disaster whose seeds had been sown long before his accession to office and which undoubtedly would have come had his opponent triumphed in 1928." As these feelings intensified, the name "Hoover" became a pejorative adjective: Empty pockets became "Hoover flags," newspapers were "Hoover blankets," and shacks, "Hoovervilles." The vilification of Hoover would broaden and intensify, and by the time he campaigned for the presidency in 1932, many of his speeches were punctuated by catcalls and insults or were received in sullen silence.

Adversity had not frozen Hoover into inactivity. He worked with his usual intensity, burning the midnight oil at the White House in an attempt to pull the nation's economy from the deep morass into which it

125

had plunged. He made decisions, issued presidential proclamations, and initiated legislation. But nothing seemed to work, and not only did the economy fail to respond to his blandishments, it got worse.

If Hoover's laissez-faire capitalism and shy stoicism were qualities that had brought him to the top, they would, ironically, contribute to his political demise. His philosophy and personality, so well suited to his earlier endeavors, worked to his disadvantage in these baffling times, which knew no parallel in the history of the nation.

The president was limited in his ability to improve the economy by the conviction that federal interference was a dangerous thing and that economic salvation could come only from the private sector. He resisted outright relief, judging it to be "economically unsound" as well as "morally offensive, sapping the initiative of the working class." Although he encouraged private charity, he just could not stomach the idea of a public dole. The economy was "fundamentally sound," said Hoover, and would right itself if only the nation remained confident. Author Cabel Phillips wrote:

> The President and his spokesmen tried desperately to coax good times back by incantation. It was firmly believed in most important quarters in Washington and Wall Street that if confidence could be restored, the banks would lend money again, factories would open their doors, businessmen would buy and sell, workers would be hired, and life would return to normal.

But one of the biggest problems in restoring the nation's confidence was Hoover himself. Because he was a private man, he had neither the desire nor the ability to communicate with the public on a personal basis. Hoover was totally lacking in what would later become a popular word to describe a politician's ability to identify with and persuade people— charisma. For Hoover, going on the radio to have a heart-to-heart chat with the American people would have been just as much anathema to him as it would be grist for the mill of Franklin Roosevelt two years later. So Hoover toiled behind the closed doors of the White House, and his public communications were not directed at the plight of the average man on the street. As a result, people began to think that he did not care about them, and as this conviction spread, it would—perhaps even more than the Depression itself—bring about Hoover's political downfall.

🖝 BUSINESS

Despite falling stock prices, Wall Street had emerged from the 1929 fiasco in surprisingly good shape. According to author Geoffrey Perrett:

It was not until the spring of 1931 that Wall Street, where legend has it that the Depression began, saw its first economic collapse. For a year and a half, brokerages weeded out the players who had lost, known in the parlance of customers' men as "pushing the dead ones overboard." The commission on selling was the same as the commission on buying. But in April, 1931, Pynchon and Company, one of the biggest, most respected firms, went bust. To many on Wall Street, this was almost as stunning as the crash itself.

It was still possible to make considerable amounts of money in the market by selling stocks short, and the bears were out in force, precluding any serious upturn. The New York Stock Exchange finally turned on the bears and took their honey away, eliminating any further short sales of securities that were trending downward.

Since the 1929 crash, the Harvard Economic Society had been making prognostications in its newsletter, the *Weekly Letter*, which could not have been further off the mark:
• November 16, 1929. "A severe depression like that of 1920–21 is outside the range of possibility."
• January 18, 1930. "With the underlying conditions sound, we believe that the recession in general business will be checked shortly and that improvement will set in during the spring months."
• May 17, 1930. "General prices are now at the bottom and will shortly improve."
• August 30, 1930. "Since our monetary and credit structure is not only sound but unusually strong . . . there is every prospect that the recovery which we have been expecting will not be long delayed."
• September 20, 1930. "Recovery will soon be evident."
• November 15, 1930. "The outlook is for the end of the decline in business during the early part of 1931, and steady . . . revival for the remainder of the year."
In 1931, the Harvard Economic Society discontinued publication of the *Weekly Letter*. Its reason: insufficient funds.

☛ FOREIGN NEWS

France
British novelist Arnold Bennett loved Paris and bristled when it was suggested that the city's water was not potable. To demonstrate his faith in his adopted city, Bennett quaffed some *eau de Paris*. Whether the water

did him in or not is a question better left to forensic experts. At any rate, shortly after Bennett's drink of faith he developed typhoid fever and died.

Safecracker Henri Charrière had a butterfly tattooed on his chest, hence his nickname, "Papillon," the French word for that colorful insect. Apprehended in Paris for killing a pimp in 1931, he was sentenced to hard labor for life, his claim that he had been framed falling on deaf ears. Fourteen years later, after eight futile attempts, he would escape from the penal colony in French Guiana called Devil's Island by using a raft made out of bags of coconuts to keep him afloat in the treacherous waters surrounding the island.

Holland
Prima ballerina Anna Pavlova was celebrating New Year's Eve at the Cannes restaurant when a pigeon flew in through an open window and perched on her shoulder. Pavlova became *distrait,* mindful of a Russian superstition that held that a bird flying into a room meant death. The ballerina cut short her revelry, leaving the restaurant before midnight.
Less than three weeks after the incident, Pavlova was stricken with pleurisy while in The Hague. The lung infection worsened, and she went into a coma, regaining consciousness some hours later to make the sign of the cross and to say to her maid, "Get my swan costume ready." A half hour later she died, just a week short of her forty-ninth birthday.

Germany
Balloonists Auguste Piccard and Charles Kipfer ascended from Augsburg in a hot-air balloon that had a pressurized cabin, a first in ballooning. The duo stayed aloft for sixteen hours, reaching a height of 51,775 feet, the highest altitude ever achieved in a balloon.

Japan
Beginning in 1931, the Japanese naval academy initiated an exercise that would be part of its curriculum for the next decade. Each student was required to answer the following question: "How would you carry out a surprise attack on Pearl Harbor?"

☛ REGIONAL NEWS

New York
The Empire State Building was completed, becoming the tallest office building in the world. Although it was originally conceived as a modest structure of thirty stories, Joseph Raskob and his fellow investors had gotten caught up in a height competition. The Metropolitan Life

Insurance Building had held the prize at 700 feet but was topped by 100 feet by the Woolworth Building. Then along came the Bank of Manhattan at 900 feet, only to be bested by the Chrysler Building in 1930, breaking the magical 1,000-foot mark by a scant 36 feet.

Raskob sent his architects back to their drawing boards with orders to raise the Empire State Building to 1,250 feet. An extraordinary construction feat, the 102-story building was finished in under a year because Raskob wanted it completed by May 1, 1931, the date when many New York City office leases came up for renewal. Built with 10 million bricks, the building was constructed on the two-acre site of the old Waldorf-Astoria. City zoning laws required high-rise structures to narrow as they increased in height, resulting in only one quarter of the building's square footage being in the upper stories. A television tower would be added in 1950, adding another 222 feet, and it would remain the world's highest office building for thirty-nine years.

• On the morning of July 28, 1945, a B-25 bomber crashed into the building in pea soup fog, killing three crew members and ten early morning pedestrians below who were hit by falling debris. The seventy-eighth and seventy-ninth stories of the structure were heavily damaged.

• On March 31, 1956, lights were turned on atop the building. They were so powerful they could be seen from an aircraft as far away as 300 miles.

• Christmas 1977 found John Helms despondent and without funds. He jumped off the eighty-sixth floor of the Empire State Building, lost consciousness, and woke up a half hour later on a ledge one floor below, the wind having blown him back onto the building. He tapped on the window of an office and attracted the attention of an employee named Bill Steckman. Steckman recalled, "I couldn't believe it. You don't see a lot of guys coming through the window of the eighty-fifth floor. I poured myself a stiff drink. . . ." The story of Helms's abortive suicide attempt brought scores of calls offering him lodging for the holidays.

• Lightning strikes the Empire State Building on an average of twenty-three times a year.

• Mohawk Indians contributed heavily to the construction of the giant skyscraper, riveting the lengths of steel together as the frame stretched skyward. Their total lack of fear of heights and catlike agility enabled them to move easily and quickly across the narrow beams. This unique facility had been discovered in 1866 when some members of the Caughnawaga reservation had been hired to work on a bridge being built across the St. Lawrence River. To the astonishment of their employers, the Mohawks had moved about on the superstructure as easily as they had on the ground below. No major New York skyscraper would be built without their aid.

1931

Nevada

The State of Nevada had traditionally suffered from a low tax base because of its low population, lack of industrial development, and abundance of untaxable federal lands. When the Depression added to their revenue problems, the state sought other means of generating funds. Legislators came up with one way of improving the state's economy, enacting a law requiring only a six-week residency to obtain a divorce. There were 5,260 divorces granted in Nevada in 1931, and Reno would soon be known as the Divorce Capital of the World as wealthy would-be divorcées settled in at local dude ranches to wait out the residency requirement.

Alabama

Nine black youths, between the ages of thirteen and twenty, went on trial in Scottsboro, Alabama, for the alleged rape of two white women on a freight train. Victoria Price, nineteen, and Ruby Bates, seventeen, concerned that they were about to be arrested for vagrancy, accused the boys after a fight had broken out on the train between them and a group of whites. The attorney assigned to defend the blacks did so reluctantly, was drunk during most of the trial, and called no witnesses in his clients' defense. Although an examination of the two women revealed that they had not had sexual intercourse recently, the prosecutor told the jury, "Guilty or not, let's get rid of these niggers," and it concurred, returning a guilty verdict. Eight of the boys were sentenced to death, the ninth to life imprisonment because he was underage.

The verdict created the greatest worldwide protest since the execution of Sacco and Vanzetti; there were riots in Harlem and attacks on our embassies in Europe, and an American bank was bombed in Cuba. There were six more trials and three appeals to the Supreme Court, but the prisoners remained behind bars even when Ruby Bates later admitted to having fabricated her charges. It would not be until 1937 that charges against five of the defendants were withdrawn, the other four remaining in jail until the 1940s. The nine boys would spend a total of over 100 years in prison for a crime that they had not committed.

• In 1977, the judiciary committee of the Alabama legislature voted against a proposed bill that would have compensated defendant Clarence Willie Norris with $10,000 after his pardon in 1976 by Governor George C. Wallace.

☛FOLKWAYS AND MORES

The Council of Churches of Christ in America came out in favor of birth control in 1931.

130

The Metropolitan Insurance Company released figures showing that there had been 20,000 suicides in 1931, far exceeding the twelve-month period following the Wall Street crash.

☛ SCIENCE

Scientist Charles S. Ford wrote a book submitting proof that the world was flat. Ford must have suspected that his work would not be received sympathetically by the scientific community, his introduction reading as follows: "To me the truth is precious . . . and I should rather be right and stand alone than run with the multitude and be wrong. [My views have] already won the scorn and contempt of some of my fellow men. I am looked upon as being odd, strange, peculiar. . . . But truth is truth and though all the world reject and turn against me, I will cling to the truth still."

☛ MARRIAGE AND COURTSHIP

Briton Glynn de Moss Wolfe married his first wife in 1931 and would marry for the twenty-fourth time in 1980—never taking a bride over the age of twenty-five, and siring forty children along the way. Wolfe kept several wedding dresses stashed away in various sizes so that no untoward delay would be forthcoming should matrimonial opportunities present themselves.

Across the Atlantic, an American named Tommy Manville was also married in 1931; he would eventually go to the altar a total of eleven times. The son of the founder of the Johns-Manville Corporation had taken his first wife when he was seventeen after a five-day courtship. Divorcing her in 1922, he had married his father's secretary, Lois Arline McCoin, twenty-three, in 1925. Sadly, the marriage was a short one, his wife expressing an opinion that would be shared by other Manville spouses: "Tommy never enjoyed being married. For him, the fun was in the chase. I took exactly three days to realize it."

Babe Ruth predicted that Manville's 1931 union would not last a month, but Manville proved the Babe wrong since the couple did not separate for thirty-four days. "Never again," said the disillusioned husband after his fourth wife failed to pass muster in 1937, but he succumbed once again in 1941 and took spouse number five, a chesty blonde. But Manville's tolerance for domesticity did not improve, and his fifth marriage dissolved after seventeen days, his sixth after two months,

1931 and marriage number seven lasted just eight hours. Manville's eighth, ninth, and tenth wives were similarly dispatched, and his eleventh and final choice was a waitress named Christine Erlen, whom he married in 1960 when he was sixty-six. They were still together when Manville died in 1967.

• Manville received a note from an Iowa farmer after his seventh marriage had failed. The farmer wrote, "My brother is in a mental institution. They ought to let him out and put you in."

• Discussing the cost of his numerous divorces in an interview with columnist Ed Sullivan, Manville commented, "Every penny was well spent. I know some of the biggest men in the country who spent a lot more on hobbies and ended up with a lot less."

☛ MUSIC

On November 3, 1929, Ripley's "Believe It Or Not" cartoon, a national favorite, had startled Americans with the news that the country had no official national anthem. Furthermore, announced Ripley, the anthem that the country had unofficially adopted was an old English drinking song, an unusual choice for a nation that had fought Britain in two wars and had banished alcoholic beverages.

Ripley's cartoon galvanized Americans into action as over 5 million concerned citizens petitioned Congress to establish a national anthem once and for all. The old English drinking song that Ripley had referred to was "To Anacreon in Heaven," written about 1780 as the official song of a London musical society. "The Star-Spangled Banner," a poem that Francis Scott Key had written while observing the bombardment of Baltimore's Fort McHenry during the War of 1812, had been set to the music of this ballad, which despite wartime antagonism, was then an extremely popular tune in the United States.

In 1931, many Americans were opposed to adopting "The Star-Spangled Banner" as the country's national anthem. Some found it difficult to sing, others disliked the emphasis that the lyrics put on war. Among the other contenders were "America," dashed off in just a half hour by a Baptist minister, and "America the Beautiful," inspired by Katherine Lee Bates's first visit to Colorado's Pikes Peak. Not a contender at the time was Irving Berlin's "God Bless America," which Berlin had written but did not introduce until 1938.

After much debate, Congress made "The Star-Spangled Banner" America's official national anthem, but it is not alone in having music that

132

was composed across the Atlantic. "The Battle Hymn of the Republic," "Yankee Doodle," and "Hail to the Chief" all share that distinction.

• "Hail to the Chief" is a tune well known to Americans, although it is doubtful whether even the most patriotic citizen could sing the first verse. It goes like this:

> Hail to the Chief who in triumph advances!
> Honored and bless'd be the evergreen pine.
> Long may the tree, in his banner that glances,
> Flourish, the shelter and grace of our line.

Its source is Sir Walter Scott's story in verse *The Lady of the Lake*, and the "chief" in the title is actually Roderick Dhu, fictional chief of a Highland clan. The pine was Roderick's clan badge.

ENTERTAINMENT

On Christmas Day 1931, a cultured and somewhat hushed voice came across the nation's radio airwaves: "Good afternoon, opera lovers from coast to coast." Listeners sat back to listen to live opera from New York's Metropolitan Opera House for the first time, introduced and commented on by Milton Cross. These Texaco-sponsored broadcasts bore Cross's imprint for the next forty-three years and 800 broadcasts on Saturday afternoons.

In 1922, Cross had sung ballads on Newark's station WJZ, having studied music at the Damrosch Institute, later to become the Juilliard School of Music. He then turned to announcing, hosting broadcasts of Chicago's Civic Opera. His broadcasts from the Met were an immediate success, Cross projecting a blend of conservatism and enthusiasm as he unfolded the convoluted plot of yet another comic opera or melodrama.

Cross made few mistakes, but one of them bears noting. At the end of one broadcast, he intended to tell his audience not to switch their dials to another station or to turn off their sets, because the news would follow. Instead, Cross announced, "Stay stewed for the nudes."

Actress Helen Hayes appeared in her first movie in 1931, after having established herself as a distinguished stage actress. The film was called *The Sin of Madelon Claudet,* and when Hayes went to the first screening of the movie, she was so appalled by her acting that she begged the studio to sell her the film so that she could prevent its distribution. The studio turned her down, distributed the movie to theaters across the country, and Hayes won an Academy Award for her performance.

133

1931 *The Little Show* opened on Broadway, featuring the song "Mad Dogs and Englishmen," conceived by England's Noel Coward in 1930 while motoring from Hanoi to Saigon.

Dracula was a film that achieved great acclaim in 1931, starring Bela Lugosi. The Hungarian-born Lugosi was so successful in the role that he was typecast as the prototypical diabolical madman in one Hollywood film after another, maintaining his image offscreen by holding interviews with the press while reclining in a coffin. Lugosi became a drug addict and died at seventy-three in 1956, appropriately laid to rest in the same cape he had worn as Dracula.

Another classic horror movie made its debut in 1931, the film *Frankenstein*, starring Boris Karloff. Preparing Karloff for the role was a task that took makeup man Jack Pierce five hours each filming day. The monster's head had to be formed into a square, with a large scar across the forehead. Karloff's arms were made to look long by shortening the sleeves of his coat, while his legs were stiffened by steel supports. Pierce used black shoe polish on Karloff's fingernails, and greasepaint of a bilious blue-green hue was used to cover his face.

• *Frankenstein, or the Modern Prometheus* had been first published in 1818, written by twenty-one-year-old Mary Wollstonecraft Shelley under somewhat unusual conditions. She and her husband, the poet Percy Bysshe Shelley, were staying at Lord Byron's villa in Geneva with Byron and a friend. As a lark, Byron suggested that all four try their hands at writing a ghost story, and young Mary's tale of scientist Victor Frankenstein and his ghoulish creation was declared the winner.

☛ SPORTS

Alpine skiing championships for women were inaugurated at Murren, Switzerland. The winner of both the downhill and slalom events was a young woman named Esme MacKinnon from largely snowless Great Britain.

Tennis fans at Wimbledon were shocked when a female competitor named Lili de Alvarez took to the court in short trousers instead of the traditional knee-length skirt. Although they appreciated the increased mobility that the novel costume offered, onlookers predicted a short life for the abbreviated trousers because they were convinced that most women would find them too ugly to wear.

On February 2, 1931, a horse named Brampton was driving for the **1931** wire in a race in Dargaville, New Zealand, comfortably in the lead. Forty feet from the finish line, Brampton fell, rolled over several times with his jockey clinging frantically to his back, and crossed the line the winner.

Major league baseball made a rule change, deciding that hits that bounced into the stands would no longer be counted as home runs but would henceforth be ruled as two-base hits.

On February 17, 1931, the first sporting event ever to be telecast took place in Japan: a baseball game between members of the Waseda University Baseball Club in Tokyo. Four months later, Britain's Derby was televised from Epsom Downs, with the *Daily Telegraph* reporting that "all the Derby scenes were easily discernible. The parade of the horses, the enormous crowd, and the dramatic flash past the post."

On March 31, 1931, Notre Dame football coach Knute Rockne dined with friends at a Chicago hotel and then took a cab to the airport to catch a plane to Los Angeles to attend a Studebaker sales meeting and discuss a football film with a Hollywood studio. Later that night, his Trans-Continental and Western Airways flight crashed near the town of Bazaar, Kansas, killing all on board. Knute Rockne's Notre Dame squad had enjoyed a perfect season in 1930, going undefeated in ten games, bringing his thirteen-year record in South Bend to 105 wins, 12 losses, and 5 ties.

1932

☛ NATIONAL NEWS

In William Manchester's book *The Glory and the Dream,* the author tells of a *Saturday Evening Post* writer who asked the eminent British economist John Maynard Keynes if he could think of a historical event similar to the Depression. "Yes," replied Keynes. "It was the Dark Ages, and it lasted four hundred years."

Both Manchester and Frederick Lewis Allen refer to 1932 as the "cruelest year," and it is doubtful whether there has been another in our nation's history that recorded as much human misery. Perhaps even worse than the hunger and deprivation was the average man's feeling of helplessness, of not understanding why all this was happening to him, what was being done to stop it, or when it was going to end. Author Peter Drucker writes, "Depression shows man as a senseless cog in a senselessly whirling machine which is beyond human understanding and has ceased to serve any purpose of its own." Frederick Lewis Allen adds:

136

Perhaps the worst thing about this Depression was its inexorable continuance year after year. Men who have been sturdy and self-respecting workers can take unemployment without flinching for a few weeks, a few months, even if they have to see their families suffer; but it is different after a year . . . two years . . . three years. . . . Among the miserable creatures curled up on park benches or standing in dreary lines before the soup kitchens in 1932 were men who had been jobless since the end of 1929.

☞ DEPRESSION VIGNETTES

Some vignettes of the Depression in 1932 follow:
• A Brooklyn, New York, writer answered his doorbell one morning, expecting to find the postman making his usual delivery. "Instead of the postman, however, I was confronted by two children, a girl, as we afterwards learned, of ten and a boy of eight. Not very adequate for the season and the weather, their clothing was patched but clean. They carried school books. 'Excuse me, Mister,' said the girl in a voice that sounded older than she looked, 'but we have no eats in our house and my mother said I should take my brother before we go to school and ring a doorbell in some house'—she swallowed heavily and took a deep breath—'and ask you to give us something to eat.'"
• Emigration outpaced immigration as it would throughout the decade. Applicants for jobs in Russia averaged 350 a day.
• There was so great an overabundance of unemployed college graduates that New York department stores could require applicants for the position of elevator operator to have a bachelor's degree.
• The University of Chicago's Special Committee on Garbage Dumps reported: "Garbage eating was reported at Cicero and 31st Street, at the I.C.C. Railroad at 25th Street, at Fulton and Randolf markets, at 40th and Ashland, and at the large dump at Summit."
• Not only people were broke in 1932. Many states, counties, and towns were also feeling the pinch. When an Ohio county was forced to cut off aid to the poor because of lack of funds, a crowd desperate for food invaded Toledo stores and seized goods from the shelves.
• "Brother Can You Spare a Dime?" was a hit song.
• The *New York Times* announced that a new organization had come into being called the Association of Unemployed College Alumni.
• Mr. and Mrs. Joseph Jacobs named their newly arrived baby girl Norma Depression Jacobs.
• The Jones family went to court to change the name of their four-year-old son from Herbert Hoover Jones to Franklin D. Roosevelt Jones,

1932 stating a desire to "relieve the young man from the chagrin and mortification which he is suffering and will suffer."

- By the autumn of 1932, approximately 25 percent of the nation's banks were no longer operating.

- In 1932, 56 percent of blacks and 40 percent of whites were without jobs.

- Two hundred fifty thousand children under the age of twenty-one were estimated to be "roaming the country," using freight trains as their means of transportation.

Against this somber background, a presidential campaign was waged in 1932. It pitted the incumbent, still believing that the tide of economic events would turn in his favor, against two-time New York governor, Democrat Franklin Delano Roosevelt.

The fifty-year-old Roosevelt's patrician background provided him with social and financial credentials more common to the Republican Party than to his own. He had been born in Hyde Park, New York, the son of lawyer and financier James Roosevelt and the former Sara Delano. His parents between them numbered no fewer than twelve ancestors who had come to America on the *Mayflower*, and FDR was related to eleven former presidents when he took office in 1933. His father was a Democrat who had served Hyde Park as town supervisor and hospital trustee, having turned down opportunities to run for the legislature and Congress, regarding politics as "an occupation for those who were willing to deal with immigrants."

As the couple's sole issue, Franklin lacked neither possessions nor diversions and was doted on by his parents, whom he called "Popsie" and "Sallie." He received his early education from private tutors, learned to speak French and German, and enjoyed country life on his father's 187-acre estate, playing with his red setter, his pony, and his sailboat, and collecting stamps. When he went to the village, it was usually to get his hair cut, instructed by his governess not to converse with the locals. He first traveled to Europe at the age of two and spent most of his summers in England and Germany until he reached the age of fourteen. At five, he had been taken to the White House, where a disgruntled President Cleveland, suffering the exigencies of his office, had said to young Franklin, "My little man, I am making a strange wish for you. It is that you may never be president of the United States."

When FDR left home in September 1896, he was not abruptly intermingled with the great unwashed; he was sent to prep school at Groton, where his fellow students came from families listed in the *Social Register*, just like his own. After graduation, he went to Harvard in the fall of 1900, where he enjoyed mixed academic, social, and extracurricular

138

success, becoming editor of the *Crimson*, the student newspaper, but was turned down by the club of his choice, Porcellian, which he described nearly two decades later as the "greatest disappointment of my life." He had been seen as a bit too eager to curry favor with his peers, a touch "pushy," but his shortcomings could not have been serious ones, for, upon graduation, he was elected permanent chairman of the class committee.

Roosevelt's family ties had not been weakened during his absence from Hyde Park. After his father's death in 1901, his mother took up residence in Cambridge to be near her son. His cousin Theodore had been elected president in 1901, abetting FDR's social standing, and he had attended the debut of Teddy's daughter Alice at the White House in 1902. Also while at Harvard, he had fallen in love with his cousin Eleanor, the daughter of the president's deceased brother Elliott.

Roosevelt's mother had not been at all pleased by her son's affection for Eleanor, a shy and distinctly plain girl whom she regarded as an unsuitable potential spouse for her tall, handsome son. Between the ages of eight and ten, Eleanor had lost her father, mother, and a brother, and was brought up by her grandmother before being sent away to school; she had been nicknamed "Granny" by her fellow family members because of her serious demeanor. As Franklin and Eleanor's relationship blossomed, Sara Roosevelt had become more active in her opposition, taking her son away on a Caribbean cruise in the hope that fate might intervene on her behalf in the form of a shipboard romance. But Franklin was charmed by his cousin's sincerity and intelligence, choosing Columbia Law School for his graduate work so that he could be near her. They were married in the spring of 1905, President Roosevelt himself giving away the bride. But if Eleanor had hoped that matrimony might bring her independence from her mother-in-law, she was sadly mistaken. The couple's wedding gift from Franklin's mother was a townhouse at 125 East Thirty-sixth Street, just three blocks away from Sara Roosevelt's home at 200 Madison Avenue. Their next New York City residence would find them even closer, living in side-by-side townhouses that shared common living and dining rooms.

Roosevelt had failed to distinguish himself at Columbia, cutting classes frequently and failing several courses, leaving law school before receiving his degree. However, he had absorbed enough law to pass the bar examinations, and joined the prestigious Manhattan firm of Carter, Ledyard & Milburn as a clerk.

Since birth, the future quintessential egalitarian had lived in a hothouse environment of extreme ease and privilege, enjoying the fruits of his upbringing. Consistent with his background, he might well have continued along this path—lawyer, husband, father, clubman, sportsman, traveler—perhaps even returning to Hyde Park in the role of country squire that his mother wished for him. Perhaps it was the influence of his

1932 serious new wife, perhaps that of his presidential cousin, because early in his fledgling legal career, Roosevelt made a startling confession to a fellow law clerk. He announced that he wanted to be elected to the state assembly, then to serve as assistant secretary of the navy, to be followed by becoming governor of New York and then president of the United States!

The career path that Roosevelt had outlined was the exact route that his cousin had taken to the White House and, with only a minor variation, would be FDR's path as well. But at the time, it must have seemed like a highly quixotic set of goals for a young man who had recently failed to obtain his law school degree, content to have his income supplemented by a doting mother so that he could live in a townhouse waited on by three servants. But with the faint embers of Roosevelt's ambition suddenly brought to blaze, his goals gradually came to pass.

In 1907, Democratic officials in his Dutchess County home district were looking for a candidate for state senator. Because only one Democrat had been elected in the district since 1856, party stalwarts were not clamoring to become cannon fodder in yet another hopeless cause, forcing Democratic bigwigs to look beyond the ranks of their more prominent members. Despite his political inexperience, Roosevelt had some desirable credentials: youth, good looks, a name that was a proved vote getter, and perhaps of even greater importance, the ability to finance his own campaign, since party politicos were reluctant to tap their meager treasury for such a seemingly futile cause. So FDR won the nomination and waged a vigorous house-to-house campaign in a rented red Maxwell. When the votes were counted on election night, he had won by a narrow plurality.

In Albany, FDR undertook no liberal reforms, mindful of his Republican constituency, and pleased his district well enough to win a second term. As an early supporter of Woodrow Wilson, he was delighted when the New Jersey governor won the presidency in 1912, even more so when the second step in his self-prophecy came true, and he was appointed assistant secretary of the navy.

Down to Washington went the Roosevelts, aglow at the prospect of living in the nation's capital with the movers and shakers of government. Having proved himself an able vote getter, FDR now developed administrative skills and broadened his contacts, while his good looks and charm opened up an extensive social life. Words like "matinee idol" and "twentieth-century Apollo" were used to describe him at the time, and Washington hostesses showered invitations upon the couple. But then Fate stepped in, having decided that young Roosevelt would not be allowed to leap from peak to peak but would have to test the valleys below, as FDR faced a crisis on the home front of no mean proportions.
140

Eleanor Roosevelt's lack of interest in sex is well documented, and she later told her daughter that the physical intimacies of marriage were an "ordeal." Her lack of ardor could only have been exacerbated by giving birth to seven children in nine years (one of whom, the first Franklin, Jr., died in 1909). After delivering for the seventh time in 1916, "Eleanor put her foot down," in the words of her son James, and she and Franklin would not share the same bed for the rest of their marriage.

In 1918, Eleanor found some letters that left no doubt that her husband had been carrying on an affair with her part-time social secretary, Lucy Rutherford. Confronted with her discovery, Roosevelt considered divorcing Eleanor and marrying Rutherford, but there were too many pitfalls in his path. A divorce with adultery as grounds would have sounded the death knell for his political career; furthermore, Rutherford was a Catholic, unable to marry a divorced man in her church; finally, Roosevelt's mother opposed his divorce, and thwarting her might have brought an end to her financial assistance. And so Roosevelt sought conciliation with his spouse, and she, for the sake of the children, agreed to remain his wife. FDR broke off his affair with Lucy Rutherford, although they would meet without Eleanor's knowledge until his death.

Many historians believe that Roosevelt's White House secretary, Missy LeHand, later became the president's mistress. Roosevelt's son Elliott concurs, his son James does not, but the truth seems unimportant as it applies to the relationship between Franklin and Eleanor. Theirs would be a platonic relationship, which obviously suited her best. It would strengthen from this low point as years passed, particularly after Roosevelt was stricken with polio. It would be based solely on their respect for one another's abilities, values, and ideals.

Roosevelt's prospects were bright indeed when he journeyed to the family's Canadian summer home at Campobello in early August 1921. His stint at the Department of the Navy had been a success, and presidential candidate James Cox had selected him as his running mate in the 1920 election. Although a Republican landslide had been inevitable, FDR profited politically by waging an effective campaign. Returning to New York City after the election to practice law, Roosevelt found his earning power enhanced by his government contacts, leaving him plenty of time to scan the political horizon, looking for an opportunity to launch his next foray. But when he returned to New York from Campobello six weeks later, it was not to his home but to Presbyterian Hospital. Roosevelt had contracted poliomyelitis, which left him paralyzed from the waist down.

FDR thought that he would soon regain the use of his legs, a belief that he would harbor for the next several years. But in March 1922, he was fitted with the seven-pound braces on each leg that would be his cumbersome companions for the rest of his life; no treatment or therapy

1932 would significantly improve his condition, although he would assiduously pursue them. How could anyone contemplate furthering one's political career with such an affliction? What gave FDR the strength to resume his quest?

First and foremost was his own character. Author Ted Morgan writes, "Out of his pain came personal renewal, greater understanding, and surprising reserves of strength." FDR cast off the last vestiges of youth. He had more than enough time to think, to contemplate the cruel card that had been dealt him, and he finally decided that he would not let polio do him in.

The second factor was a chance opportunity that came his way in 1924. Presidential candidate Al Smith asked his former campaign manager, Joseph Proskauer, whom he would recommend to place his name in nomination for president at the upcoming Democratic Convention to be held at New York's Madison Square Garden. Proskauer suggested Roosevelt, and the surprised Smith asked him to explain his choice. Proskauer replied, "Because you're a Bowery mick and he's a Protestant patrician, and he'd take some of the curse off you." Smith agreed to the political expediency of Proskauer's choice, and the two went to see Roosevelt, who said that he would be happy to nominate Smith but that he was too busy dealing with the delegates to write a speech, suggesting that Proskauer write it for him. But when Proskauer returned with a draft, Roosevelt did not like it and wrote one himself. To resolve which speech was better, newspaper editor Herbert Bayard Swope was asked to read them both and select the best one. Swope read Roosevelt's speech first and pronounced it "lousy." He then read Proskauer's, proclaiming it the "greatest nominating speech" since the silver-tongued William Jennings Bryan had nominated Grover Cleveland. FDR was highly miffed at Swope's choice but agreed to give Proskauer's speech, saying, "All right, I'll make the goddamned speech, and it'll be a flop."

Getting to the podium at Madison Square Garden was no easy task for FDR. His son James helped him to the rear of the platform, and then he used his crutches to struggle to the microphone as every set of eyes in the hushed crowd followed each step. Just over a half hour later, Roosevelt finished Proskauer's speech, which paraphrased a quote from Wordsworth at its finish, supplying a nickname for Smith that would be his for years to come:

> Who is the Happy Warrior? Who is he
> That every man in arms would wish to be.

Those final words brought forth a forty-minute demonstration, many observers later commenting that Roosevelt's nomination for the presiden-

142

cy in 1932 had been assured at just after midnight on June 27, 1924, at
Madison Square Garden.

Author Paul Conkin writes, "Polio made the aristocratic Roosevelt into an underdog. For him it replaced the log cabin." Whether Conkin's words are altogether true, Roosevelt did turn adversity into triumph, going on to be elected governor of New York twice, the last victory by the greatest plurality in the state's history. When it came time for the Democratic Convention in Chicago in 1932, FDR was the front-runner, his aides James Farley and Louis Howe having done excellent advance work with the delegates. James Nance Garner released delegates pledged to him in return for the vice presidential nomination, putting FDR over the top. Roosevelt flew to Chicago from Albany, abandoning the traditional custom of waiting for a delegation to visit him personally to inform him of his nomination. His acceptance speech contained the words, "I pledge you, I pledge myself, to a new deal for the American people," and the New Deal was born.

Roosevelt's nomination, however, was not greeted with enthusiasm by many of the pundits of the day. Journalist Walter Lippmann, who had earlier written off FDR as "an amiable Boy Scout," wrote that Roosevelt was a "pleasant man who, without any important qualifications for the office, would like to be President." H. L. Mencken described the event as a "great convention . . . nominating the weakest candidate before it." A politician loyal to Garner said, "It's a mule ticket, stronger in the hindquarters than in the front."

If the New Deal had been declared, its eventual ideology had not emerged. Roosevelt campaigned for a balanced federal budget and frugality in government spending (both of which he would blatantly violate), inspiring one newspaper to write, "We have another Hoover." But these responses to Roosevelt's nomination did not faze John Nance Garner, who saw the handwriting on the wall, suggesting that the ticket, "sit down—do nothing—and win the election." And he did exactly that, contributing just one radio speech, while the handicapped presidential candidate stumped 13,000 miles back and forth across the country, in what hindsight proved to have been an unnecessary use of his energies. FDR won by a 7-million-vote plurality, taking forty-two of forty-eight states. In a massive bit of understatement, Herbert Hoover in his *Memoirs* later wrote, "General prosperity had been a great ally in the election of 1928, but was a major enemy in 1932."

• A bit of doggerel circulated by the Democrats in 1932:

> Mellon pulled the whistle,
> Hoover rang the bell.
> Wall Street gave the signal,
> And the country went to hell.

1932 No person in the United States was more adored than was Charles Lindberg, conqueror of the skies. When his infant son was kidnapped on the night of March 1, 1932, the nation gave forth an outpouring of outrage and sympathy, reacting as though a member of their own family had been snatched away.

A ladder had been used to reach the second story of the Lindberghs' Hopewell, New Jersey, home to remove Charles, Jr., from his crib. A note was left, advising the child's father that the twenty-month-old boy would be in good care and that $50,000 in ransom money would be required to gain his release; the note carried a curious symbol of two intersecting circles. Details of how the funds were to be delivered were to follow, and Lindberg was advised not to contact the police.

But the police were called in, and the news was picked up by the press. Newspaper sales saw a 20 percent gain, President Hoover pledged the aid of federal authorities, and a jailed Al Capone offered a $10,000 reward. The next day, Anne Morrow Lindbergh gave the press a list of the foods that made up the baby's diet so that the kidnapper(s) could provide proper nourishment for the child. Roads around the Lindbergh house were jammed, and what clues the police might have been able to find were soon obliterated by curiosity seekers. A shady ex-Department of Justice agent assured millionaire Evalyn Walsh McLean that he could arrange for the baby's release for $100,000; she provided the funds, and McLean turned out to have been bilked.

The first break in the case came when a retired Bronx schoolteacher named John Condon wrote a letter to the *Bronx Home News* offering $1,000 for the return of the child and his services as an intermediary between the kidnapper(s) and the Lindbergh family. Soon he received a note that contained a duplicate of the symbol on the note left in the nursery of the Lindbergh home, which had not been publicized. The note contained a message for Lindbergh advising him on how to deliver the ransom money. Like the original letter, it appeared to have been written by a German, based on certain word usages and misspellings and the transposition of the dollar sign: 1000$. Lindbergh obtained the funds and accompanied Condon to a Bronx cemetery where contact was made, the money delivered, and a note received advising that the child could be found on a boat off Martha's Vineyard. But after two days of searching the island and its environs, no trace of the baby was found.

On May 12, 1932, a truck driver came upon the body of a child not far from the Lindberghs' house, buried in a shallow grave, dead of a fractured skull. It would not be until September 1934 that the police got an important lead in the case. The ransom had been paid in gold certificates, and when the nation had gone off the gold standard, all gold certificates were recalled, police asked filling station attendants to record the license plate number of anyone using one of the bills for payment.
144

And so it was that a man paid for his gas with one of the gold certificates **1932** used as ransom in the kidnapping, his license plate was duly recorded, and several days later the police traced the automobile to Bruno Richard Hauptmann, a German-born carpenter, with a criminal record in his own country, who lived at 1379 East 222nd Street in the Bronx. More than $13,000 of the ransom money was found in his garage, his handwriting and spelling were identical with that on the various ransom notes, and the ladder left behind on the night of the kidnapping was matched exactly to a missing piece from the floor of Hauptmann's attic. John Condon identified Hauptmann's voice as the one he had heard in the cemetery, and New Jersey prosecutors started mounting their case.

The press flocked to Flemington, New Jersey, for the trial, over 300 reporters attending the proceedings, including Edna Ferber, Damon Runyon, Walter Winchell, and Alexander Woollcott. The jury deliberated for eleven hours and then pronounced Hauptmann guilty. The *New York Times* wrote:

> The charge of the judge and the verdict of the jury established a crime but did not clear away a mystery. We do not yet know exactly what happened on the tragic night at Hopewell. . . . The presiding judge . . . told the jury that the State had been unable to present positive evidence identifying the prisoner at the time and place of the original crime, and that circumstantial evidence had to be depended upon.

In 1936, the Lindbergh family took up residence in England in an attempt to seek some relief from the publicity that had focused on them for nine years and did not return to the United States until the 1940s. Then in 1950, a man knocked on the door of their Darien, Connecticut, home and claimed to be Charles Lindbergh, Jr. He was to return again, as did many others like him, to reopen the Lindberghs' old wounds.

☛ FOREIGN NEWS

France
French author Tristan Bernard was a prolific writer who would turn out fifty novels and forty plays. He wrote a two-character play in 1932 called *The Exile*, which must be a candidate for the briefest stage work ever written. Here is how it goes:

> The curtain rises on the interior of a mountain cabin located near the frontier. The mountaineer is seated before his fireplace. There is a knock on the door. The exile enters.

145

1932 EXILE: Whoever you are, have pity on a hunted man. There is a price on my head.
MOUNTAINEER: How much?

The exile hastily leaves, as the curtain falls.

Soviet Union
A meat shortage in the Soviet Union had led to rabbit breeding. The government announced that the 1.5 million rabbits on hand were expected to grow to 7 million in the next twelve months and to 25 million by 1934. The Soviet newspaper *Izvestia* warned, "Eschew those who underestimate the rabbit."

☞ MEDIA

The *National Police Gazette* had fallen on hard times and published its last edition in February 1932. The publication has been described by author George Gipe as "*Playboy,* the *National Enquirer, True Detective,* and *Sports Illustrated* all wrapped up in one—sixteen pale pink quarto pages of sex scandals, crime, cheesecake, and lurid advertising, profusely illustrated with magnificently detailed woodcuts." Respectable newspaper vendors had refused to sell the *Gazette,* but the paper had developed a healthy circulation through saloons and barbershops. Alas, Prohibition had dried up their bar business. And when women invaded barbershops in the 1920s to have their hair bobbed, another bastion of masculinity had been breached, leaving the *Gazette* with no adequate channel of distribution.

☞ BOOKS

Lawyer Erle Stanley Gardner wrote a mystery novel called *The Case of the Velvet Claws,* introducing fellow barrister Perry Mason. Gardner found time to practice law and turn out 140 novels between 1933 and 1938, spewing out some 1 million words a year.

Author Pearl Buck was awarded the Pulitzer Prize in 1932 for her novel *The Good Earth.* She earned over $7 million, turning over a substantial portion of her income to an organization that cared for illegitimate children conceived in Asia by members of the American armed forces.

146

☞ FOOD AND DRINK

A Texan named C. Elmer Doolin entered a San Antonio eatery and ordered a sandwich that came with some corn chips on the side. Finding them particularly tasty, he bought the recipe from the restaurant's Mexican owner for $100 and opened a family business that turned out the chips in quantity, calling his product Fritos.

☞ SPORTS

In 1932, the Dallas-based Employers Casualty Company decided to enter a team in the women's national amateur track championships, sponsored by the AAU. The team was unusual in its composition, consisting of a single competitor, a 105-pound dynamo named Mildred Didrikson, who performed like a full squad of athletes, scoring points in seven events, winning five of them, and establishing three world's records. "Babe" Didrikson went on to win three medals in the 1932 Olympics in Los Angeles, taking a gold in both the javelin and high hurdles, and a silver in the high jump.

Didrikson, who married professional wrestler George Zacharias in 1938, became the finest woman athlete of the first half of the twentieth century, excelling in a host of sports. In addition to track and field, she toured with an all-male professional baseball team, establishing a women's record that still stands by throwing a baseball 296 feet. She took a stab at boxing before turning her attention to golf, at which she would excel both as an amateur and a professional. As a pro, she won over fifty major tournaments, including fifteen in a row, and one day smashed a wind-aided drive that came to rest 346 yards away. After a cancer operation, she won her third U.S. Open in 1954, two years before her death at the age of forty-three.

Another star of the 1932 Olympics was Poland's Stanislawa Walasiewicz, who later Americanized her name to Stella Walsh when she moved to the United States. She won the 100-yard dash and became the first woman to run the distance in less than 11 seconds when she was timed in 10.8. Walsh enjoyed success in track into her forties and died in 1980, when she was killed in a robbery. An autopsy revealed the presence of small, nonfunctioning male sex organs, and subsequent chromosome tests, conducted by a coroner's office, indicated that Stella Walsh was predominantly male.

1932 Several baseball records were established in 1932:
• Cleveland shortstop John Burnett got nine hits in one game, an eighteen-inning contest on July 10.
• The New York Yankees managed to negotiate the entire season without being shut out by an opposing team.
• Lou Gehrig matched an 1896 record by hitting four home runs in a single game. Gehrig would have had five, but Philadelphia Athletics outfielder Al Simmons ran down his towering fly ball to deny him the fifth.

German heavyweight boxer Max Schmeling lost to Jack Sharkey in a tightly contested fifteen-round bout. Schmeling's manager felt that the wrong fighter had been awarded the decision, summing up his disagreement in three words, which would stand the test of time. Manager Joe Jacobs said, "We wuz robbed."

☛ ENTERTAINMENT

Manhattan late-night revelers flocked uptown to Harlem's Cotton Club, where talented black musicians, dancers, and show girls provided exciting entertainment. Until 1932, all female entertainers had to be light-skinned, a rule that was dispensed with when Louis Armstrong's wife Lucille Watson was added to the club's roster of black stars. But the club did not relax its segregation rule, and blacks continued to be banned from patronizing the club.

A man named Charles Urban Yeager came up with a gimmick to attract more patrons to his movie theater, initiating "Bank Night," a particular evening during the week when cash prizes were awarded to lucky patrons. Yeager's idea spread like wildfire and soon Bank Night was packing in movie patrons at theaters all over the country.

Rin Tin Tin died at the age of fourteen, the four-legged film star having acted in fifty movies. The dog's estate filed suit against Michael Winner in 1976, alleging that Winner's film, *Won Ton Ton, the Dog That Saved Hollywood,* was taken from the life of Rin Tin Tin. Winner commented, "It's absurd to be sued by a dog, especially by a dog who's been dead for the past twenty years."

☛ SCIENCE

Physicist John D. Cockcroft walked through the streets of Cambridge, England, repeating, "We've split the atom," shaking his head in
148

amazement. He and his associate E. T. S. Wilson had used a homemade **1932**
proton gun to unravel the "first clue to the release of atomic power."

☞ EDUCATION

Time reported that a teacher marking College Board examinations in biology came across one student's interesting answer to the following:

QUESTION: Define and clearly distinguish between a spore and sperm.
ANSWER: A spore grows right straight up into adultery but a sperm does not.

1933

In the spring of 1933, we faced a crisis. . . . We were against revolution. And, therefore, we waged war against those conditions which make revolution—against the inequalities and resentments that breed them.

—FDR

☛ NATIONAL NEWS

During the four-month interregnum between Roosevelt's election and his inauguration (on March 4—he was the last president to be sworn in on that date), a power vacuum existed in the presidency that very nearly resulted in the collapse of the nation's banking system. Serving in the White House was a lame duck president beset by worsening economic conditions, a man who lacked both a popular mandate and the support of Congress. Waiting in the wings was the president-to-be who rejected Hoover's pleas for joint action on pressing issues, claiming that he lacked the legal authority to do so. A more compelling reason for Roosevelt's not wishing to give Hoover his public support was FDR's unwillingness to be associated with the president's unpopular record. Rebuffed by Roosevelt, Hoover believed that FDR was willing to send the nation to the very edge of disaster so that he alone would be acclaimed the nation's savior when Salvation was achieved.

150

Congress had returned to Washington in early December to be **1933** greeted by a crowd of several thousand people on the steps of the Capitol chanting, "Feed the hungry, tax the rich." State and city officials hinted at the possibility of a revolution, and Will Rogers wrote, "These rascals in Russia . . . have got mighty good ideas." A senator and several respected magazines suggested a dictatorship, while many states declared bank holidays, gold was hoarded by those who distrusted the long-term value of the currency and the solvency of the banks. As March approached, there was serious doubt that the federal payroll could be met.

On the morning of the inauguration, President Hoover remarked, "We are at the end of our string. There is nothing more we can do." It was a cold, bleak day in Washington, mirroring the nation's spirits. Journalist Arthur Krock described the mood of the city as "that which might be found in a beleaguered capital in wartime"; General Douglas MacArthur had prepared his troops for a possible riot.

In his inaugural address, Roosevelt delivered his now famous words, "Let me first assert my firm belief that the only thing we have to fear is fear itself—nameless, unreasoning, unjustified terror which paralyzes needed efforts to convert retreat into advance." But the biggest cheers came when he hinted that he might have to use almost dictatorial powers: "I shall ask the Congress for . . . broad executive power to wage a war against the emergency, as great as the power that would be given to me if we were invaded by a foreign foe."

The avalanche of legislation that marked the period from March 9 to June 16 is well known, as is the declaring of a bank holiday, the calling in of gold, and the creating of an "alphabet soup" of new government agencies. Just before the inauguration, *Editor and Publisher* magazine wrote, "What this country needs if we are to shake off the torpor of fear and hopelessness is a series of blinding headlines proclaiming action, resolute leadership, a firm grip at the controls." This happened, at the direction of the president, assisted by his Brain Trust, a group of advisers who were predominantly liberal college professors. Roosevelt also began what would be known as his fireside chats, in which he explained his actions to the public in simple terms. Confidence was built, people turned in their gold, and 70 percent of the banks were able to reopen. Cabell Phillips writes, "All across the country there was a sudden upsurge of support and enthusiasm for the President. At last, people told one another, *something* was being done. . . . They deluged him with messages of fealty and good wishes." Some 14,000 letters and telegrams poured into the White House mail room during the first week alone. The *New York Daily News*, which had not backed Roosevelt in the election, grudgingly conceded it might have been wrong and wrote: "The newspaper pledges itself to support the policies of FDR for a period of at least one year; longer if circumstances warrant."

151

Alfred M. Landon of Kansas stated: "If there is any way in which a Republican governor of a midwestern state can aid the President in the fight, I now enlist for the duration of the war." When the first Hundred Days came to an end, the *New York Times* wrote:

> He [Roosevelt] seemed to the American people to be riding the whirlwind and directing the storm. The country was ready and even anxious to accept his leadership. From President Roosevelt it got a rapid succession of courageous speeches and efforts and achievements which inclined millions of his fellow citizens to acclaim him as the heaven-sent man of the hour.

Early in 1933, Chicago's Mayor Anton Cermak was worried about his city's worsening financial situation. If he could not get help fast, he foresaw the worst, but how could he cry out to Roosevelt for help when he had actively opposed FDR's nomination at the Democratic Convention? When he was urged by Alderman Paddy Bauler to seek peace with the president-elect, Cermak replied: "I don't like the sonofabitch." "For crissakes," Bauler argued, "you ain't got any money for the Chicago schoolteachers, and this Roosevelt is the only one who can get it for you. You better go . . . kiss his ass or whatever you got to do. Only you better get the goddam money for them teachers, or we ain't goin' to have a city worth runnin'."

Unable to dispute the wisdom of Bauler's reasoning, Cermak decided to go to Florida and seek an audience with Roosevelt, who would be in Miami on his return from a fishing trip. Cermak went up to the President to greet him after a speech at Bay Front Park, and as the two chatted, thirty-two-year-old Joseph Zangara fired six pistol shots at Roosevelt, missed FDR, but twice hit Cermak. The mayor died two weeks later.

☛ FOREIGN NEWS

Scotland

In the spring of 1933, a "monster" was sighted at Scotland's Loch Ness, and the *Daily Mail* decided to investigate, engaging a big-game hunter to track down the beast. Sure enough, he found some strange footprints along the shore of the lake in December of that year, which he had cast in plaster and sent to the British Museum for precise identification. While the museum's scholars analyzed the findings, the nation's newspapers trumpeted the story across the British Isles, capturing the imagination of millions of people, who debated what the investigation would reveal. It did not take the museum officials long to identify the footprints, which were judged to have "been made by a dried hippopotamus foot, perhaps a Victorian umbrella stand from someone's front hall." Periodic sightings have been reported since and even photographs have been produced, yet the elusive Loch Ness Monster remains "at large" to this very day.

Germany

While President Roosevelt was taking the helm of the American ship of state, Adolf Hitler assumed power in Germany. Author John Toland writes that a major speech by Hitler to the Reichstag "was remarkable for its prudence and moderation. He vowed to respect private property and individual initiative; promised aid to peasants and middle class alike. He would end unemployment and promote peace with France, Britain, and even the Soviet Union."

• One week later, Hitler announced a boycott of Jewish business in Germany, stating: "I believe that I act today in unison with the Almighty Creator's intention: by fighting the Jews I do battle for the Lord."

• Also in 1933, Albert Einstein's bank account was seized when German authorities found a dangerous weapon in his house—a bread knife.

• Hitler also undertook the removal of "dangerous foreigners" from German soil. One American banned from the country was Mickey Mouse. The Soviet Union followed suit in 1936, Italy in 1938, and East Germany banned the offensive rodent in 1954. Today, Mickey Mouse is known in West Germany as Michael Maus, in France as Michel Souris, in Italy as Topolino, in Japan as Kiki Kuchi, in Denmark as Mikkel Mus, and in Spain as Miguel Ratoncito.

Britain

For as long as anyone could recall, all sailors in the British navy had received a daily tot of rum, although abstainers could opt for tuppence instead. In 1933, the British Admiralty reported that 60 percent of the tars were "passing up the rum for the tuppence," a new high.

☞ REGIONAL NEWS

New York

Gas station attendants in Poughkeepsie were slack-jawed when a man drove into their stations and asked that his gas tank be filled with water. They complied each time, and each time the man dropped a pill into the tank full of water, explaining that he had found a way to convert water into gasoline. When his engine started right up, skeptical onlookers turned into enthusiastic purchasers of the pill, which just happened to be for sale. They had become victims of a much-repeated scam, the con man having poured the water into a dummy gas tank, which he would empty

153

before proceeding to the scene of his next demonstration of the "magic pill."

Illinois

Fan dancer Sally Rand did her part to relieve the Depression blues by performing at the Century of Progress Exposition at Chicago to the music of Debussy's "Clair de Lune," covered at times by some fast-moving ostrich plumes. The fair's organizers credited the agile Rand with making the event a financial success. In discussing her career, Rand commented that she had "never made any money until she took off her pants."

The Farm Belt

On November 11, 1933, a dust storm took place from the Texas panhandle to the Canadian border. The storm would be known as the "great black blizzard," turning the sky dark as far away as Albany, New York.

The huge demand for wheat during World War I had seen farmers neglecting crop rotation, planting every acre they could as wheat prices escalated. And there was very little vegetation to hold the soil because cattle had been allowed to roam free in the early part of the century, consuming every bit of greenery they encountered. When the tractor arrived, farmers could plant even more land. In 1933, a drought came to the area, turning the soil into dust. So when big winds arrived on Armistice Day in 1933, the soil just blew away. In the *Saturday Evening Post*, R. D. Lusk wrote:

> By mid-morning a gale was blowing, cold and black. By noon it was blacker than night, because one can see through night and this was an opaque black. It was a wall of dirt one's eyes could not penetrate, but it could penetrate the eyes, the ears, and nose. It could penetrate to the lungs until one coughed up black. If a person was outside, he tied his handkerchief around his face, but he still coughed up black; and inside the house, the Karnstrums [a South Dakota family] soaked sheets and towels and stuffed them around the window ledges, but these didn't help much. They were afraid because they had never seen anything like this before. When the wind died, and the sun shown forth again, it was on a different world. There were no fields, only sand drifting into mounds and eddies that swirled in what was now an autumn breeze. There was no longer a sectionline road fifty feet from the front door. It was obliterated. In the farmyard, fences, machinery, and trees were gone, buried. The roofs of sheds stuck out through drifts deeper than a man is tall.

154

An ad in the *Cincinnati Enquirer's* classified section read as follows: "Have complete course, 'How to Become a Success.' Will swap for room rent."

New Jersey

A West Orange, New Jersey, employer posted the following notice:

President Roosevelt has done his part: now you do something. Buy something—buy anything, anywhere; paint your kitchen, send a telegram, give a party, get a car, pay a bill, rent a flat, fix your roof, get a haircut, see a show, build a house, take a trip, sing a song, get married. It does not matter what you do, but get going.

☛ PROHIBITION

Utah, a state with a fairly low incidence of alcohol consumption because of its large Mormon population, became the thirty-sixth state to ratify the Twenty-first Amendment, which replaced the Eighteenth, a Utah legislator named S. P. Thurman bringing joy to the nation's spirits-lovers when he cast the deciding vote. News of the end of Prohibition reached New York at 5:33 P.M., and comedian Joe Fields of the Weber and Fields vaudeville team hoisted a glass of champagne at the Astor Hotel, claiming to be the first legal imbiber after thirteen years, ten months eighteen days, and a few hours of Prohibition.

☛ ENTERTAINMENT

Playing opposite Maurice Chevalier in the 1933 comedy *A Bedtime Story* was Baby LeRoy, a beguiling scene-stealer who later incurred the wrath of comedian W. C. Fields. Since LeRoy was but six months old, he could not legally sign a contract, nor could his mother, who was only sixteen, also underage. LeRoy's grandfather was finally pressed into service to act on the infant's behalf.

People who knew Richard Hollingshead, Jr., thought that he had taken leave of his senses in 1933 when he set up a movie projector in his yard and, using a nearby building for a screen, watched a film from his

1933 automobile. But Hollingshead had an idea that would come to fruition on the night of June 6, 1933, when the first drive-in movie theater opened on Admiral Wilson Boulevard in Camden, New Jersey. The film shown on that history-making night was *Wife Beware*, but it was parents who would beware as drive-in theaters proliferated across the nation, posing yet another threat to the morals of the young. They came to be known by the young as "passion pits," and many a teenage daughter was interrogated the morning after visiting a drive-in as to the precise plot of the film that she had gone to see.

Shirley Temple received 730,000 fan letters in 1936, but it fell short of the record set in 1933 by an actor to whom 800,000 pieces of mail were sent. The beneficiary of this tremendous show of affection was Mickey Mouse.

"Why don't you come up and see me sometime?" is a line rightfully identified with Mae West, whose sexual innuendos had done much to make her one of the most popular movie stars in the country. Actually, West did not say exactly that to Cary Grant in the 1933 film *She Done Him Wrong*. What she did say was, "Why don't you come up sometime and see me?" but repetition over time would slightly alter her invitation.

☞ SPORTS

British jockey Gordon Richards won the last race at Nottingham on October 3, 1933. Moving to Chepstow the next day, Richards won all six races on the card, and the following day at the same track he took the first five events, giving him a total of twelve victories in a row, a record that still stands. He was later knighted, becoming Sir Gordon Richards.

Racing fans at the Kentucky Derby were amazed when a lightly regarded colt named Broker's Tip won the big event. Prior to the Derby, Broker's Tip had never won a race, having entered the Churchill Downs classic as a maiden. Broker's Tip never won again after his day in the sun in Louisville, retiring with only that one victory to his credit.

Tennis ace Helen Wills Moody took the Wimbledon title, defeating Dorothy Round two sets to one. Although she had lost, Round had accomplished something that none of Moody's opponents had managed since 1927: She had won a set. During the period, Moody had won five Wimbledon titles, four French Opens, and four U.S. Opens.

A seventeen-year-old jockey named George Edward Arcaro won the **1933** first race of his career on a horse inappropriately named No More, for Arcaro would cross the finish line a victor in 4,778 more races, which included two Triple Crowns, five Derbies, six Preaknesses, and six Belmonts, finding him aboard such legendary horses as Whirlaway, Citation, Assault, Nashua, and Kelso.

• In 1942, Arcaro was nearly knocked off his mount by a jockey named Vincent Nodarse. Incensed, Arcaro retaliated by smashing Nodarse and horse into the rail, bringing about an inquiry by the track's stewards. When the stewards asked if he had deliberately made contact, Arcaro replied, "Deliberately? I was trying to kill that son of a bitch!" He was suspended from riding for a year.

Francis Wistert played tackle for Michigan's football team in 1933 wearing uniform number 11 and was named to the All American squad, starting a family tradition. His brothers Albert and Alvin both wore the same number while playing tackle at Michigan. Albert was an All-American in 1942, Alvin in both 1948 and 1949.

Babe Ruth continued to add to his list of accomplishments in 1933:
• Babe hit a two-run homer to lead the American League to victory over the National League in the first All-Star Game, held at Chicago's Comiskey Park. The game, which was the brainchild of Chicago sportswriter Arch Ward, was played for the benefit of retired players.
• The thirty-eight-year-old Babe pitched the last game of his career against the Boston Red Sox, edging the Sox 6–5 to win the ninety-fourth victory of his career against forty-six losses.

☞ ENTERTAINMENT

Eugene Gladstone O'Neill's new play, *Ah, Wilderness!*, a comedy, opened in New York City on October 2. However, it would be O'Neill's tragedies that would bring him recognition as the century's preeminent American playwright, whose works included *Desire Under the Elms, Strange Interlude, The Iceman Cometh,* and *Long Day's Journey into Night*. He had won the first of three Pulitzer prizes in 1920, had received an honorary degree from Yale in 1926, and won the Nobel Prize for literature in 1936.

Expelled from Princeton for throwing a beer bottle through the office window of the university's president, Woodrow Wilson, O'Neill had worked as a seaman, dockworker, and reporter, having once attempted suicide after bouts of alcoholism; he had begun writing plays while recuperating from tuberculosis. Critic Brooks Atkinson commented that

1933 writing plays was "not so much his profession as his obsession." His plays plumbed the depths of human misery, reflecting his own tormented life.

O'Neill's father had been an embittered actor who found success in only one play, *The Count of Monte Cristo*, playing the role of the count over 5,000 times. His mother was a morphine addict, his brother a hopeless alcoholic who had died in 1923; his son, Eugene Jr., became addicted to heroin, and his grandson, Eugene III, would die in his crib in 1946. O'Neill and his daughter Oona became estranged when she eloped with actor Charlie Chaplin at eighteen. He married three times, his last a love-hate relationship that brought him more pain than happiness. O'Neill suffered from Parkinson's disease, his hands shaking so badly before he died that he could not write or light his own cigarettes.

In 1945, O'Neill took the manuscript of *Long Day's Journey into Night* to his publisher, Bennett Cerf, at Random House. The play was placed in the company's safe, unread by anyone other than O'Neill, with instructions that it was not to be removed until twenty-five years after his death, because he did not want the play to be published or performed while members of his family were still alive. After his death, his wife did not respect his wishes, and the play was published just three years later, in 1956.

• "He has redeemed the American theater from commonplaceness and triviality." (Yale professor William Lyons Phelps)

• "It was a great mistake my being born a man, I would have been so much more successful as a sea gull or a fish. As it is, I will always be a stranger who never feels at home, who does not really want and is not really wanted, who can never belong, who must always be a little in love with death." (Edmund in *Long Day's Journey into Night*)

• O'Neill's epitaph for himself, which does not appear on his gravestone, was this:

EUGENE O'NEILL

There is something
to be said
for being dead.

Ma Perkins and *The Romance of Helen Trent* joined the growing list of daytime radio soap operas that were available to listeners eager to forget their problems for a while and involve themselves in someone else's trials and tribulations.

The king and queen of radio soap opera writers were Frank Hummert and Anne Ashenhurst, who became Mrs. Hummert in 1935. Their programs included *Amanda of Honeymoon Hill*, *Backstage Wife*, *John's Other Wife*, *Just Plain Bill*, *Our Gal Sunday*, *The Romance of Helen Trent*, *Stella Dallas*, and *Young Widder Brown*, just to name a few,

158

and by 1938 their shows would account for one eighth of all radio airtime. **1933**
The Hummerts first worked up a title and theme for each show and then
wrote a summary of the plot and key happenings over the next half dozen
episodes. Then they turned the skeleton of the show over to one of their
twenty writers, who fleshed it out. The Hummerts also employed six
editors and a clerical staff of sixty.

In their delightful book, *The Soaps,* Madeleine Edmondson and
David Rounds describe the prototypical soap opera male and female:

> Soapland women are strong and able in many areas. They may
> put careers aside when they marry in order to devote them-
> selves fully to wifehood, but this should not for one moment
> be taken to imply that they could not do all kinds of other
> things if they happened to want to. . . . Wives and mothers
> frequently have business acumen as well as insight into personal
> and psychological problems, and fortunately they do not hesitate
> to set their sons, husbands, and lovers straight, though usually
> in a tactful way, of course. Their judgments are likely to be
> correct, and when trouble comes, they, being more resourceful
> and flexible than men, are often able to come up with a solu-
> tion. . . . Men are rarely shown helping women out of their
> difficulties. It is the other way around. The truth is, men may
> seem strong, but they all have their weakness. Not only do
> they lack confidence in themselves, but they are often, for one
> reason or another, in need of practical help from women.

A few of the most popular shows:

• *Stella Dallas,* based on the 1923 novel by Olive Higgins Prouty,
was "the true to life story of mother love and sacrifice, in which Stella
Dallas saw her own beloved daughter, Laurel, marry into wealth and
society and, realizing the differences in their tastes and worlds, went out
of Laurel's life."

• *Mary Noble, Backstage Wife* was "the story of an Iowa stenog-
rapher who fell in love with and married Broadway matinee idol Larry
Noble."

• *The Romance of Helen Trent* was the story of a woman "who sets
out to prove to herself what so many women long to prove, that because a
woman is thirty-five or more . . . that romance can live in life at thirty-
five and after."

• *Our Gal Sunday* was "the story of an orphan girl named Sunday,
from the little mining town of Silver Creek, Colorado, who in young
womanhood married England's richest, most handsome lord, Lord Henry
Brinthrope. The story asks the question: Can this girl from a mining town
in the West find happiness as the wife of a wealthy and titled
Englishman?"

159

1933 • *Portia Faces Life* was "a story reflecting the courage, spirit and integrity of American women everywhere."

☞ BOOKS

Two books that censors were attempting to keep out of circulation were given a clean bill of health in 1933:
  • A New York court found in favor of Erskine Caldwell's *God's Little Acre* in a suit lodged by the New York Society for the Prevention of Vice.
  • Random House publisher Bennett Cerf had sued the government to allow publication of James Joyce's *Ulysses* in the United States, and New York's district court upheld his suit, judging the four-letter words in the novel to be consistent with the subject matter and not inserted for the sole purpose of titillating readers of the work.

☞ CRIME

In July 1933, oilman Charles Urschel was playing bridge at his home when he was forcibly abducted by two men, his family later receiving a demand for $200,000 for his safe return. The ransom was duly paid and Urschel released unharmed nine days later.

Urschel's kidnappers had not realized that they were dealing with an imaginative and highly resourceful man. Because he had been blindfolded while in custody, he could not identify his captors, but he carefully stored a number of valuable clues away in his brain. When a plane passed overhead, he asked the time and began to establish a pattern in the flights, also carefully noting a day on which no planes were heard because of bad weather. He also noted conversations about the weather, the sounds of various animals, and the noise from a squeaky well. The FBI carefully pieced together the information and surmised that Urschel had been held captive near Paradise, Texas. A search of the area turned up a farm belonging to the Shannon gang, and two weeks after Urschel had been released, the FBI moved in, capturing a gaggle of Shannons, who had indeed served as Urschel's guards, and one Harvey Bailey, whom the FBI accused of the kidnapping. Unfortunately for their vaunted reputation, they had the wrong man, although they never admitted it, and Bailey, who was a wanted bank robber but had no connection with Urschel, was sentenced to life imprisonment. After serving time on that sentence and for other crimes that he *did* commit, Bailey was paroled in 1965, at the age of seventy-eight.

Urschel's careful observations had led the FBI to the small fry, but

160

the two kidnappers were still at large. They were soon captured, but nowhere near Texas, in completely unrelated events. One of them, Albert Bates, was taken at his own home in Denver, probably on a tip from his wife. Then the second kidnapper, no other than George "Machine Gun Kelly" Barnes, was captured when the FBI traced a wire sent by a confederate to him in Memphis, his old home town. Both kidnappers were convicted for life; Bates died at Alcatraz, Kelly at Leavenworth. Ora Shannon, the Texas farm's owner, sent money for Kelly's funeral, according to his cellmate, and the body was shipped to the family plot there.

☛ PEOPLE

When Evelyn Venable was signed to a contract by Paramount Pictures, her father took no chances that his daughter's morals would be corrupted by the salacious love scenes that were the order of the day in Hollywood. On his insistence, Venable's contract released her from any scenes that required her to kiss.

Ringgold Wilmer Lardner died at his home in East Hampton, New York, which he called No Visitors, N.Y. An accomplished sportswriter, "Ring" Lardner had also distinguished himself writing poetry and fiction. Once when asked to list the ten most beautiful words in the English language, he submitted the following list:

> blute
> crene
> fit
> gangrene
> guzzle
> mange
> McNaboe
> scram
> smoot
> wretch

The Mellon brothers, Andrew and Richard, were two of the acknowledged business leaders in the United States; the family's Pittsburgh-based fortune had also benefited many eleemosynary causes. Although both brothers were conservative in demeanor, they had been playing practical jokes on each other all their lives.

In 1933, when Richard Mellon was dying, he summoned his brother to his bedside, signaling Andrew to draw close. When Andrew did, his

1933 brother was not satisfied, asking him to come even closer. When he did, writes author Jay Robert Nash, "Richard Mellon, using up his last ounce of strength, again raised his arm and brushed Andrew's shoulder, his final breath hissing out the words; 'last tag.' With that, the tycoon died, and left his brother permanently 'it.'"

1934

ANDY: *Is you been keepin' yo' eye on de stock market?*
LIGHTNIN': *Nosah, I ain't never seed it.*
ANDY: *Well, de stock market crashed.*
LIGHTNIN': *Anybody git hurt?*
—Amos 'n' Andy

☞ NATIONAL NEWS

After visiting the United States, British playwright George Bernard Shaw declared that his most abiding recollections of America would be Niagara Falls, the Rocky Mountains, and *Amos 'n' Andy*.

Although *Amos 'n' Andy* may seem like a strange choice for the erudite Shaw, radio in America in the 1930s was a national obsession, an inexpensive means of combating the Depression blues. And in the halcyon days of radio broadcasting, no program so captivated listeners as the goings-on in the lives of Amos, Andy, George "Kingfish" Stevens, Sapphire, Ruby, Lightnin', Madame Queen, and Shorty the barber, frequenters of the Fresh Air Taxi Company and the Mystic Knights of the Sea Lodge.

The show concerned the lives of urban blacks and was written by two whites, Freeman Gosden and Charles Correll, who played five of the major parts, for it was common for whites to portray blacks—in the

163

1934 tradition of the minstrel shows. White actor Marlin Hurt portrayed the popular Beulah, a black maid, the audience never questioning that his was the voice of a black female.

The show was first aired in Chicago as *Sam and Henry,* and then *Jim and Charlie,* before its creators settled on *Amos 'n' Andy* after hearing this exchange in an elevator one day.

> ELEVATOR OPERATOR: Well, well, famous Amos.
> PASSENGER: Hello, handy Andy.

The NAACP complained that the show unfairly stereotyped blacks, but *Amos 'n' Andy* appealed to whites and blacks alike. With the industrious Amos juxtaposed against the slothful Andy, involved constantly in get-rich-quick schemes that required no work on his part, the show was a morality play of sorts, which was usually resolved in favor of the righteous. *Amos 'n' Andy* also came to the support of President Roosevelt in the early days of the New Deal, when he imposed a bank holiday in March 1933. Andy reflected:

> De President of de United States is fightin' fo' more dan just 'mergency bankin' relief—he is workin' out a plan to have a system in de banks dat will not he'p now, but will he'p 'em fo' all time to come, an' dis banker says dat dat's zackly whut's goin' happen an' Mr. Roosevelt means bizness, an' he's gittin action, so yo' see, dis bank holiday is really a great thing fo' de country.

The show was first heard on network radio at 11:00 P.M. Eastern Standard Time but was switched to 7:00 P.M. when Eastern listeners complained that the show went on too late. In its new time slot, however, fans on the West Coast received the show at 4:00 P.M., when a good portion of its listeners had not arrived home from work. Gosden and Correll solved this problem by agreeing to do two live shows daily so that both coasts could receive the broadcast at 7:00 P.M. in their respective time zones.

Between 7:00 and 7:15 P.M. on weekdays, the country virtually came to a standstill. Jack Benny recalled "walking past motion picture theaters and seeing signs promising to stop the movie and turn on the radio when it came time for the show." Department stores piped in the show for evening shoppers, and telephone use during these fifteen minutes declined sharply. Sanitation engineers reported that sewer pipes were almost flow-free while the show was on the air but were extremely active just after the program was over.

When Amos and Ruby had a child, nearly 2.5 million listeners wrote in to suggest a name for the infant; when Ruby was ill, some 65,000 get-well letters and cards were sent to the patient; and when Ruby's health further deteriorated, 18,000 irate listeners threatened to boycott Pepsodent toothpaste, the show's sponsor, should her condition worsen. In its palmy days, *Amos 'n' Andy* was heard by 74 percent of the listening audience, bringing expressions such as "I'se regusted" and "check and double check" into use by tens of millions of Americans. First aired in 1926, it was heard on week nights until 1943, when it changed to a half-hour weekly format. The program was converted to television in 1951.

☞ FOREIGN NEWS

Soviet Union

Soviet leader Joseph Stalin declared that henceforth children over the age of twelve would have to pay the same penalty as adults for committing certain crimes. Stealing corn or potatoes brought a sentence of eight years in a labor camp, while stealing cucumbers was not deemed to be as heinous an offense, resulting in only a five-year sentence.

Poland

There were suddenly three more mouths to feed in the Andzurka family of Crusyna, Poland. On February 5, 1934, Anna Andzurka, her daughter, and her granddaughter all gave birth on the very same day.

Canada

In the multiple-birth department, no one could top Elzire Dionne, who gave birth to five girls on May 28, 1934, on a rural southern Ontario farm, between the hours of three and six in the morning. The twenty-four-year-old mother and thirty-two-year-old father already had six children, the eldest of whom was seven. The new babies were named Annette, Cecile, Émilie, Marie, and Yvonne, and all together, they weighed 11.5 pounds.

The Dionne house had only four rooms and no electricity. Before Dr. Allan R. Dafoe could get there, three of the children had been born with the help of two of Elzire Dionne's female neighbors. The doctor, who improvised an incubator from a butcher's basket until authorities could provide a proper one, doubted that any of the infants would live, and the mother herself was in serious condition. Quintuplets are a rare phenomenon—estimated as occurring once in 41 million single births—and it was rarer still for all five to live.

But live the Dionnes did, mother and daughters, and soon the lives of the Dionne family would undergo a drastic change. The Quints became as popular a tourist attraction in Canada as Niagara Falls, 3 million

165

1934 tourists visiting the farm between 1934 and 1943. *Time* magazine called the quintuplets "the world's greatest news-picture story." In 1939, visitors to Canada from the United States, filling out tourist questionnaires in Ottawa, would still cite the quintuplets as the most popular tourist attraction in Canada.

The Dionne farm was transformed into an amusement-park-like setting, with the Quints on display. Although Dr. Dafoe tried to assure a normal life for them, the public and the media made that impossible. They were celebrities, always on stage. Émilie died of an epileptic seizure in 1954, and the other four sisters became estranged from their parents. In a book called *We Were Five*, the remaining Quints aired their family grievances for all the world to read. Whether or not they were right in their accusations seems irrelevant, for their chances of living normal lives had probably ceased to exist the day the world learned of their birth and near miraculous survival.

Switzerland

The Swiss parliament passed the Swiss Bank Secrecy Act that allowed banking transactions to be highly secretive, replacing the use of signatures with account numbers as a means of effecting transactions. Guarding the identifications of depositors would protect many European Jews fleeing the Nazis. Depositors were not required to furnish background information, and banks would not assist authorities in investigating their customers. Thus, in time, users of these accounts would include a host of criminals, tax evaders, deposed heads of state, and miscellaneous possessors of ill-gotten gains.

Japan

An American all-star baseball team visited Japan and received a tremendous reception, greeted by cries of "Banzai Babe Ruth!" and "Banzai Lou Gehrig!" ("Long live Ruth!" "Long live Gehrig!"). Ruth hit thirteen home runs to help his team win all sixteen games against Japanese competition, securing his position as Japan's most famous foreigner then and for years to come. In World War II, Japanese soldiers attempted to demoralize American combat troops by screaming, "To hell with Babe Ruth!"

France

In 1895, Pierre Curie had married a fellow student in Paris named Marja Sklodowska from Poland, and he and "Marie" began to work together, Pierre as a physicist, Marie as a chemist. The couple discovered radium in 1898 and were awarded the Nobel Prize for physics in 1903.

Pierre died in 1906 when he was run over in a street accident, but Marie Curie continued their work in the field of radioactivity, again in

1911 winning the Nobel Prize. In 1934, Madame Curie was still putting in sixteen-hour days in the laboratory, although she was in ill health.

She had bad vision, constant ringing in her ears, and an abnormal blood count, finally dying on July 4, 1934, totally unaware that her close contact with radioactive material had brought about her death. Her estate's major asset was a gram of radium that had been given to her on a visit to America, and she willed it to the University of Paris, stipulating that her daughter have the right to use the radium in her research. Her daughter later died of leukemia.

☞ REGIONAL NEWS

New York

Vassar College removed a 42,000-pound World War I tank from its Poughkeepsie, New York, campus, perhaps regretting the acceptance of the unusual gift by the French government after the war in gratitude for contributions made to its cause by Vassar alumnae.

Texas

J. F. Cantrell opened a "washateria" in Forth Worth, Texas, with four washing machines available for public rental, unaware that his establishment was the first laundromat in the United States.

California

Alcatraz opened its doors in 1934. It was located on a small island in San Francisco Bay for which the prison was named (Aloatraz is the Spanish word for "pelican").

"The Rock" was the strictest of all federal prisons: Prisoners were not allowed to talk to one another, weapons searches were frequent, and guards were instructed to fire their weapons at the slightest sign of trouble.

The surrounding bay was hardly conducive to escape because water temperatures were low, currents powerful, and sharks frequently in evidence. Yet at least thirty-five convicts risked their lives in escape attempts—seven to be killed by guards, twenty-two to be captured, and the rest assumed to have drowned.

☞ WEATHER

Although only 6,288 feet high, New Hampshire's Mount Washington rivals mountains twice its size for the foulness of its weather, which has claimed many lives. Meteorologists blame the mountain's location, which

1934 is often the point at which tropical and arctic air masses collide. On an April day in 1934, Mount Washington had the dubious honor of experiencing winds measured at 231 mph, a world's record.

☛ FUN AND GAMES

Known in vaudeville as the King of the Unicycles, Walter Nilsson decided to ride his 8½-foot-high bike from New York to San Francisco, a distance of over 3,300 miles. Although he made the journey in 117 days, he never was the same again, the trip leaving him with a myriad of physical problems that remained with him until his death. Some consolation might have come from Robert Ripley, who cited Nilsson for the "Most Unbelievable Feat of the Year."

A seventeen-year-old girl entered a dance marathon in West Palm Beach. Three thousand six hundred hours later, or around five months in elapsed time, she was declared the winner, having celebrated her eighteenth birthday on the dance floor. Her name was June Hovick; she later changed it to June Havoc and enjoyed a successful career as an actress. Her sister also saw her name in lights, working as a stripper under the name of Gypsy Rose Lee.

The first All-American Soapbox Derby was held in Dayton, Ohio, in 1934, as boys between the ages of eleven and fifteen vied to see whose homemade motorless minicar was the fastest. The all-male event was later opened to girls, and in 1975, an eleven-year-old girl by the name of Karen Stead took the top prize, maneuvering her vehicle with her left arm in a cast.

☛ ENTERTAINMENT

Hearst columnist Louella Parsons, born Louella Oettinger, had received some very bad news in 1925. Told that she had tuberculosis, she was given only six months to live, so she moved to Hollywood in hopes that the sunny climate might reverse her condition. Indeed, the California weather seemed to agree with her, and she recovered, starting an interview program in 1934 called *Hollywood Hotel,* on which stars appeared to plug their films. Parsons later wrote a movie column that would be carried by some 400 newspapers until 1965. She became so powerful in Hollywood that a word from her for or against a member of the film community could seriously affect that person's career. As a result, most stars worked hard to stay in her good graces.

168

Frank Capra had considerable difficulty finding stars who wanted to act in his romantic comedy, *It Happened One Night*. Robert Montgomery declined the starring male role, and Myrna Loy, Margaret Sullivan, Constance Bennett, and Miriam Hopkins all demurred when offered the female lead. Capra plunged ahead anyway, making do with Clark Gable and Claudette Colbert. The film made glittering stars out of them both, and they each won an Oscar for their performances.

A committee of American Catholic bishops founded the Legion of Decency to evaluate the effect of individual films on the morals of the viewing public. Their ratings, published in Catholic newspapers, ranged from A-1 ("morally unobjectionable for general patronage") to C ("condemned"), and church members were urged to boycott the movies that the legion found wanting. The Legion of Decency remained a powerful influence on the film industry until the 1960s.

Because she had become a film actress, Mrs. Ogden Ludlow and spouse were unceremoniously dropped from Philadelphia's *Social Register*. Mrs. Ludlow's professional name was Katharine Hepburn.

Moviegoers welcomed the first of six Thin Man films that starred William Powell, Myrna Loy, and their savvy dog Asta. *The Thin Man* was not Nick Charles, played by Powell, but the murdered man in one of Charles's cases.

☛ BOOKS

Roger Tory Peterson published his first book on birds, a field guide containing all species found in the eastern United States. The twenty-six-year-old former schoolteacher supplied the illustrations as well as the text, and the book was both an artistic and a commercial success as over 500,000 copies were sold by 1970. Peterson went to work for the Audubon Society, and the air force adapted his methods for identifying birds to plane spotting during World War II. His books eventually covered birds found in all areas of the country and became a basic text for bird lovers.

☛ AUTOMOBILES

In the spring of 1934, Henry Ford received unsolicited testimonials from two well-known Americans extolling the excellence of his automobiles:

1934 • "While I still have got breath in my lungs, I will tell you what a dandy car you make. I have drove Fords exclusively when I could get away with one." (Clyde Barrow)

• "Hello old pal: Arrived here at 10 A.M. today. Would like to drop in and see you. You have a wonderful car. Been driving it for three weeks. It's a real treat to drive one. Your slogan should be: Drive a Ford and watch the other cars fall behind you. It can make any other car take Ford's dust. Bye-bye." (John Dillinger)

☛ BUSINESS

Proof of the power of the movies in affecting the buying habits of Americans was demonstrated in 1934:

• In the film *It Happened One Night*, Clark Gable removed his shirt and, lo and behold, was not wearing an undershirt, whereas most American men did. As a result of Gable's appearing naked from the waist up, undershirt sales plummeted.

• Gangster movies were extremely popular during the 1930s, often showing toughs wearing caps, leading to a precipitous drop in that informal type of head covering.

☛ POLITICS

As Roosevelt prepared for the 1934 congressional elections, he regretted a speech that he had made in 1932 in which he vowed to cut federal spending if he were elected. FDR instructed speech writer Samuel Rosenman to review the speech and find a means of interpreting the remarks in his favor. After rereading Roosevelt's earlier words, Rosenman could find no way to whitewash FDR's promise, advising him as follows: "Mr. President, the only thing you can say about that 1932 speech is to deny categorically that you ever made it."

☛ PEOPLE

A legendary figure in America was Tommy Hitchcock, who missed receiving a ten-goal rating in polo only once between 1922 and 1940. Turned down by the army because he was only seventeen, he had joined France's Lafayette Escadrille in World War I, bagging his first German plane before he had reached his eighteenth birthday. When he was shot down behind German lines, he made a dramatic escape by jumping from a moving train.

170

At a party one night, Hitchcock was dancing with a young woman whom he had just met, who was unaware that she was in the arms of the famous polo player. In an attempt to make casual conversation, Hitchcock remarked, "I'm afraid I am not dancing very well this evening, I'm a little stiff from polo." His partner replied icily, "It doesn't make any difference to me where you come from."

1934

1935

The bullet hasn't been made that can kill me.

—Jack "Legs" Diamond, who was shot dead in his Albany, New York, apartment by members of the Dutch Schultz gang

☞ NATIONAL NEWS

When the new decade had begun in 1930, gangsters were front-page news. In the eyes of a cynical public, they appeared to operate with impunity within their spheres of influence, risking retribution only from their peers. Americans regarded institutions of law enforcement with disdain, believing them to be either corrupt or ineffective. The first few years of the 1930s had witnessed a series of events that only strengthened that conviction:

• In 1930, "Legs" Diamond had taken a breather from his feud with Dutch Schultz, traveling to Europe, where, to his surprise, no country would receive him, causing the American press to comment that there were more restraints placed on Diamond outside the country than within America's borders.

• Vincent "Mad Dog" Coll's bullets hit five children when he was warring with the Schultz gang on a New York City street in 1931, and one

172

died. Coll went free, however, when the state's case against him collapsed because the prosecution introduced testimony from a suborned witness.

• Schultz informed reporters that he would see that justice was done, and Coll was gunned down in 1932 in a telephone booth.

• When Al Capone was sentenced to eleven years in prison in 1932, press and public regarded it as a hollow victory for the forces of justice. The *Boston Globe* wrote, "It is ludicrous that this underworld gang leader has been led to the doors of the penitentiary at last only through prosecutions on income tax and conspiracy charges."

Author Richard Gid Powers noted that such was the frustration of the nation over the absence of law and order that "Will Rogers suggested that the tradition of lynching public offenders should be revived," and the *Washington Post* wrote that "public authority as now constituted is impotent. Vigilante committees should be organized in every community to cooperate with the law authorities."

Hollywood's introduction of a number of gangster movies only made matters worse. By the time Roosevelt took office, "the country was used to the idea that some sort of national mobilization was going to be necessary if the country was going to survive its 'war' with the organized underworld."

In 1933, Franklin Roosevelt had responded to public opinion by creating a crime-fighting organization under the wing of Attorney General Homer S. Cummings's Department of Justice. It was called the Federal Bureau of Investigation—a merger of the Prohibition Bureau, the Bureau of Identification, and the Bureau of Investigation—and was headed by John Edgar Hoover, thirty-eight, director of the Bureau of Investigation since 1924. A law school graduate, Hoover had disappointed his parents by not becoming a minister. Two years later, the FBI was an organization revered by the public. Hoover became one of the most respected public servants in America, aided by a self-controlled publicity machine that kept him and the bureau in the public eye for the next three decades.

The first publicity windfall came in 1934 when FBI agents in Chicago shot and killed John Dillinger, the most sought-after criminal at large in the United States and perhaps the most imaginative bank robber ever to ply his trade in America. A navy deserter, Dillinger had turned to robbery in 1924 and was soon jailed; in prison, he met several fellow convicts whom he identified as excellent potential gang members. Since Dillinger was the first of the group to be paroled, he vowed to return after his release to free his friends. But before he could fulfill his promise, Dillinger was caught in an attempted robbery and found himself back in jail in Lima, Ohio. However, his future partners-in-crime managed to escape without his aid, returning the favor that Dillinger had meant to grant them by shooting their way into the Lima jail and freeing him, killing a guard in the process.

173

1935   Over the next year, the gang executed a series of imaginative and precisely planned bank robberies that netted them more money than Jesse James had stolen in a lifetime. Three examples of the gang's inventiveness follow:

• Dillinger and a fellow gang member dropped in at the Peru, Indiana, police station one day, saying they were reporters from a detective magazine. The flattered officers were delighted to show their auspicious guests around, taking them on a tour of their weapons arsenal and giving them a full briefing on police procedures. A day later, the two "reporters" returned and made off with the department's cache of ammunition, guns, and bulletproof vests.

• One day, Dillinger paid a visit to the president of a bank, pretending to be a salesman, offering a system that could supply air to the bank's vault in the event employees were accidentally locked in. After Dillinger gave the executive a grisly account of the horrors of death from suffocation, he was allowed to make a detailed inspection of the vault. Dillinger promised to return soon and was as good as his word, emptying the vault in the process.

• A member of the Dillinger gang went to Sioux Falls, South Dakota, posing as a movie producer, getting the word around that his company would be coming to town to do some filming. The following day, townsfolk and police stood idly by, watching what they would later realize was the real-life Dillinger gang robbing a bank.

Apprehended once again, Dillinger was jailed in Crown Point, Indiana, where the press flocked to write about the legendary bank robber who had finally been put behind bars for good. But Dillinger escaped once more, holding guards at bay with a pistol that they claimed was a .45, while he made his getaway. But what Dillinger had actually brandished as a weapon was a gun that he had carved out of wood. When his father and sister revealed this to the press, newspapers had a field day ridiculing law officers once again.

Enter J. Edgar Hoover and the FBI, but they had no better luck bringing Dillinger to justice than did their local confreres. Twice they had him trapped, and both times he escaped. But finally the FBI got a break when a woman came forth and promised to deliver Dillinger into the bureau's hands. Her name was Anna Sage, a Romanian-born madam of an Indiana brothel, whom the government was attempting to deport because of her unsavory activities. She went to Melvin Purvis, head of the FBI's Chicago office, and offered to set up her friend and customer in return for her freedom. And so it was that Sage told Purvis that on the night of July 22, 1934, she would accompany Dillinger to a movie at the Biograph Theater in Chicago, wearing a red dress to identify herself. (*Manhattan Melodrama* was playing, whose female lead, Myrna Loy, was Dillinger's favorite.) When the show was over at 10:30 P.M., the crowd poured out of the theater, and sure enough, there was the woman in red with her companion. Purvis moved in on Dillinger and gunned him down as he attempted to reach for a weapon to defend himself.

The publicity attending Dillinger's death was voluminous, and the FBI was extolled for hunting down the man who had defied law and order so brilliantly, killing ten people in the process. But to Hoover's consternation, the spotlight fell not on himself and the bureau but on Purvis and Anna Sage. Hoover soon removed Purvis from key cases, and Purvis went to Hollywood to supervise several radio shows on law enforcement. After his departure, Hoover put together the FBI's official account of Dillinger's undoing, with Purvis and Sage totally removed from center stage.

Perhaps even more valuable to Hoover and the FBI than the Dillinger shooting was a film made in 1935 called *G-Men*, starring James Cagney as an FBI man, which heaped credit on the bureau. Latching on to a good thing, Hoover oversaw the content of numerous movies, radio, and television programs, books, articles, and comic strips, often hiring ghostwriters to assure that he and the bureau were depicted to his liking. An example was *Fed*, a slick detective magazine that in its September 1937 issue featured "G-Men vs. Crime," with the subhead "Are Your Fingerprints on File? How J. Edgar Hoover's FBI Can Help You Protect Yourself and Your Family." Hoover also became a close friend of columnist and radio broadcaster Walter Winchell, who kept his name constantly in the news in exchange for an occasional scoop.

Although Hoover was mercilessly debunked after his death, he should be credited with putting together an organization manned by highly efficient and courageous agents, as well as with establishing state-of-the-art training and scientific investigation techniques. But he was a stern taskmaster, initiating a dress code for his agents that could not be deviated from—dark suits, white shirts, black shoes, and short haircuts. Hoover fired one agent for marrying an Arab, another for having a "clammy" handshake, and a third for wearing a necktie that he thought garish. He also dismissed another agent whose line-of-duty wounds had scarred his face, saying, "Get rid of him. He doesn't look like an FBI man!" Hoover also resisted efforts to integrate his organization, and for years the only blacks in the bureau were his chauffeur and his receptionist.

But beyond the publicity he received, he gathered so much material on the most intimate details of the lives of Washington officials that no president wanted to risk Hoover's wrath by asking him to step down. President Lyndon Johnson summed it up as follows: "I'd rather have him on the inside of the tent pissing out, than on the outside pissing in."

Encouraged by gains in the congressional elections of 1934, Roosevelt made plans for a rash of new legislation in the spring of 1935.

175

1935 Presidential adviser Harry Hopkins said, "We've got to get everything we want—a works program, social security, wages and hours, everything now or never . . . a complete ticket to provide security for all the folks of this country up and down and across the board." And FDR got most of what he asked Congress for, including the Social Security Act, providing up to $15 a month to retirees over the age of sixty-five. But the president had his problems, and two of the thorniest ones were named Father Charles E. Coughlin and Senator Huey Pierce Long.

Coughlin had started out modestly enough, delivering sermons on a Detroit radio station. According to author William Manchester, Coughlin was heard on over sixty stations, and "outdrew 'Amos and Andy,' 'Dr. Fu Manchu' and Ed Wynn." Moderate at the outset, Father Coughlin began to sound not unlike Hitler and Mussolini as his mushrooming popularity made him more and more powerful. He opposed freedom of speech, called the New Deal the "Jew Deal," and suggested that "the use of bullets" would not be a bad way of getting rid of FDR. He praised Mussolini and talked of "nationalization of banking and currency and of national resources." Fortunately, Coughlin could entertain no presidential ambitions because he had been born in Canada.

But the man whom FDR feared the most was Huey Long, senator and former governor of Louisiana. Born poor, Long had dropped out of high school to peddle shortening before completing Tulane's three-year law course in eight months. Such was his brilliance that he once argued a case before the U.S. Supreme Court without the aid of fellow lawyers, consulting only a single page of notes.

Long had avoided service in World War I by claiming to be a "public official" needed at home, using his appointment as a notary public to obtain his exemption. He practiced law successfully and became wealthy, then turned his attention to politics. Although defeated in his first try for the governorship, he was elected in 1927, commencing what Jay Robert Nash called a "reign . . . a period of terror, intimidation, and corruption never equalled in American history." *American Heritage* adds:

> The Kingfish . . . proceeded to build within his domain the nearest thing so far to an American version of a police state. Opponents were first cajoled and offered bribes, but if they remained obdurate, they were threatened and sometimes beaten by the state police and their businesses destroyed. . . . He beat back an attempt to impeach him by bribing a number of state senators to announce in advance that they would vote for acquittal regardless of evidence. . . . He could buy a legislator, he chortled, "like a sack of potatoes."

Long used his Share Our Wealth program to gain a national constituency, offering an annual income of $2,500 to all. And in early 1935, it looked as though he could mount enough support in the 1936 presidential election to force a "no-decision," which would leave the choice up to the House of Representatives.

Journalist Hodding Carter recalls an enemy of Long's saying, "Good God, I wish somebody would kill the son of a bitch." And on the evening of September 8, 1935, Carl Austin Weiss, disgruntled because Long had ruined his father-in-law's career, stepped out from behind a pillar in the rotunda of the Louisana state capitol and fired a single shot into Long's stomach. The assassin was cut down by sixty-one bullets from the guns of Huey Long's bodyguards, but Weiss's one shot had found its mark, and the Kingfish was dead.

Writer Clifton Fadiman supplies this anecdote about Long:

Before beginning his electoral campaign in southern Louisiana, Long was reminded by a colleague that a large number of the voters there were Catholics. In accordance with this advice, he opened his first speech with the words: "When I was a boy, I would get up at six o'clock in the morning on Sunday, and I would hitch our old horse up to the buggy and I would take my Catholic grandparents to mass. I would bring them home, and at ten o'clock I would hitch the old horse up again, and I would take my Baptist grandparents to church." "Why Huey," remarked his colleague later, "you've been holding out on us. I didn't know you had any Catholic grandparents." "Don't be a fool," replied Long. "We didn't even have a horse."

☛ FOREIGN NEWS

Venezuela

American pilot Jimmy Angel had been told by a local prospector that gold could be found in a stream at the top of the Auyan Mesa plateau in southeastern Venezuela. But the prospector had died before telling Angel the exact location of the precious metal, and his efforts to find the stream on foot had proved unsuccessful, so Angel decided to reconnoiter the area in an airplane. Although he did not find the elusive river, he did discover the highest waterfall in the world, descending 3,212 feet into the valley below, some 800 feet higher than the falls at California's Yosemite National Park. It was named Angel Falls in his honor.

1935

Germany
- The Hitler regime instructed German radio stations not to play jazz music attributed to either Jews or blacks.
- The Nazi government decided to issue a postcard carrying a picture of Chancellor Hitler in the company of the perfect Aryan child. Hitler's aides combed the country and came up with a handsome, blond, apple-cheeked lad, who was duly photographed with Herr Hitler. Thousands of postcards were sold before a shocking discovery was made: The young man who had posed with Hitler was the grandson of a man named Wedell, a Dusseldorf rabbi.

Soviet Union
Joseph Stalin, general secretary of the Soviet Communist Party, said, "Gaiety is the most outstanding feature of the Soviet Union."

☛ ARMED FORCES

The last two surviving carrier pigeons to serve in World War I died in 1935. One bird named Mocker had distinguished himself in the Allies' attack on Germany's Hindenburg Line. When the Allies had been pinned down by a single German artillery piece, Mocker was given a message to carry to headquarters, pinpointing the location of the weapon. Flying over enemy lines, the bird sustained a shrapnel wound but continued his flight, successfully delivering the message. A few minutes later, the gun was put out of commission, and Mocker earned the Distinguished Service Cross and France's Croix de Guerre for his act of heroism. Just short of his twenty-first birthday, his health began to deteriorate, and he was given periodic doses of whiskey and water to ease his discomfort before he died on June 14, 1935.

☛ MARRIAGE AND COURTSHIP

Woolworth heiress Barbara Hutton divorced husband number one and married for the second time in 1935. Eventually she would have seven spouses and would dispense millions of dollars in divorce settlements before dying in 1979. Her first husband was a Russian *poseur* who called himself Prince Alexis Mdivani. The ersatz prince was jettisoned on May 13, 1935, the distraught Hutton stating, "I shall never marry again." She stuck to that vow for a mere twenty-four hours before marrying Count Haugwitz-Reventlow, who was replaced by actor Cary Grant. (The couple were soon nicknamed Cash and Cary.) After that unsuccessful union terminated, Hutton returned to royalty in 1947, pledging her troth to a Lithuanian prince, Igor Troubetzkoy, who would soon regain bachelorhood, settling for a weekly allowance of $1,000 for the rest of his life. In 1951, the thirty-nine-year-old Hutton went to the altar once more with Dominican Republic playboy Porfirio Rubirosa, whose talents in the bedroom were attested to by scores of international lovelies, including actress Zsa Zsa Gabor, who stated that Rubirosa was "to lovemaking what Tiffany is to diamonds," a considerable accolade from such an acknowledged connoisseur. Seventy-three days later, Rubirosa was once again back in circulation, and Hutton's sixth husband would be former German tennis star Baron Gottfried von Cramm. Divorced in 1961, the five-and-dime-store heiress took her seventh and last husband in 1964, a Laotian painter named Raymond Doan Vinh Na Champassak, the happy bride resplendent in an Indian gown with gold rings adorning each toe, the soles of her feet painted red. Champassak would be $3 million richer when the couple split up in 1966. The fifty-three-year-old Hutton bypassed matrimony for the rest of her life, living in a Beverly Hills hotel until her death in 1979 at the age of sixty-six.

• "Spring must be here. Barbara Hutton is doing her husband cleaning." (Bob Hope)

☞ SPORTS

New York's Downtown Athletic Club awarded its first Heisman Trophy to University of Chicago halfback Jay Berwanger. The trophy presented to the nation's finest college football player was named for John Heisman, athletic director of the club and former University of Pennsylvania football coach. Heisman had introduced many innovations to football: the center snap, the vocal "hike" as a signal to start play, and the hidden-ball trick; and he had been influential in breaking the game into quarters rather than halves and in legalizing the forward pass.

• Only players from teams east of the Mississippi River were eligible for the award in 1935, and only sportswriters from eastern states were allowed to vote.

• Berwanger became the first player drafted by the National Football League in its initial 1936 draft, but he declined to play. For ten years, "Breakaway Jay's" Aunt Gussie used the trophy as a doorstop.

• Football had come a long way since 1873 when Cornell's president refused to let the university's team travel to Cleveland to play a game with the University of Michigan. President White said, "I will not permit thirty men to travel four hundred miles merely to agitate a bag of wind."

179

1935   Perhaps the most productive forty-five minutes in the history of track and field was turned in by a young Ohio State athlete named Jesse Owens at the 1935 Big Ten championships at Ann Arbor, Michigan. Buckeye fans were not looking for too much from the young speedster, who was suffering from a case of the flu that had kept him in bed for several days. In Owens's first event, he ran the 100-yard dash in 9.4 seconds, equaling the world's record. Ten minutes later, Jesse broad-jumped 26 feet 8¼ inches on his first try, breaking the world's record for that event. With but nine minutes of rest, Owens took the 220-yard dash in 20.3 seconds— world's record number three. And just twenty-six minutes after that, Owens won the 220-yard high hurdles, establishing yet another world's record, his fourth in just three quarters of an hour.

But wait. Owens had also been timed at 100 and 200 meters at the same time that he ran the 100-yard and 200-yard races. When all the stopwatches were checked, it turned out that Owens had broken these world's records as well, swelling his total to six.

• In 1960, a broad jumper named Ralph Boston finally broke Owens's broad-jump record, which had survived for twenty-five years.

🐾 EDUCATION

Members of Princeton's senior class were requested to specify the greatest playwright and the best painter who had ever lived. Noel Coward beat out William Shakespeare for the best playwright award, while a magazine illustrator named McClelland Barclay bested Rembrandt in the painting category.

🐾 MUSIC

In February 1935, premier violinist Fritz Kreisler admitted to having taken certain liberties with his recitals, having performed his own compositions while purporting that they were the works of famous composers. His rationale: If he had told his audiences that he had written the music, they would not have paid attention.

🐾 CRIME

The expression "Crime does not pay" was seriously challenged in 1935 when the mothers of Clyde Barrow and Bonnie Parker, the notorious "Bonnie and Clyde," made a highly lucrative vaudeville tour with John
180

Dillinger's father, J. W. Dillinger, recounting personal vignettes of their
deceased progeny's lives.

☞ MONEY

The top income earner of 1935 was reported to be newspaper mogul
William Randolph Hearst. The runner-up was movie actress Mae West.

☞ FUN AND GAMES

Parker Brothers introduced the game Monopoly, which it had turned
down on first inspection as taking too long to play and having "fifty-two
fundamental errors." The game was the brainchild of out-of-work
engineer Charles B. Darrow, who, when Parker Brothers initially
rejected his game, had had the game privately manufactured and
distributed in Philadelphia, where it was a great success, causing Parker
Brothers to take on Monopoly after all. It became the best-selling board
game of all time, and more Monopoly money was printed annually on a
total dollar basis than was printed by the U.S. Treasury.
• All Monopoly properties are named for actual streets in Atlantic
City, New Jersey. Yes, Virginia, there *is* a Marvin Gardens.

☞ QUOTES

Sports manager and fan Joe Jacobs had been ill, but nothing could
prevent him from leaving his bed of pain to attend the World Series. After
seeing his team lose, and a substantial wager go down the drain, he gave
vent to his feelings in a remark that would be repeated often: "I should
have stood in bed."

"All modern American literature comes from one book by Mark
Twain called *Huckleberry Finn*." (Ernest Hemingway, *The Green Hills of
Africa*, 1935)

New York gangster Dutch Schultz, born Arthur Flegenheimer, was
gunned down in a Newark bar, in an oft-repeated act of gangland
retribution. Schultz's last words confused even his closest friends: "A boy
has never wept, or dashed a thousand krim."

"Just a fad, a passing fancy," said Philip Wrigley, owner of the
Chicago Cubs, when the first major league night game took place at

1935 Crosley Field in Cincinnati. In 1987, his team was the lone holdout against night games.

🐾 PEOPLE

The year 1935 saw the end of the active playing career of Babe Ruth, and the finale was carried out with typical Ruth pyrotechnics. The pudgy forty-year-old slugger hit three home runs on behalf of the Boston Braves against Pittsburgh at Forbes Field, and the victim, pitcher Guy Bush, recalls Ruth's swan song:

> I sure as hell remember everything about that day and those homers. After Ruth hit that first homer off me, my catcher, Earl Grace, said, "Is that the kind of cheap homers he always hits? He must be able to hit harder than that." Well, I guess Ruth proved it the next time around. I throwed about six inches over the outside of the plate and he hit that ball deep to right center, the longest damn ball I've ever seen hit, off me or anyone else. He got ahold of that good fastball and hit it off the fat part of his bat and there was no wind to help, either. And it didn't need no help, no way.

🐾 DRESS

Forty-two men were prosecuted at Atlantic City, New Jersey, for wearing bathing suits without tops. Said a town representative, "We'll have no gorillas on our beaches."

1936

I have found it impossible to carry the heavy burden of responsibility and to discharge my duties as King as I would wish to do without the help and support of the woman I love.
—The Duke of Windsor

☛ NATIONAL NEWS

"Deeds, not deficits" was the Republican Party's credo as Kansas governor Alfred Mossman Landon jousted with Franklin Roosevelt in the presidential campaign of 1936. Landon's campaign symbol was the sunflower, Kansas's state flower, and FDR regarded it as an appropriate choice, noting that "it was yellow, had a black heart, was useful only as parrot food, and always died before November." Landon was a likable, folksy man who had operated his state's budget on a break-even basis as required by law and planned to do likewise with the country's. Not to be outdone, FDR promised a balanced budget as well, although he had nearly doubled the country's deficit during his first administration.

An improving economy gave a boost to FDR's campaign, the Federal Reserve Board's Adjusted Index of Industrial Production having worked its way up from early Depression lows to nearly 1929 levels by election time. But Roosevelt had to deal with an increasingly hostile press as well

183

1936 as the ire of businessmen and the well-to-do, who accused him of a multitude of sins, including deficit spending, increasing the size of the federal government, and restricting business growth. Apart from these public admonishments, the list of private charges was a good deal longer: Roosevelt was a "traitor to his class," a man who had never known honest toil and had lived off his mother's money; a "Jew" whose real name was "Rosenfelt"; a "dictator," a "Stalin" who would make America just like Russia. Well-dressed men reclining in deep leather chairs in men's clubs became apoplectic at the mere mention of his name, considering FDR a threat to the capitalistic society that they held sacred. Meanwhile, he had become a hero to the less fortunate: Many children and schools were named after him, and blacks would turn to the Democratic Party for the first time since they were given the vote.

As the election approached, newspaper publisher William Randolph Hearst's political antenna signaled a Landon landslide, declaring, "I'll stake my reputation as a prophet on it." But nothing so gladdened Republican hearts as the preelection poll conducted by the *Literary Digest,* a magazine respected for the accuracy of its political prognostications. The magazine relied heavily on the telephone to contact the staggering total of 2.5 million prospective voters. Based on its results, the *Digest,* like prophet Hearst, forecast a Landon sweep, predicting an electoral vote margin of 370–161.

Few Americans paid much attention to a new pollster on the block, George Gallup, whose results indicated a far different outcome, an electoral vote romp for Roosevelt by 477–42. Gallup had conducted far fewer interviews than the *Digest,* contacting potential voters in person rather than by telephone, believing that phones were a Depression luxury that millions could not afford, biasing the results in favor of the more well-to-do. And Gallup's forecast was right: FDR won all states but Maine and Vermont, racking up 523 electoral votes and 61 percent of the popular tally, sweeping in a Democratic Congress with a 3 to 1 majority.

During the Depression, many Americans sought temporary refuge from the times in escapist literature set in faraway places and days gone by. Pearl Buck's *The Good Earth* topped fiction sales in 1931–1932, as did Hervey Allen's *Anthony Adverse* in 1933–1934. But the success of these books was dwarfed by a novel published in 1936 that became the best-selling work in the history of the United States, eclipsing the previous titleholder, *Uncle Tom's Cabin,* in only six months. It was called *Gone with the Wind,* the first and only book by a five-foot-tall housewife from Atlanta, Georgia, named Margaret Mitchell.

Mitchell had grown up in Atlanta, traveling north to Smith College to study medicine. When her mother died, she terminated her studies and returned home to live with her father, becoming a newspaper reporter on the *Atlanta Journal*. Not long afterward, she married, and **1936** when a broken ankle failed to respond to treatment, she quit her job. At her husband's urging, she began to write a novel about the Civil War and its aftermath. Mitchell was well grounded for the task, since her father had been a past president of the Atlanta Historical Society. Increasingly crippled by arthritis, she labored at her typewriter for ten years before the story of her heroine, Pansy, and her devotion to her plantation, Fontenoy Hall, was completed.

Mitchell was shy about her work and initially refused to show it to a representative of the Macmillan Publishing Company when he came to Atlanta seeking potential writing talent. But she had a change of heart, stuffed the hefty manuscript into a suitcase, and delivered it to the executive at the railroad station just as he was boarding a train back to New York.

Weighing 3 pounds, the 1,037-page novel was published in 1936. In the editing stage, the heroine's name was changed from Pansy to Scarlett, and Fontenoy Hall became Tara. Priced at $3.00, the book became an instant success, with 1.5 million copies sold in the first twelve months. It has since been translated into twenty-seven languages, total sales having exceeded the $25 million mark.

• The titular phrase, *Gone with the Wind*, is an excerpt from a poem by Ernest Dowson, but when Margaret Mitchell had submitted the manuscript to the publisher, the title was *Tomorrow Is Another Day*. Other titles considered were *Ba! Ba! Black Sheep, Bugles Sang True, Jettison, None So Blind, Not in Our Stars, Milestones,* and *Tote the Weary Load*.

Some definitions of various political ideologies made the rounds in 1936:

SOCIALISM: If you have two cows, you give one to your neighbor.

COMMUNISM: If you have two cows, you give them to the government, and then the government gives you some milk.

FASCISM: If you have two cows, you keep the cows and give the milk to the government; then the government sells you some milk.

NEW DEALISM: If you have two cows, you shoot one and milk the other; then you pour the milk down the drain.

NAZISM: If you have two cows, the government shoots you and keeps the cows.

CAPITALISM: If you have two cows, you sell one and buy a bull.

England

Britain's King George V died at the age of seventy after a long illness, concluding twenty-six years on the throne. *The Times* of London reported that the king's death had been "a peaceful ending," but it was not until fifty years later that the details of the monarch's passing would be revealed.

As reported in the *New York Times* on November 28, 1986, the notes of the deceased Lord Dawson, the attending physician, were finally revealed in London, showing that the doctor had injected the king with doses of morphine and cocaine to hasten his death, having then instructed his wife, "to advise *The Times* to hold back publication"—to hold the presses so that the august morning paper could be the first to carry the news of the monarch's death instead of the "less appropriate evening journals." Lord Dawson had written in his notes: "It was evident that the last stage might endure for many hours, unknown to the patient but little comporting with the dignity and serenity so richly merited and which demanded a brief final scene." Dawson's notes also revealed that the king's last words had not been "How is the Empire?" as previously reported, but "God damn you."

News of Dawson's intended act of kindness was not well received. Kenneth Rose, a biographer of the king, said of the euthanasia, "In my opinion the King was murdered by Dawson," adding that he was "appalled" by the revelation.

George V was succeeded by his son, the Prince of Wales, who became King Edward VIII, Emperor of India. The consensus of historians is that the new king was a weak man who had never wanted to ascend to the throne, having found his princely duties both restricting and onerous.

Author Christopher Warwick tells us that George V held his eldest son in low regard and that he

> . . . heartily disapproved of the modern trend-setting way in which his son dressed; he despised this circle of friends. Given the dynastic hopes invested in the Heir Apparent, the prince's fondness of other men's wives was, not unnaturally, another source of disappointment. So badly did father and son clash on one memorable occasion that a courtier overheard the King bellow at the Prince of Wales, "You dress like a cad. You act like a cad. You *are* a cad. Get out!"

It is fairly well documented that the Prince of Wales had made up his mind to marry an American woman named Wallis Warfield Simpson in 1934. It is unfortunate that he had not mustered the courage then to tell his father of his intention, for it might have spared the royal family the disgrace of abdication. The king would probably have welcomed the opportunity to remove the heir apparent from the line of succession, but as it was, he went to his grave convinced that his son would take the throne and "ruin himself" before the first year of his reign was out. In the eyes of many, his prophecy was fulfilled.

The Prince of Wales had met Mr. and Mrs. Ernest Simpson at a house party in the country in 1930. Mrs. Simpson was the former Wallis Warfield of Baltimore, Maryland, and she had ended her first marriage to an American aviator, Earl Spencer. Her second husband, an ex-Grenadier guardsman, was engaged in the shipping business in London and was the product of an American mother and an English father. The prince was immediately taken with the outspoken American woman, enjoying her assertive and dominating nature. Depending on the source, Edward VIII's wife-to-be is portrayed either as crass, cold, aggressive, and overbearing—or as effervescent, intelligent, and charming, with a marvelous sense of humor. Photographer Cecil Beaton initially described her as "a brawny great cow or bullock in sapphic blue velvet. . . . To hear her speak was enough. Her voice was raucous and appalling. I thought her awful, common, vulgar, strident, a second-rate American with no charm." Yet Beaton changed his mind and later spoke of her as "all that is elegant. . . . I am certain that she has more glamour and is of more interest than any public figure."

When the Prince of Wales became Edward VIII in January 1936, it was not long before Wallis Simpson became a frequent visitor to Buckingham Palace. As the year wore on, his relationship with the married American woman became big news in the foreign press, and the twosome was frequently photographed together during several vacations in Europe. In Britain, however, it was not until a few days prior to the king's abdication that Fleet Street ceased protecting the monarch's privacy. Only those Britons with friends or relatives abroad were alerted to the relationship; when Wallis Simpson was granted a decree nisi (a tentative divorce to become absolute in six months) in October, her suit was only accorded brief mention in the section of the newspaper given over to legal notices.

As fall came to an end, the pace of events began to quicken:

• On November 16, the king informed Prime Minister Stanley Baldwin of his intent to marry Mrs. Simpson. Although the king was permitted to marry a commoner under the British Constitution (but he was forbidden to marry a Roman Catholic), Baldwin advised him that

Parliament would not sanction a union with a twice-divorced woman with two living husbands.

• On November 20, a compromise was offered to Baldwin by advisers to the king: a morganatic marriage that would have excluded the king's wife from becoming queen and prevented any issue from their union from succeeding to the throne. This option was also rejected.

• On December 3, the news of the king's dilemma finally appeared in the British press, arousing considerable sympathy for his cause. Edward VIII was urged by close friends to use this show of popular support to persuade Parliament to change its mind, but declined, saying that it would be divisive for the country to prolong debate over the matter.

• Faced with a storm of publicity, Mrs. Simpson left for Cannes the same day. There she issued a statement announcing her intention "to withdraw from a situation that has been rendered both unhappy and untenable." She called the king to tell him that at the request of the prime minister she was giving up her divorce suit, but Edward VIII was not dissuaded, telling her that the Instrument of Abdication was being drafted.

• On December 10, the king signed the Instrument of Abdication. The following day, he broadcast his decision to the nation and departed the next day for France, having become His Royal Highness Prince Albert Christian George Andrew Patrick David, Duke of Windsor, the seventh and last name he would have. Born Prince Edward of York, he had been Prince Edward of Cornwall and York, Prince Edward of Wales, the Duke of Cornwall, the Prince of Wales, and King Edward VIII, prior to becoming the Duke of Windsor.

• The couple were married in France on June 3, 1937, after Wallis Simpson's divorce became final. The Church of England refused to put its stamp of approval on the nuptials, so a minister of the Episcopal church presided.

• *Time* named Wallis Warfield Simpson its Woman of the Year for 1936. Queen Elizabeth II and Corazon Aquino are the only other women to be so honored.

Hungary
There was some good news and bad news for a young Hungarian girl. The good news for Zsa Zsa Gabor was that she was awarded the title of Miss Hungary; the bad news was that she was forced to relinquish her title when it was revealed that the quick-blooming child had not yet become sixteen, the minimum age one had to be to enter the contest.

India
The Indian Rajah of Kolanka contributed a silver cup to be awarded annually to the team that won the Bangladore Limited Handicap Polo

Tournament. It is difficult to imagine the winning team toasting their victory by drinking champagne from the trophy; the rajah had not skimped on the prize, purchasing a cup that stood six feet tall.

Germany
Four thousand German troops moved into the Rhineland, disregarding the provisions of the Treaty of Versailles by occupying the demilitarized zone. England and France protested the action but took no military steps to confront the Germans.
- "Germany has no desire to attack any country in Europe." (David Lloyd George)
- "We rule by love and not by bayonet." (Joseph Paul Goebbels)

Soviet Union
Government officials in the USSR were concerned about the increase in the number of abortions performed since the operation had been legalized in 1920, allowing women who were less than two-and-a-half-months pregnant to obtain abortion on demand. Seven hundred thousand abortions had been performed in 1934, convincing the government that the practice should be restricted to life-threatening situations, an edict that would stay in effect until 1955.

REGIONAL NEWS

Kentucky
The last public execution in the United States was held in Owensboro, Kentucky, on June 10, 1936. A crowd estimated at 20,000 gathered to watch the hanging of Rainey Bethea, a young black man sentenced to death for killing a white woman. Hanging was the state's penalty for criminal assault, with counties given the local option of conducting the execution either in public or in private. The county sheriff elected to open the event to the public.

The morning of the hanging found many people in the virtually all-white crowd intoxicated and in a celebratory mood, shouting, "Take him up!" and "Let's go!" as they waited in a three-acre lot for the proceedings to begin. Author George Gipe writes, "When the hangman sprung the trap there was a large cheer from the crowd. Then, despite the presence of armed guards around the scaffold, many persons rushed forward, attempting to grab the hood from Bethea's dangling form, tear off bits of his clothing, even cut pieces of flesh from his body as souvenirs."

1936

Arizona and Nevada

In one of the greatest engineering feats known to man, Hoover Dam was completed; it began to generate electricity and to supply water for towns as far away as Los Angeles. Construction of the dam had created Lake Mead, 115 miles long, the world's largest man-made body of water.

The dam stretched 1,300 feet across the Colorado River at the Arizona-Nevada border. Concrete had been poured to a thickness of 600 feet at the base of the dam; at the top—726 feet above—the dam was 45 feet thick.

• The project had been known as Hoover Dam since its inception. However, President Roosevelt changed its name to Boulder Dam in a show of partisan petulance, and it would retain the name until 1947, when it was returned to its original name.

Utah

Mormons refused to avail themselves of federal financial aid and would stick to this decision during the entire Depression, believing "that the Lord alone giveth and the Lord taketh away."

☛ ENTERTAINMENT

The January 4, 1936, edition of *Billboard* provided the first ranking of best-selling records. Topping the list were:

"Stop, Look and Listen"	(Joe Venuti and his orchestra—Columbia)
"Quicker Than You Can Say"	(Ozzie Nelson and his orchestra—Brunswick)
"The Music Goes Round"	(Tommy Dorsey and his orchestra—RCA Victor)

Mildred and Patty Hill collaborated on a little ditty that was to become a song that is sung perhaps more often than any other in the United States and still generates royalties today. They call it "Happy Birthday to You."

An often repeated line was first spoken by Gary Cooper to his costar Madeleine Carroll in the 1936 film *The General Died at Dawn*. Cooper said: "We could have made beautiful music together."

Another bit of dialogue delivered in a 1936 film caught the attention of Bob Clampett, creator of cartoon character Bugs Bunny. When Carole Lombard said, "What's up, Duke?" to William Powell in *My Man*

Godfrey, it inspired Clampett to give Bugs the signature line "What's up, Doc?"

Luise Rainer won an Oscar as best actress for the 1936 film *The Great Ziegfeld,* an accomplishment that she would duplicate for her role in *The Good Earth* the following year. In 1967 and 1968, Katharine Hepburn would also be awarded back-to-back Oscars for her performances in *Guess Who's Coming to Dinner?* and *The Lion in Winter.*

Humphrey Bogart appeared in no fewer than eighteen movies during the period from 1936 to 1938. Some can still be seen on predawn television. His output during this three-year period is as follows:

1936
The Petrified Forest
Bullets or Ballots
Two Against the World
China Clipper
Isle of Fury

1937
Black Legion
The Great O'Malley
Marked Woman
Kid Galahad
San Quentin
Dead End
Stand-In

1938
Swing Your Lady
Crime School
Men Are Such Fools
The Amazing Dr. Clitterhouse
Racket Busters
Angels with Dirty Faces

The ten top draws at movie box offices in 1936 were as follows:

Shirley Temple
Clark Gable
Fred Astaire and Ginger Rogers
Robert Taylor
Joe E. Brown

1936

Dick Powell
Joan Crawford
Claudette Colbert
Jeanette MacDonald
Gary Cooper

The movie *Show Boat* revived the popular Broadway musical, all its songs, save one, by Jerome Kern and Oscar Hammerstein II. The exception was the popular song "Bill" with lyrics supplied by P. G. (Pelham Grenville) Wodehouse, author of over one hundred novels, many featuring an unflappable valet named Jeeves.

➤ BOOKS

Author Zane Grey died, but sales of his books would continue, reaching 30 million copies by the 1960s. Born Pearl Grey in Zanesville, Ohio, he had taken his mother's maiden name as his first name. An opportunity to play baseball brought him to the University of Pennsylvania, where he had earned a degree in dentistry in 1896. But practicing dentistry had bored Grey, and he soon turned to writing. After several novels, he had begun to take his material from the Old West, and *Heritage of the Desert* and *Riders of the Purple Sage* created an appetite for Westerns that lives on today. His theme of the lone gunfighter inspired numerous films and television shows.

➤ SPORTS

On May 8, 1936, jockey Ralph Neves was riding a horse named Flanakins in a race at San Francisco's Bay Meadows racetrack. Suddenly he was caught up in an accident that brought four horses and their jockeys to the ground in front of him. When Neves tried to avoid the melee, his horse reared, sending him hurtling through the air. When doctors reached Neves, they could detect no sign of either the jockey's pulse or heartbeat, and he was pronounced dead. His body was removed by ambulance to a hospital not far from the track and placed in a holding room until it could be taken to the mortuary. At the track, the sad news was announced to the crowd.

Approximately thirty minutes later, Neves awoke and, upon finding himself in a dark room, screamed for help. When he got no answer, he located the door and stepped outside, garbed only in his riding boots and a sheet. He flagged a cab and returned to the track, where the same doctors who had pronounced him dead reexamined him and found him

192

totally fit, suffering only from some cuts and bruises and shock. He was
back riding again the next day and produced more winners that year than
any other jockey at Bay Meadows.

In the early days of surfing, Tom Blake was the best there was on a
board. Then, as now, a ride of 200 yards was considered a good one, and
in early June 1936, Blake and several fellow surfers were waiting for a big
one at the outer reaches of Waikiki Bay. Suddenly Blake saw a series of
giant waves about a half mile away and moved his board into position.
Pushing off on the second wave of the group, he found himself propelled
toward the beach atop a mammoth wave that spanned the width of
Waikiki Bay. His companions wiped out, but Blake rode the wall of water
for a full mile before it dissipated on the shore.

Horton Smith won more money than any other professional golfer on
the PGA tour in 1936, although his take for the year was but an average
weekend's work for top golfers today. Smith's winnings: $7,682.

Tennis star Helen Wills Moody submitted to an experiment. She and
former Davis Cup player Howard Kinsey hit a single ball back and forth
2,001 times without error, concluding their rally only because Kinsey had
an engagement to give a tennis lesson. The rally took one hour and
eighteen minutes, and both players had experienced eye fatigue about
halfway through the exchange, although they each commented that it had
quickly gone away.

The story of Jesse Owens's success at the 1936 Olympics in Berlin is
well known, when he and other American black track stars caused Aryan
supremist Adolf Hitler some uneasy moments. Some lesser known
highlights of the Berlin Olympics and their aftermath follow:
• This was the first Olympics for which the Olympic flame was
carried from Greece to the site of the games, a tradition that has been
continued. This practice was conceived of by Adolf Hitler.
• Although Jesse Owens was given ticker tape parades in New York
and in Cleveland, his home town, President Roosevelt failed to acknowledge Owens's four gold medals with even a congratulatory letter;
nor did the AAU honor Owens with the Sullivan Award, given to the
year's best amateur athlete, in either 1935, when he established six
world's records, or in 1936, the year of his Olympic triumphs. Golfer
Lawson Little and Olympic decathlon champion, Glenn Morris, were the
respective recipients.
• When Owens set a world's record in the 200-meter dash, a black
Californian named Mack Robinson was second. Robinson's younger

1936 brother, Jackie, would be the first to break the color barrier in major league baseball.

• During the New York ticker tape parade, someone threw a paper bag into Owens's car as it worked its way up Broadway. Thinking it was probably just some cookies, Owens paid it little mind until the parade concluded. When he opened it up, he found the bag contained $10,000 in cash.

1937

These cool cats they say my music's old-fashioned. They say they study music. Funny they got to and I don't have to go into no rudimentals.

—Louis Armstrong

☛ NATIONAL NEWS

The miseries of the Depression were acted out to the accompaniment of some of the century's most spectacular American popular music. Broadway, Hollywood, Tin Pan Alley, the radio, the phonograph, the big bands, the crooners—all were contributors to an incredible variety of melodies, lyrics, arrangements, and styles, many of which endure today and give promise of becoming indigenous to our culture.

When one discusses the composers at work in the 1930s, one begins with George Gershwin, who was equally at home on Broadway, in Tin Pan Alley, in Hollywood, and at the concert hall. On February 11, 1937, Gershwin was playing his Piano Concerto in F with the Los Angeles Philharmonic when, writes pianist Oscar Levant, "I noted he stumbled on the very easy passage in the first movement. Then in the *andante,* in playing four simple octaves that conclude the movement above the

195

sustained orchestral chords, he blundered again." Gershwin recalled "that his mind went blank and he smelled burning rubber," but a subsequent medical examination revealed nothing alarming. By early June, he was bothered by dizziness and headaches, and submitted to a neurological examination, which indicated that his sense of smell had been impaired, but he opted not to have a spinal tap to determine if there were further complications.

On July 9, Gershwin fell into a coma and was rushed to Cedars of Lebanon Hospital in Los Angeles, his illness diagnosed as a brain tumor. Doctors performed a craniotomy the following day from which Gershwin never recovered, dying five hours after the operation.

His thirty-seven years had been incredibly productive, and at the time of his death, his future plans included collaborating on a film ballet with George Balanchine, taking a concert tour of Europe, and composing a symphony. But while no popular composer tackled as many forms of musical expression as did Gershwin, there were a host of other gifted composers and lyricists at work. There were some common threads among them: Many, like Gershwin, were Jewish, were the sons of musicians (Harold Arlen, Irving Berlin, and Kurt Weill were the sons of cantors), were brought up in New York City (Berlin, Howard Dietz, Gershwin, Oscar Hammerstein, Lorenz Hart, Jerome Kern, Richard Rodgers, and Arthur Schwartz), and were educated there (Dietz, Hammerstein, Hart, Rodgers, and Schwartz all studied at Columbia).

A discussion of the careers of all these talented men could easily fill a volume, but it is worth looking at two in particular:

Irving Berlin was born Israel Baline in Russia, in 1888, his family emigrating to Manhattan two years later. After selling newspapers, Berlin held jobs as a singing waiter and a song plugger before writing his own words and lyrics, and by 1911 he had fifty songs to his credit. That year he wrote "Alexander's Ragtime Band," which enjoyed sheet-music sales of over 1.5 million copies.

Two of Berlin's most popular songs were ones that he wrote and then put aside, to be resurrected at a later date. The first was "God Bless America," which he had composed in 1918 for a Broadway revue, but he decided that the show was a bit too frivolous for a serious patriotic song. Had it surfaced then, it would surely have been a contender for America's national anthem when Congress debated that issue in 1931. As it was, Berlin waited two decades before the song was introduced by Kate Smith on Armistice Day in 1938.

The second song that Berlin shelved was "White Christmas," which he would write in 1939, but put away in a trunk, to surface in 1941 in the movie *Holiday Inn* with Bing Crosby and Fred Astaire. When Berlin had written the original version, the opening line was, "I'm sitting in a pool in

196

Beverly Hills dreaming of a white Christmas." He simplified the line, Crosby recorded it in just eighteen minutes, and the crooner's version sold over 25 million records, while renditions by other artists produced sales of another 100 million. Some other Berlin hits were "A Pretty Girl Is Like a Melody," "Always," "Easter Parade," "Say It with Music," and "There's No Business Like Show Business."

• Berlin donated his royalties from "God Bless America" to the Boy Scouts and the Girl Scouts; royalties from "Always" he gave to his wife.

• The only key in which Berlin could play the piano was F-sharp.

• "Irving Berlin has no place in American music. He *is* American music." (Jerome Kern)

Cole Porter was a composer from an entirely different background. Porter had been born in Peru, Indiana, of wealthy parents. His maternal grandfather had made a fortune in the lumber business in West Virginia. The precocious Porter had composed two songs by the age of ten, one of which his proud mother had published in Chicago. At Yale, he had written two college songs, "Bingo Eli Yale," and the "Yale Bulldog Song," which nostalgic Elis still sing at football games today. Porter went on to graduate school, his grandfather having stipulated that he become a lawyer if he were to qualify for a handsome inheritance. When Porter showed no flair for the world of briefs and torts, his law school dean suggested that he transfer to the Harvard School of Music, which he did after having secured his grandfather's reluctant permission.

At Harvard, Porter wrote his first musical comedy with a fellow student. Not long after it failed, he joined the French Foreign Legion, transferring to the French Artillery School at Fontainbleau during World War I. Porter developed a fondness for Paris that kept him there after the war, studying music at the Schola Cantorum, while living on an allowance from his grandfather. When that munificent gentleman died in 1923, Porter inherited close to a million dollars, commenting that he could then afford to "go to Venice." Porter married an American woman and to Venice he did go, as well as to many other pleasant watering spots, and his productivity as a composer during the 1920s was meager.

In 1928, Porter was coaxed home by producer E. Ray Goetz to write songs for a musical that included "Let's Do It," its lyrics touching upon the mating habits of "bluebirds, bluebells, sponges, oysters, clams, jellyfish, electric eels, shad, sole, goldfish, dragonflies, centipedes, mosquitoes, katydids, ladybugs, moths, locusts, bees, fleas, chimpanzees, kangaroos, giraffes, hippopotamuses, sloths, guinea pigs, bears and Pekinese dogs," in addition to certain human species. The erudite Porter drew from his education, travels, and social contacts to produce a host of sophisticated songs. "What Is This Thing Called Love?" was inspired by a native Moroccan chant, while "Begin the Beguine" came from music that Porter

1937 had heard on an island in the Dutch East Indies; he could even compose songs for musicals from Shakespeare and Greek mythology and make them popular successes. During the 1930s, he wrote songs for a host of successful shows with stars like Ethel Merman and Fred Astaire, his hits including "Love for Sale," "Night and Day," "You're the Top," "I Get a Kick Out of You," and "Anything Goes."

• In 1937, Porter was involved in a riding accident that resulted in both his legs being crushed. Over the next twenty-one years, he would have thirty-one operations in an attempt to save his legs, but in 1958 he finally had to have his right leg amputated. (He called the injured limbs Geraldine and Josephine.) However, his convalescence did not reduce his musical output, and he continued to compose in his Waldorf Towers apartment.

The year 1933 had found the record business in a shambles, with the previous year's sales just 5 percent of what they had been in 1927. Author Roland Gelatt writes, "You did not buy luxuries when banks were foundering on all sides; you saved whatever hard cash you had for groceries." But in the mid-1930s, the market began to turn around; improved technology accounted for records with much better sound, and the high in-home incidence of radio sets induced manufacturers to turn out low-cost phonograph attachments. But the biggest boon to the industry was cheaper disks, as record companies decided to lower their prices in an attempt to move from high margins, low sales to the reverse, by pricing their records so that they were within the reach of every consumer.

Record sales had also been inhibited by the abundance of live music that poured forth, at no cost, from the family radio. Not only popular music, but hours of classical music and opera each week. While radio initially retarded record sales, it would prove to be a long-term blessing in disguise by creating a national interest in classical music that resulted in huge record purchases in the late 1930s when lower costs brought phonograph record prices down. By 1938, 33 million records were sold, and the record industry came alive. Unfortunately, it would have to take a hiatus in its growth during World War II when shellac (a key ingredient in record production, produced for the most part in India) was available only in small quantities for nonmilitary use. But records came back after 1945, and postwar growth would be fueled by popular music, not classics, aided by a new arbiter of taste, the disk jockey, who was already making his presence felt in the late 1930s.

On the night of August 21, 1935, Benny Goodman and his orchestra were finishing up a less than spectacular engagement at the Palomar

Ballroom in Los Angeles. Tired of catering to the crowd's requests for bland music, Goodman decided to play the sound that he and the boys in the band preferred: the free-wheeling, driving arrangements of one of his associates, Fletcher Henderson. The crowd went wild, danced up a storm, and the King of Swing was on his way.

Two years later, swing had given birth to a variety of expressions that his young fans used to urge the Goodman band on: "Swing it, Benny"; "Feed it to me," "Spank the skins," "In the groove," and "Killer diller" are just a few. "Bugle Call Rag," "And the Angels Sing," and "Sing, Sing, Sing" were but a few of Goodman's hits, and his band members were so talented that there would be frequent personnel changes as one after another went on his own. Lionel Hampton, Harry James, Teddy Wilson, and Gene Krupa were some of the Goodman alumni who prospered.

Competing for the crown of the King of Swing were leaders of many other great bands. Tommy Dorsey, the Sentimental Gentleman of Swing, had hits such as "Marie" and "Who"; clarinetist Artie Shaw produced favorites such as "Begin the Beguine" and "Lover Come Back to Me"; Glenn Miller delighted audiences with "Moonlight Serenade," "Little Brown Jug," "In the Mood," and "Tuxedo Junction"; Duke Ellington's popular songs included many of his own compositions, like "Mood Indigo," "Sophisticated Lady," and "In a Sentimental Mood." Swing was indeed king, and fans followed their favorite bands to dance at places like Frank Daily's Meadowbrook and the Glen Island Casino.

If you could not afford to dance at one of the so-called log cabins, you could tune into your Philco, Atwater Kent, or Stromberg Carlson, which brought popular music from roadhouses, hotels, and ballrooms in or near the big cities. "From high atop the Roosevelt Hotel in beautiful downtown New Orleans, we bring you the music of the swing-and-sway man himself, Sammy Kaye."

Accompanying the bands were vocalists such as Ella Fitzgerald, Ray Eberle, Martha Tilton, Connie Haines, and Skinny Ennis, plus a gaggle of family combinations like the Andrew, Boswell, and Pickins sisters. But for women, perhaps the most popular of all the music makers were the crooners, the favorites of the decade being Rudy Vallee, Russ Columbo, and Bing Crosby. By the end of the decade, another kid on the block was pressing for attention. His name was Frank Sinatra, and he had performed on *The Major Bowes Amateur Hour* with a group called the Hoboken Four. He would be hired by Harry James when his wife heard him sing on the radio, move to the Tommy Dorsey Band, and then strike out on his own in 1942, inspiring Frank Swoonatra Clubs in many cities. Author Louise Tanner writes:

There had always been a comic quality to Bing Crosby's oglings. One felt that acquiescence on the girl's part would send him back to Dixie and the kids. A mother sensed instinctively that Rudy Vallee was the sort of boy who would kiss her daughter good night at the door. (One could imagine him wrestling manfully with those hormones he learned about at Yale.) No parent in her right mind could look with equanimity on the hollow Sinatra cheeks, sunken eyes, large ears, which gave the wartime adolescent her first taste of the mother-instinct. Even mother herself might suppress the feeling, "I certainly would like to fatten that boy up." . . . If Vallee was the boy who kissed your daughter at the door, Frankie was the boy she would go upstairs with.

One would have thought that Franklin Roosevelt's overwhelming electoral mandate in 1936 would have given the chief executive clear sailing in 1937. Yet it was perhaps FDR's most difficult year in the White House, for he sustained two major setbacks that inflicted serious damage upon his presidency:

• On the budget front, the president gave in to his secretary of treasury, Henry Morganthau, who convinced FDR that he must finally come to grips with an upwardly spiraling federal deficit and put the country's budget in balance. But without the accustomed plasma of above-average government spending, the country fell into a recession—yes, a recession—right in the middle of a Depression. Industry shaved production, resulting in 2 million jobs lost, and the stock market gave up hard-won earlier gains. The following year, FDR would abandon his brief attempt to reduce the deficit and used government spending once again as a means of getting the economy's heart beating.

• Since his inauguration, Roosevelt's programs had been put into law by a responsive Congress that bent to his will. But not so the Supreme Court, which had ruled several of his pet New Deal projects unconstitutional, and in early 1937, Roosevelt decided to tailor that body more to his liking.

Armed with his electoral mandate at the polls, FDR moved to alter the Supreme Court without first bothering to preview his plan with Congress, an oversight he would later regret. Quite out of the blue came Roosevelt's announcement that he would propose legislation to increase the size of the court by six justices. While he gave as his reason an increasingly heavy court calendar, it was patently obvious to the Congress, the press, and the public that he intended to pack the court with pro–New Deal justices who would take the liberal side in cases that came before them.

A dominant Democratic Congress had no problem with FDR's intent; it was his heavy-handed, dictatorial power play that offended

200

them. Soon many of those legislators whom the president had not consulted joined with Republicans in a coalition to defeat his plan. Having seen the handwriting on the wall, Roosevelt could have backed down gracefully and sustained little damage. But this unforeseen opposition only steeled his resolve, and he attempted to bully certain legislators and bend them to his will, exacerbating the situation even more. They stuck to their guns, however, and the bill never gained headway. Ironically, attrition on the court achieved Roosevelt's goal in a fairly short time, but he had won the battle while losing the war. Congress would never be as willing an ally again.

☛ FOREIGN NEWS

England

On June 20, 1937, Daisy Alexander made out her will, put it into a bottle, and threw it into the Thames River near London. The will was a simple one, which read as follows: "To avoid any confusion, I leave my entire estate to the lucky person who finds this bottle, and to my attorney, Barry Cohen, share and share alike—Daisy Alexander (June 20, 1937)."

Two years later, Daisy Alexander died, the paper that she had ensconced in the bottle representing her only will. If Alexander had been a lady of limited means, her unusual will would probably have attracted little interest. But born Daisy Singer, she was a member of that fortunate family that had prospered in the sewing machine business, and her estate was valued at $12 million.

As the years passed, it would have been quite natural if Attorney Cohen had said a daily prayer asking that the bottle not be smashed to bits on some rocky shore but miraculously found, so that he and the fortunate retriever could share the bequest. Whether he did so or not, one day in March 1949, one Jack Wrum strolled along a San Francisco beach, jobless and out of cash. He spotted the will-bearing bottle, broke it open, and read the dramatic message—later to find that the paper was not a cruel joke or the work of a lunatic, but the real thing.

How had the bottle made its way to San Francisco? Oceanographers speculated that it had floated down the Thames into the North Sea, then proceeded north and east above Sweden, Russia, and Siberia, through the Bering Strait into the Pacific Ocean, where it bobbed leisurely across that vast expanse of water, before a wave deposited it safely upon the California shore.

Finland

According to Irving Wallace, David Wallechinsky, and Amy Wallace, a *Donald Duck* comic book recorded how Donald had assumed the

201

guardianship of three ducklings named Huey, Dewey, and Louie. The youthful water fowl were delivered to Mr. Duck in 1937 by a "Miss Duck," whose role was never explained, nor did she ever make another appearance in the life of the Duck family. While the ducklings' origins were never explained, they were raised as "nephews" by their bachelor "uncle." Readers accepted them as legitimate members of the Duck clan until 1978, when a youth club in Helsinki canceled its subscription to the *Donald Duck* comic book on the grounds that the parentage of the ducklings was dubious and that their so-called uncle had been squiring about one Daisy Duck for over four decades without having made an honest woman out of her. Furthermore, the committee was offended by Donald Duck's lack of propriety in not covering his from-the-waist-down extremities with trousers. Not until a Donald Duck fan club in Germany "offered comic-book documentation that Donald didn't indulge in unsavory habits or have sex with Daisy" were the exonerated comic books purchased once more by the Finnish youth group.

☛ AIR TRAVEL

Amelia Earhart was dubbed Lady Lindy in May 1932 when she had become the first woman to match Charles Lindbergh's solitary conquest of the Atlantic. Not resting on her laurels, Earhart had added a number of other noteworthy aeronautical achievements to her dossier over the next several years, including setting a coast-to-coast speed record for women in 1932 and becoming the first woman to fly solo from Hawaii to California, Los Angeles to Mexico City, and Mexico City to Newark—all in 1935.

In 1937, Earhart set out to fly around the world, her venture financed by her publisher-husband, G. P. Putnam. In May, she took off from Oakland, California, with an ex-Pan American Airways pilot, Fred Noonan, in a twin-engine Lockheed Electra called the Flying Laboratory, their flight plan including stops in Miami, Puerto Rico, Brazil, Africa, New Guinea, Howland Island in the Pacific, and Hawaii, before returning to Oakland. By July 2, they reached New Guinea and then took off for Howland Island, some 2,500 miles to the east. At Howland Island, a U.S. Coast Guard cutter was positioned to offer Earhart radio contact, and an airstrip had been constructed solely for her visit.

Early on July 3, the Coast Guard cutter received a garbled message from the Electra, interrupted frequently by static. A number of other messages were sent, but of insufficient duration to allow a precise fix on her position. Just before 8:00 A.M., Earhart radioed, "We are circling but cannot hear you. . . ." and at 8:45 A.M. came her last message, "We are on a line of position 157 dash 337. We are moving north and south."

The U.S. Navy launched a three-week search for the Flying Laboratory, using a number of ships and sixty planes from an aircraft carrier, but not a trace of the plane was found.

What happened to Amelia Earhart, Fred Noonan, and the plane?

The most obvious conclusion was that the plane simply could not find Howland Island and ran out of gas, crashing in the Pacific and leaving no trace. The Coast Guard cutter's commander said that Earhart's flight preparations were "casual, to say the least," and that in her eagerness to get started, she had not waited for proper radio equipment. This is the government's "official version."

This may well have been true, but it has not kept a number of investigators from publishing a variety of theories and "findings" disputing Washington's version. Just a few follow:

• Earhart and Noonan were spying for the government by overflying Japanese islands along their route and somehow fell into Japanese hands.

• Earhart's plane was found on the island of Saipan by an American soldier, but later "destroyed."

• Earhart was captured and then held in Tokyo during the war.

• After World War II, American military personnel in Tokyo unearthed a file on Amelia Earhart, which also later disappeared.

• In 1966, U.S. Admiral Chester W. Nimitz, World War II hero in the Pacific, said, just prior to his death, "I want to tell you, Earhart and her navigator did go down in the Marshalls and were picked up by the Japanese."

Only one thing seems certain. At least in some circles, a question will continue to be asked that may never be answered to everyone's satisfaction: "What became of Amelia Earhart?"

Millionaire aeronautics enthusiast Howard Hughes had worked on both the design and the construction of an airplane called the H-1. Boasting that it could attain higher speeds than any other American aircraft, Hughes had proved his point by flying from California to New Jersey at an average speed of 332 mph.

In 1937, the United States government turned down Hughes's plane for army use, but the speed and maneuverability of the aircraft did not escape the discerning eye of the Japanese. Mitsubishi Ltd. developed a dead ringer of the H-1, which would perform brilliantly in World War II. It was called the Zero.

☛ SPORTS

Joseph Louis Barrow (Joe Louis) had been born in Alabama in 1914, the son of a poor black sharecropper. As he reached maturity, his rock-

203

hard physique led him to the ring, and he turned pro in 1934, fighting his first bout for $52. His first defeat as a professional did not come until 1936.

In 1937, Louis challenged James J. Braddock for the heavyweight championship. Despite his formidable record, knowledgeable white sportswriters portrayed Louis as lazy, totally unsuited to the demanding training required of a world-class pugilist. So disparaging were their comments that they left little doubt about their choice in the upcoming bout, from either a talent or a racial standpoint:

• Bill Corum wrote in the *New York Journal*, "There isn't an ounce of killer in him. Not the slightest zest for fighting. He's a big, superbly built Negro youth who was born to listen to jazz music, eat a lot of fried chicken, play ball with the gang on the corner, and never do a lick of heavy work he could escape. The chances are he came by those inclinations naturally."

• Jack Miley of the *New York Daily News* wrote, "Joe was never used to easy living and he loves it. Not that he dissipates or goes to extremes, so far as I know. But any young fellow, accustomed to earning his bread by the sweat of his brow, who now sleeps ten or twelve hours a day and stuffs himself full of food like a gourmand isn't the kind of guy I wish to bet my dough on."

• Finally, some words from R. G. Lynch of the *Milwaukee Journal:* "The hulking brown body might have been lolling in a cabin doorway in Alabama, listening to somebody inside making mouth music . . . an uninformed visitor would never have thought that anybody had ever called this smooth-faced, placid, slightly sullen Negro youth a jungle killer."

Louis dominated Braddock in the fight, winning on a TKO in the eighth round to become the youngest man to hold the heavyweight championship, and only the second of his race to do so. To the accolades of an enlightened press? Not at all. Most sportswriters wrote of Braddock's courage in withstanding the attack of the Negro; many took an opposite posture to their prefight remarks on Louis's laziness, portraying him as a calculated killer, *Time* citing his "cool, poised cruelty."

If Louis's success failed to please the white press, it was a tonic for blacks. Author Richard Wright comments, "From the symbol of Joe Louis's strength, blacks took strength, and in that moment all fear, all obstacles were wiped out, drowned. They stepped out of the mire of hesitation and irresolution and were free! Invincible! A merciless victor over a fallen foe! Yes, they had felt all that. . . ."

Louis would retain the heavyweight crown until 1950. Although he made over $4 million in the ring, he would have little to show for his efforts when he quit fighting. But by then, he had gained the admiration
204

of whites as well as blacks as a magnificent champion and, perhaps of greater importance, a superior human being.

• "Joe Louis is a credit to his race—the human race." (Jimmy Cannon)

☞ FOOD AND DRINK

In 1937, spinach was a popular crop for many farmers in Crystal City, Texas, and town fathers decided to build a statue to honor the American who had done much to popularize the vegetable. The honoree was Popeye.

Margaret Fogarty Rudkin was well known in her Westport, Connecticut, community for the tastiness of her homemade bread. In 1937, she decided to set up ovens in the stable of the family farm to produce loaves in large quantities—first for her neighbors and then for local retailers. Her bread would eventually be sold across the United States, and the resourceful Rudkin later sold her Pepperidge Farm business to the Campbell Soup Company for $30 million.

Grocery-market owner Sylvan Goldman reasoned that he could sell more food to his customers if they could carry more food away from the shelves. Goldman took some folding chairs on which he mounted shopping baskets, and then he put the strange-looking contraption on wheels. Soon women were pushing his "shopping carts" down the aisles of his Oklahoma City store, guiding the back of the chair to maneuver the vehicle.

☞ ENTERTAINMENT

The movie *Snow White and the Seven Dwarfs* had its premiere, and the film would both charm and terrify many generations of American children. Developing a cartoon of standard movie length was an awesome task for Walt Disney and his associates, requiring some 2 million individual drawings for animation. Some of the rejected names for the dwarfs were Gaspy, Doleful, Awful, Gabby, and Helpful.

Love Is on the Air was released, marking the film debut of radio announcer Ronald Reagan, who played the role of Andy McLeod in the film, himself a radio announcer. June Travis was the female lead.

1937   Would-be actor Anthony Quinn wangled a part as an Indian in the film *The Plainsman* by purporting to be a member of the Cheyenne tribe and by disclaiming any knowledge of the English language.

It is Hollywood legend that Lana Turner was observed while perched on a stool at the soda fountain of Schwab's Drug Store in the film capital and promptly offered a film contract. Actually it was not Schwab's but Currie's Ice Cream Parlor where *Hollywood Reporter* publisher Billy Wilkerson spotted Julia Turner; as Lana Turner, she made her film debut in 1937 in *They Won't Forget*.

☞ MEDICINE

A New York state senator opposed legislation proposed to curb syphilis, believing that the publicity surrounding the bill's passage would familiarize many citizens with both the name of the malady and its meaning, and thereby "corrupt the innocence of children, and . . . create a shudder in every decent woman and man."

☞ PEOPLE

Thus spoke Katharine Hepburn in *Stage Door:* "The calla lilies are in bloom again. . . ."

When Fred Astaire and Ginger Rogers performed together in the film *Shall We Dance* in 1937, one of their dance numbers was done on roller skates. Soon roller skating gained great popularity in the United States, and grateful rink owners credited the two dancers with sparking the sudden public interest.

When *The New Yorker* magazine wrote an article about William Sidis, he was not pleased and went to court claiming invasion of privacy.
The New Yorker had portrayed Sidis as a brilliant screwball, which is just what he was. He had been admitted to Harvard at eleven, a year younger than the youngest previously admitted student—Cotton Mather in 1674. Sidis's father was a professor of psychology at Harvard, and his parents had taught him how to read before he was six months old. As a freshman, he had lectured an audience consisting mostly of Harvard faculty on the mathematics of four-dimensional space, but he was proficient in so many fields that it was only a question of which one he
206

would choose to make his mark in. But perhaps the burden of carrying so much information in his young brain was too much for him, for he suffered a nervous breakdown shortly after graduating from college and spent a good portion of his later life gathering a collection of streetcar transfers.

1937

1938

By all these lovely tokens,
September days are here.
With the summer's best of weather
And autumn's best of cheer.
                    —Helen Hunt Jackson

☛ NATIONAL NEWS

On the morning of September 21, 1938, New York and New England weather reports called for more rainy weather and some clouds. A few thorough readers of local newspapers saw rear-page squibs about a tropical storm that was working its way up the Atlantic Coast, but few paid much attention. Hurricanes were not considered a threat at that time because a major storm had not battered the shores of New England since 1815.

The tropical storm was first reported in the Bermuda Triangle, heading toward Florida, and the Jacksonville weather bureau had broadcast storm warnings. Floridians battened down the hatches, being well trained for the devastation that could be wrought by a hurricane. Some residents remembered that 780 lives had been lost in Florida in the hurricanes of 1926 and 1935 and breathed a sigh of relief when the storm veered to the north and east, leaving them unscathed.

208

When the hurricane passed several hundred miles to the east of **1938**
Cape Hatteras, responsibility for monitoring the storm was transferred
from the weather bureau in Jacksonville to the one in Washington, D.C.
The meteorologists there completely misjudged the strength of the
hurricane, although reports coming in attested to the power of the storm.
The captain of an offshore Cunard liner had radioed a dangerous
barometer reading of 27.85, while the Empire State Building was already
recording winds of up to 120 mph. Forecasters had been deceived by
somewhat better conditions at Cape Hatteras where winds of only 61 mph
were recorded with the barometer at 29.26. It was later revealed that
conditions in the direct path of the storm were something else again, with
barometric pressure at 27.75 and winds gusting up to 100 mph.

By the early afternoon of September 21, the Washington, D.C.,
weather bureau had stopped using the word "hurricane" in its reports,
noting that the "tropical storm" was headed out to sea. The first warnings
that the hurricane would pass over land came too late and were heard by
too few to allow more than token preparations. Trapped between two
ridges of high pressure, the storm had gained even more strength as it
bore down on Long Island. And when the hurricane hit, the land failed to
reduce its momentum, previous rains having so moistened the ground
that the storm behaved just as it had over the ocean.

Some examples of the impact of the storm on Long Island follow:

• The first wave accompanying the storm crashed upon the shore
with such force that it was recorded on a seismograph in Alaska.

• The Bellport, Long Island, Coast Guard Station later reported that
its barometer fell to 27.94, the lowest reading ever recorded on land in
the Northeast.

• Of Westhampton's 179 houses, 153 completely vanished, and
twenty-nine people were killed in that community alone.

Author William Manchester writes:

> . . . [a] Long Islander had bought a barometer a few days ear-
> lier in a New York store. It arrived in the morning post Sep-
> tember 21, and to his annoyance the needle pointed below 29,
> where the dial read "Hurricanes and Tornados." He shook it
> and banged it against a wall; the needle wouldn't budge. Indig-
> nant, he repacked it, drove to the post office, and mailed it
> back. While he was gone, his house blew away.

The storm went on a course that took it just west of New Haven and
Hartford, Connecticut, and Northampton, Massachusetts, and into
Vermont south of Burlington. Vermonters had noticed the sea smell hours
before the storm finally arrived, as well as a strange sensation in their ears
as the barometer fell. Salt spray from the first wave to hit Long Island had

1938 been borne aloft to whiten windows in Montpelier, the state capital, 125 miles from the sea.

Although Long Island had acted as a buffer for southwestern Connecticut, the exposed coasts of eastern Connecticut and Rhode Island were devastated, a 100-foot wave rolling over Providence left thirteen feet of water in its downtown streets.

The sad aftermath left about 700 people dead and over 60,000 homeless, and those who had lost houses or buildings were reimbursed by insurance companies at the rate of only 5 cents on the dollar. The New York, New Haven, & Hartford Railroad was missing a train, and American Airlines lost a plane from its fleet at Boston's Logan Airport. New England never again went unprepared for a major storm after the "Hurricane of '38."

• In New Jersey's Palisades Park, beavers took to the dams to enlarge and strengthen them against rising water. Park officials credited the industrious animals with keeping flooding to a minimum.

Shortly after eight o'clock on Sunday, October 30, 1938, millions of Americans were relaxing with their favorite radio programs. Most of their sets were tuned in to *The Charlie McCarthy Show*, while CBS's *Mercury Theatre of the Air* was being listened to by what ratings experts would estimate to be a mere 3 percent of the radio audience. Worried that CBS would soon cancel the show, actor-producer Orson Welles had pulled out all the stops for that night's performance, hoping to attract a larger audience, a major sponsor, or at least some publicity that might work in the program's favor in the future.

The show had begun with a standard introduction: "The Columbia Broadcasting System and affiliated stations present Orson Welles and his Mercury Theatre in *War of the Worlds* by H. G. Wells." This introduction was followed by the stentorian voice of Welles intoning: "We know that in the early years of the Twentieth Century, the world was being watched closely by intelligence greater than man's." Before Wells could elaborate on this somewhat elliptical statement, he was interrupted by an announcer who delivered the weather report. Upon conclusion, the announcer then said, "We now take you to the Meridian Room at the Hotel Park Plaza in downtown New York, where you will be entertained by the music of Ramon Raquello and his orchestra."

Meanwhile, a new singer was being introduced on *The Charlie McCarthy Show*, and a portion of the audience decided to use this interlude to check on some other programs. Those who switched their dials to CBS were unaware that they were breaking in on a play when they heard an announcer say, "Ladies and gentlemen, I have a grave announcement to make. The strange object which fell in Grovers Mill,
210

New Jersey, earlier this evening was not a meteorite. Incredible as it seems, it contained strange beings who are believed to be the vanguard of an army from the planet Mars." After a brief musical interlude, another announcement told of Martians fanning out as the police headed toward the scene. Believing that they were listening to a bona fide news report, a number of listeners used their telephones to spread the news, and more and more people tuned their radios to CBS. As the program continued, there were other seemingly authentic announcements that reported a rapidly worsening situation as the "Martians" landed at various locations across the country, quickly getting the better of whatever opposition they confronted with their deadly "death-ray" guns. The play finally came to an end with a hysterical announcer proclaiming that New York City was being overrun.

Author Nigel Blundell describes the extent to which the public had been gulled:

> In New Jersey, where the Martians were first reported to have landed, the roads were jammed with cars racing for the hills. Families fled with wet towels over their heads, believing this would save them from the nauseous space gasses they had been told about. . . . In New York, restaurants emptied. . . . Sailors in the U.S. Navy were recalled to their ships. . . . In Boston there were reports of "meteors." Some impressionable people actually claimed to have seen Martians. . . . In the Deep South, weeping, hysterical women prayed in the street.

While the panic raged, Orson Welles was totally oblivious to the hysteria he and his fellow cast members had wrought. The next morning, he was dumbfounded to see the moving type on the New York Times Building spell out. "ORSON WELLES CAUSES PANIC." In the end, after lawsuits were dropped and no legal prosecution was forthcoming, Welles achieved exactly what he had set out to accomplish—a larger listening audience, a well-known sponsor, and a publicity campaign that even the most resourceful public relations man in the world could probably never have pulled off.

☞ FOREIGN NEWS

Soviet Union

Begun in 1936, Stalin's Great Purge finally came to an end in 1938. Stalin had initiated the purge when Russian farmers opposed his move from private to collective farming. The dictator later claimed that 10

1938 million farmers had been put to death, and World War II found the country seriously short of men for its armed forces.

Switzerland
Brazil had found itself with a glut of coffee beans in the early 1930s and asked Switzerland's Nestlé Company to come up with some ideas on what might be done with the huge surplus. In 1938, Nestlé developed "instant coffee," a soluble powder to which one added hot water. It was called Nescafé, and it was so simple to make that coffee consumption increased, bringing smiles to the faces of the Brazilian growers.

Germany
Hitler annexed Austria after an election that allegedly showed that 99.75 percent of the Austrian people approved of consolidating the two countries. Britain and France were reluctant to take military action against Germany and later signed a pact with Germany and Italy in Munich that guaranteed peace among the four powers. The Munich Pact horrified many because Britain and France had won Hitler's promise of nonaggression by agreeing to let him take over the Sudetenland, an area inhabited by large numbers of ethnic Germans, comprising one third of Czechoslovakia. This virtually assured that country's downfall. Nevertheless, a Gallup poll taken in the United States found a majority of the country in favor of the pact, believing that it increased the chances of avoiding another world war.
- "I believe it is peace for our time . . . peace with honor." (Prime Minister Neville Chamberlain)
- "Good man." (Franklin D. Roosevelt's cable to Neville Chamberlain after his return from Munich.)

The first Volkswagen ("people's car") was produced in 1938, envisioned by Hitler as an affordable vehicle for all Germans. The car could be obtained after a series of monthly payments had been made, but few had been delivered before the funds and car production were diverted to the war effort, leaving many thousands of disgruntled Germans out-of-pocket who had been regularly sending in their marks.

After the war, several Allied car companies could have taken over the production of the VW, but they rejected the auto as being unappetizing for the consumer market. So the Volkswagen stayed in German hands. In 1972 the feisty little Beetle would exceed the record of the Ford Model T in sales for a single model. Author John May lists just a few of the car's future accolades:

Unmodified Beetles were used in the Antarctic in sub-zero conditions throughout the fifties. A Beetle half-buried in the Libyan

212

desert for five months started on the first try. A Beetle fitted with a propeller crossed the Strait of Messina to Sicily in thirty-eight minutes—two minutes faster than the ferry service. In the United States, a "Babies-Born-in-Beetles Club" had over fifty members.

German newspaperman Carl von Ossietzky died in Berlin as a result of "treatment" that he had suffered in a Nazi concentration camp. While interned, he had been awarded the Nobel Peace Prize in 1935, becoming the first recipient not to go to Scandinavia to claim his prize.

Australia

Australians rival the British and the Germans in their fondness for beer. To cater to this extreme thirst for the malt beverage, a bar was built in Victoria, Australia, in 1938, which was 287 feet long and boasted no fewer than thirty-two beer pumps.

☛ REGIONAL NEWS

Washington

A totally unknown candidate won an election in Milton, Washington, for Republican committeeman. His name was Boston Curtis, and he had been sponsored by Milton's mayor, Kenneth Simmons, who wanted to demonstrate that the electorate often had little knowledge of those whom they supported for office. Those who had cast their ballots for Curtis were particularly embarrassed when they learned that Boston Curtis was a mule.

Illinois

In 1936, Russell W. Ballard had been appointed director of welfare for Lake County, Indiana, a position he would hold until 1941. Fortunately for future historians, Ballard began in 1938 to save amusing portions of letters sent to his department requesting aid.

Some of his favorites follow:

• "Mrs. Jones hasn't had any clothes for a year and has been visited regularly by the clergy."

• "I am glad to report that my husband who is missing is dead."

• "I am writing the welfare department to say that my baby was born two years old. When do I get my money?"

• "I cannot get sick pay. . . . I have six children. Can you tell me why?"

• "This is my eighth child. What are you going to do about it?"

213

• "Please find out for certain if my husband is dead. The man I am living with can't eat or do anything until he knows."

• "I am very much annoyed to find that you have branded my son illiterate. This is a dirty lie, as I was married a week before he was born."

• "In answer to your letter, I have given birth to a ten-pound son. I hope this is satisfactory."

• "I am forwarding my marriage certificate and my children, one of which is a mistake as you can see."

• "My husband got his project cut off for two weeks and I haven't had any relief since."

• "Unless I get my husband's money, I will be forced to lead an immortal life."

• "You have changed my little boy to a little girl. Will this make any difference?"

• "I have no children yet, as my husband is a truck driver and works day and night."

• "In accordance with your instructions, I have given birth to twins in the enclosed envelope."

• "I want my money as quick as I can get it. I have been in bed with the doctor for two weeks and he doesn't do me any good. If things don't improve I will have to send for another doctor."

☞ MEDICINE

The New York Academy of Medicine published a report by Johns Hopkins Medical School professor Raymond Pearl that read as follows: "Smoking is associated with a definite impairment of longevity. The impairment is proportional to the habitual amount of tobacco usage by smoking, being great for heavy smokers and less for moderate smokers."

☞ COMICS

In 1934, would-be writer Jerry Siegel and his aspiring artist friend, Joseph Shuster—both residents of Cleveland, Ohio—were fascinated by science fiction. On a sweltering July night, Shuster was having difficulty falling to sleep, so he turned on his creative juices and began to conceive a character called Superman. Early the next morning, he raced over to his friend Joe's house to tell him of his concept: a man garbed in "a colorful, tight-fitting costume," whose true identity would be kept secret and who opposed the forces of evil.

The two men quickly drew up a number of strips, but it was not until 1938 that they found a market for their creation. "Superman" appeared in

Action Comics in June 1938 and was so well received that comic books **1938** were soon devoted entirely to the "strange visitor from another planet, who came to Earth with powers and abilities far beyond those of mortal men. Superman, who can change the course of mighty rivers, bend steel in his bare hands, and who, disguised as Clark Kent, mild-mannered reporter for a great metropolitan newspaper, fights a never-ending battle for truth, justice, and the American way!"

Author E. Nelson Birdwell writes:

What was the appeal? Superman's exploits held something for everyone. There was his science-fiction background and his ancestry on the planet Krypton. There was high adventure in his incredible feats of strength and daring, each one topping the last. There was a maddening romantic triangle, wherein Clark Kent, reporter for the Daily Planet, fell in love with co-worker Lois Lane, who, it seemed, had eyes only for Clark's secret identity as Superman! How perplexing! Clark was his own competition for Lois's affections, his own rival.

Superman would go on radio, on television, even on Broadway, in addition to appearing in comic books and newspapers. In 1941, 200,000 youngsters became Supermen of America, promising "to aid the cause of justice," while it was estimated that 35 million people followed Superman in one medium or another. With the astounding success of Superman, one would think that Siegel and Shuster were on easy street, but the two later accepted a cash offer for rights to Superman in 1948, and afterward fell upon hard times. In 1975, Siegel toiled as a mail clerk in Los Angeles, while Shuster, nearly blind, lived with his brother in New York. The National Cartoonists Society interceded on their behalf, persuading Warner Communications, who then owned the rights to Superman, to pay each of the two sixty-one-year-old men an annual stipend of $20,000.

• Another comics character who changed his identity was Billy Batson who, upon uttering the magic word "Shazam!" became Captain Marvel. What did the word "Shazam" mean?

S	=	(Wisdom of) Solomon
H	=	(Strength of) Hercules
A	=	(Stamina of) Atlas
Z	=	(Power of) Zeus
A	=	(Courage of) Achilles
M	=	(Speed of) Mercury

Ever since Charles Lindbergh made his solo aerial conquest of the Atlantic, Douglas Corrigan had yearned to make a dramatic flight of his own. A California airplane mechanic, he had worked on the construction of *The Spirit of St. Louis* and by 1929 had saved enough money to buy a 1929 Curtis-Robin monoplane for $900. He christened the battered plane *Lizzy* and spent years getting the aircraft into decent shape.

In 1937, Corrigan, like Lindbergh, decided to fly the Atlantic alone and petitioned civil air authorities for permission to make the trip. Some say that he was turned down because of the poor condition of his plane. A government spokesman is reported to have said, "We don't authorize suicide" after having inspected the aircraft; others say that permission was withheld because worsening international conditions and the recent disappearance of Amelia Earhart had brought about a government freeze on flights over international waters. But for whatever the reason, Corrigan was rebuffed in his attempt to make the European flight. Nevertheless, he flew his plane from Los Angeles to New York, and the early morning of July 16, 1938, found him at Floyd Bennett Field, Brooklyn, declaring that he was planning a return trip to the West Coast. Gassed up and ready to go, he took off, circled the field, and headed east. Airport manager Kenneth Behr remarked to one of his men, "That man's crazy. He's supposed to be flying to California, but he's headed east instead of west."

Twenty-eight hours and thirteen minutes later, Douglas Corrigan landed at Baldonnel Airport in Dublin, Ireland. Corrigan said to an airport official, "Isn't this Los Angeles?" Told that it was Dublin, he replied, "Can you beat that? I guess I flew the wrong way."

Knowing of Corrigan's desire to match Lindbergh's accomplishment and having seen him start out in an easterly direction, New York air traffic controllers had alerted their counterparts in Ireland, and Corrigan was detained by authorities. He claimed that he had made a compass error, and lie detector tests confirmed that he was telling the truth. Also in his favor was the total absence of equipment and provisions on board for a transatlantic flight. There were no charts or maps of the Atlantic and its coastal areas, and Corrigan had little food and no warm clothing.

Whether or not Corrigan had flown to Ireland intentionally was of little consequence to the public. Corrigan's flight was a welcome respite from the gloom of the Depression, and, according to Jay Robert Nash, his "absurd antic brought back the carelessness and dash of the lost Roaring Twenties." He was welcomed in London by the American ambassador, returned to New York for a ticker tape parade, and was paid handsome **1938** fees for personal appearances and endorsements. In 1939, he played himself in a movie about the flight, *The Flying Irishman*. He ferried planes to Europe during World War II, settled down in California, and was defeated in an attempt to win a seat in the U.S. Senate in 1946. "Wrong Way" Corrigan's version of his strange flight never wavered, but even his denial of flying to Dublin, perhaps intentionally, held out the possibility of fabrication. "Wrong Way" Corrigan said, "I've told that story so many times that I believe it myself."

☞ SPORTS

Southpaw Johnny Vander Meer had not exactly taken major league baseball by storm when he had joined the Cincinnati Reds' pitching staff in 1937. So when he pitched a no-hit game on June 11, 1938, against the Boston Bees, it looked as though he was finally coming into his own.

Four days later, Vander Meer pitched for the Reds against the Brooklyn Dodgers in the first night game ever played at Ebbets Field. The twenty-three-year-old hurler once again displayed his best stuff with a steaming fastball as he repeatedly set the Dodgers down without a hit. In the last of the ninth inning, the Dodgers came to bat still hitless, but Vander Meer suddenly became wild, walking three Dodgers to fill the bases with only one out. The next play brought a force-out at the plate, and only Dodger Leo Durocher stood between Vander Meer and an incredible second consecutive no-hit game. When Durocher lofted an easy fly ball to center field, Vander Meer had established a record that most baseball experts believe will never be broken.

• Despite this feat, Vander Meer retired with a pitching record that showed 119 wins against 121 defeats.

When boxer Henry Armstrong outpointed Lou Ambers in New York City on August 17, 1938, he won the lightweight championship. Already the holder of the featherweight and welterweight crowns as well, Armstrong became the first and only boxer to hold three titles simultaneously.

Golfer Samuel Jackson Snead's ball was on the thirteenth green, a par three, while his opponent in the 1938 PGA match play tournament, Jimmy Hines, was just short of the putting surface. When Hines pitched up, his ball hit Snead's, sending it into the cup, followed by his own. Officials gave both players birdie twos.

1938 ☛ ART

Anna Mary Robertson Moses had brought up ten children, and in 1938, at seventy-eight, she decided to seek a bit of relaxation. She bought some oil paints and started copying Currier and Ives prints and picture postcards, later going on to painting local scenes at or near her upstate New York farm. She occasionally sold her work for small sums but often gave them away to anyone who wanted one.

The next year, an art collector passing through Hoosick Falls, New York, spotted some of her paintings in the window of a local drugstore. He immediately went to her farm and bought all fifteen paintings that she had on hand, three of which were later exhibited in a show called Contemporary Unknown Painters, at New York City's Museum of Modern Art. She was an immediate success and went on to paint some two thousand works in a simple style later called American Primitive. Her paintings were exhibited across the United States and in Europe. "Grandma" Moses died in 1961 at the age of 101.

• One Christmas, Cole Porter gave twenty friends some paintings that he had purchased from an elderly lady who lived near his country home. Porter's seemingly inexpensive gifts turned out to be extremely valuable when it was later determined that they were the works of Grandma Moses.

☛ BUSINESS

The first hourly minimum wage was established by Congress in 1938 at twenty-five cents an hour.

The Supreme Court ruled that "cola" was a generic word "for a soft drink based on the cola nut" and was, therefore, not the exclusive property of the Coca-Cola Company.

☛ DANCE

The Lambeth Walk succeeded the Big Apple as the popular dance of 1938. According to authors Andrew Marum and Frank Parise, the dance was created in Britain, where it had been known as the Cockney Strut. Couples "strutted forward, linked arms, reversed position, faced each other, clapped and then, as a final step, jerked their thumbs over their shoulders, saying 'Oi' for no apparent reason."

1938

Radio stations banned several songs with the verb "Do" in their titles because they were interpreted by some as being sexually suggestive. "You Do Something to Me," "Let's Do It," and "Do It Again" were three popular songs that some stations refused to play.

The good news: Spencer Tracy won an Academy Award for his role in the film *Captains Courageous*. The bad news: His Oscar had been engraved with the name "Dick Tracy."

Cartoonist and animator Walt Disney was awarded an honorary degree by Yale University in 1938. The citation: "He labored like a mountain and brought forth a mouse."

☞ MEDIA

Time magazine's Man of the Year was Adolf Hitler.

1939

The great masses of the people will more easily fall victim to a great lie than to a small one.

—Adolf Hitler

☛ THE WAR

Americans bought Rand McNally out of maps as nations around the world jockeyed for position, and portents of a global war increased. A few important and ominous events in some key countries were as follows:

Japan

The Japanese government was in the hands of militarists who had purged democratic opposition and liberal thought and were strongly committed to adding to the nation's real estate. Japan had invaded Manchuria in 1931; the Japanese then turned their attention to China, where they repeatedly sliced off pieces of territory as the decade progressed. When America came to China's aid, Japan vowed its revenge, despite having to rely on the United States for two thirds of its oil supply.

220

Spain

Spain was engaged in a civil war spawned by a Fascist general named Francisco Franco, who had turned the army against a government that he regarded as too liberal and too progressive. The Fascists were aided in their cause by Germany and Italy, the Loyalists by the Soviet Union and volunteers from all over the world. The Nazis provided the latest in military hardware, eager to test their new weaponry on civilians. When German bombs killed or wounded nearly half the population of the town of Guernica, a German official commented, "We were trying out new tactics for aerial assault. Guernica made a good laboratory." With Hitler's help, the Fascists subdued the Loyalists in March 1939 and ruled Spain with an iron fist until Franco's death in 1975.

Soviet Union

On November 30, the Soviets attacked Finland to win the Karelian Isthmus, a strategically important piece of land that would make the invasion of the U.S.S.R. more difficult. Although vastly outmanned, the scrappy Finns held out for three months before capitulating, inflicting considerable damage on the Red Army.

Italy

Italy's troops had not covered themselves with glory in the Spanish Civil War, and Mussolini "was looking for an easy mark" in order to enhance his army's military standing. He chose mountainous Albania, a nation of merely 1 million highly scattered people, a large percentage of whom were shepherds.

Germany

Prior to 1939, Hitler had limited his saber rattling to areas populated by people of German origin. In moves that he could rationalize as altruistic, he had "repatriated" 3 million Germans by occupying that area of Czechoslovakia known as the Sudetenland, and 6 million more German-speaking brothers had been returned to the fold in the Austrian *Anschluss*, or union. It was now time for Germany to broaden the scope of its efforts and export Nazism to "deserving" non-German-speaking nations as well.

March 15—Hitler, blaming the Czechs for "wild excesses" and "terror," sent his armies to occupy the rest of Czechoslovakia. The Führer boasted to his staff, "Children! This is the greatest day of my life! I shall go down in history as the greatest living German."

April 3—Hitler initiated Case White, a battle plan for the invasion of Poland that was to commence as soon as possible after September 1.

1939 *May 27*—Winston Churchill criticized Prime Minister Neville Chamberlain in the House of Commons for failing to respond to a Soviet proposal to link the U.S.S.R., France, and Great Britain in an alliance against Germany. Churchill reasoned, "Without an effective Eastern Front, there can be no satisfactory defense of our interest in the West, and without Russia there can be no effective Eastern Front." Chamberlain continued to drag his feet on the issue, dispatching envoys to the Soviet Union on a slow freighter rather than by plane.

August 23—Although Chamberlain was in no hurry to bed down with the Russians, Hitler came to the realization that a pact with the Soviets might be of significant short-term benefit to Germany. By agreeing to share his gains in the East with Stalin, he could keep the U.S.S.R. out of the war and make Britain and France think twice before taking on not one but two formidable foes. A German-Soviet nonaggression pact was signed on August 23.

August 31—News correspondent William L. Shirer was making one of his frequent visits to Germany and made this observation about the people: "Everybody against the war. . . . People talking openly. How can a country go into a major war with a population so dead against it?"

September 1—Early in August, Hitler asked that 150 Polish uniforms be procured to be worn by condemned criminals who were enemies of the Nazis in a fake raid on German troops, giving the Nazis an excuse to go to war with Poland as the aggrieved party. And so World War II began, the bogus Polish troops being killed in the process. The code word for the victims was "Canned Goods."

September 3—Britain and France declared war on Germany.

October 6—Hitler spoke in the Reichstag, stating that "Germany has no further claims against France. . . . I believe that there can only be real peace in Europe and throughout the world if Germany and England come to an understanding. Why should this war in the West be fought? It would be senseless to annihilate millions of men. No, this war in the West cannot settle any problems." The British moved troops to France, but no shooting took place, and that autumn was to be known as the period of the Phony War.

November 8—Hitler blamed the British Secret Service when a bomb exploded just after he had left a Munich beer hall, killing seven and injuring sixty-three. The "assassination attempt" would later turn out to have been cooked up by the Nazis in an effort to drum up anti-British sentiment among the German people.

December 25—William L. Shirer talked with German sailors who kept repeating the same question: "The English, why do they want to fight us?"

Although Americans followed these proceedings with interest, they **1939** supported their country's neutrality. Author Irving Werstein writes, "Who cared about those dumb Europeans? Let them blow each other's heads off. None of it was Uncle Sam's business. Thank God the war was an ocean away."

By 1939, a number of the world's most eminent physicists were privy to the fact that the mystery of nuclear fission had been solved, leading to the conclusion that it would be possible to apply that scientific knowledge to the construction of the most devastating explosive device in the history of mankind. It would take extensive experimentation, for the physics involved was still theoretical; it would also take millions and millions of dollars to fund the project. But it could be done.

By nature, physicists are both high-minded and, more often than not, apolitical. High-minded, in that they share their findings with others in their field who pursue a common goal; apolitical, in that they are not especially interested in most matters unrelated to their work. But in the shadow of impending war, those physicists knowledgeable about nuclear fission were well aware of its political and military significance. Quite simply, the first nation to have access to a weapon of this potency could either avoid a war, win a war, control the world, or destroy it, depending on its inclination.

Most of the leading physicists in the United States were recent arrivals from Europe in search of a safe haven in which to work. Enrico Fermi, a Nobel Prize winner from Italy, and Niels Bohr, from Denmark, were two of the most prominent scientists to come to the United States. They and their fellow emigrés were well aware that nuclear fission was also a subject of interest to the Germans, a recent treatise dealing with "uranium chain reaction" having been published in Germany in July 1939. Shortly thereafter, the Germans cut off from Czechoslovakia the export of uranium, an ore that had little industrial significance but that was essential to nuclear fission.

Some important physicists strongly believed that the United States government should be alerted at once. Author William Manchester describes the physicists' dilemma:

> They had no friends in power; some were still learning the
> language. Szilard and Teller went to Washington and were met
> with blank stares. Even Fermi, with his Nobel Prize, was re-
> ceived coldly. The Army and Navy needed all their energies
> to acquire conventional weapons; they had no time for Buck
> Rogers games. The State Department saw no reason for urgen-
> cy. According to their files, uranium was a rare and rather
> useless metal which was found, among other places, in Czecho-

slovakia and Belgium. Europe was in the last days of peace, armies were mobilizing, the crisis was desperate, and foreign service officers had no time for disheveled men who talked like organ grinders about splitting atoms.

Since they realized that they were totally out of their element in attempting to break through Washington's bureaucratic indifference, it is a credit to these men that they persisted. And imaginatively, too, for they realized that the only way to get attention in Foggy Bottom was to enlist the aid of a man whom even the bureaucrats could not brush off. The man they sought to enlist was Albert Einstein, originator of an equation that had changed the scientific world, $E = MC^2$, the theory of relativity.

In July 1939, they tracked down Einstein while he was vacationing, and he quickly understood the importance of their mission, agreeing to be a signatory to a letter to President Roosevelt explaining the importance of government sponsorship of a program to harness atomic energy. The letter included the sentence, "This new phenomenon would lead also to the construction of bombs."

The letter, writes Manchester, was taken to Roosevelt by Alexander Sachs, a financier known to the president. Sachs met with the president twice, and finally FDR turned to him and said, "Alex, what you are after is to see that the Nazis don't blow us up." "Precisely," responded Sachs, and what was to be known as the Manhattan Project was soon underway.

🐀 REGIONAL NEWS

New York
Twelve hundred acres of Flushing, Long Island, marshland was converted for the New York World's Fair, which attracted exhibits from all the major nations of the world except Nazi Germany. The fair had been dubbed the World of Tomorrow, and the General Motors Futurama was the most popular attraction, drawing a daily average of 28,000 visitors, who were moved in armchairs through a nearly one-acre exhibit depicting what America would be like in the 1960s. Other popular exhibits were a parachute jump with a 250-foot drop, and Billy Rose's Aquacade, featuring a spectacular water ballet. The centerpiece was an odd pair of structures: a globe some 200 feet in diameter, the Perisphere, and a 700-foot, pencil-thin tower called the Trylon (Trylon-and-Perisphere salt and pepper shakers were a popular souvenir). There was also a fountain display, intermixed with scores of "promotional gimmicks, side-shows, and downright corn." One could see Borden cows milked on a revolving platform, a robot who could speak and smoke a cigarette, and a woman who froze all of her body except her head in a block of ice. A telegram was
224

sent to Eleanor Roosevelt by using the current from electric eels to
transmit the message, and FDR became the first president to have a
speech televised. Thirty-two million people visited the fair between April
30 and October 31, and because it had been so popular, it would reopen
for five months in 1940.

Virginia

In 1938, "Carry Me Back to Old Virginny" had been proclaimed
Virginia's official state song. But in 1939, it came to light that the author
and composer, James Bland, was a black man. Despite this revelation,
Virginia stood by its guns and kept the state song, one prominent white
Virginian declaring: "What does it matter, after all? Even though a black
composed it, that's a grand old song and sure sounds like one of [Stephen
Collins] Foster's."

Pennsylvania

A Philadelphia couple receiving welfare payments won $150,000 in
the Irish Sweepstakes and, not surprisingly, applied a portion of their
winnings toward the purchase of a new house, some furniture, and an
automobile. After the federal government took its share for taxes, Pearl
and Benjamin Mason repaid the City Relief Board the $2,133.90 that they
had received in welfare payments and used the remaining $80,000 for the
renovation of tenement buildings, which they turned into a modern
housing development for families of limited means.

Georgia

Atlanta became the first city in the United States to outlaw the
playing of pinball machines. Violators were fined $20 and jailed for thirty
days.

🐀 MUSIC

A German singer named Lale Andersen recorded a song called
"Three Red Roses," which record company officials touted as a potential
hit. One night, a Radio Belgrade disk jockey became inebriated and
played the flip side of the disk by mistake, a song titled "Lili Marlene."
He was soon barraged with requests for the tune that would become a
favorite of both Allied and Axis troops during World War II.

A Montgomery Ward copywriter wrote a poem called "Rudolph the
Red-Nosed Reindeer," which the company decided to give away as a
promotion. Illustrations were added, and more than 2 million copies of

the rhyming Christmas story were distributed. The poem would be put to music in 1949 and would become a holiday favorite.

Philadelphia-born Marian Anderson had sung in her church choir as a child. Such was the beauty of her voice that the congregation had underwritten her study of music and voice, and she justified their faith by becoming a singer of such talent that Arturo Toscanini paid her the rarest of compliments, saying, "A voice like yours comes but once in a century."

In 1939, promoters were planning a concert by the black singer in Washington's Constitution Hall. Knowing that the auditorium was owned by the Daughters of the American Revolution—a group not known for its partiality to blacks—newspaper reporter Mary Johnson telephoned Mrs. Henry M. Robert, Jr., the DAR president, to get her organization's reaction to the proposed concert. Robert's reply was unequivocal: No black would ever be allowed to appear at Constitution Hall.

Informed of Robert's edict, Walter White of the NAACP decided to call attention to the organization's stand by scheduling Marian Anderson's concert at another site, free of cost and open to all comers. She agreed, and the NAACP sought the permission of the Interior Department to use the Lincoln Memorial. Secretary Harold Ickes informed President Roosevelt of the request, which he immediately granted. When Eleanor Roosevelt heard of the DAR's action, she resigned her membership in the organization and, with Ickes, headed up a committee to make the Lincoln Memorial concert a success. And a success it was, a crowd of 75,000 turning out to hear Anderson's magnificent voice.

• Despite her successes in Europe and in the United States, Marian Anderson would not be signed by the Metropolitan Opera until 1955.

☛ BUSINESS

Department store executive Fred Lazarus, Jr., convinced FDR that extending the number of shopping days between Thanksgiving and Christmas would give the economy a much needed shot in the arm. In fixing the date for Thanksgiving Day by proclamation, which was the customary procedure at the time, FDR set it for a week earlier than usual in 1939, and again in 1940 and 1941. Public opposition was strong, and the governors of many states refused to go along with the changes. The matter was finally settled when, in 1941, Congress resolved that the holiday would be celebrated in subsequent years on the fourth Thursday in November.

In order to help women make their brassiere buying more precisely gauged to size, the Warner's company instituted a new standard of measurement: cup sizes.

226

Unemployment had fallen dramatically since 1933, but there were
still 10 million Americans out of work. Those with jobs earned an average
of $2,500 a year, and a six-room Manhattan apartment rented for $75 a
month. Coffee cost 25 cents a pound, and beef about the same. On
Broadway, an orchestra ticket cost just over $2.00, and movie admission,
including a stage show that usually featured one of the "big bands," was 25
cents before one o'clock, 55 cents after.

American Tobacco Company head George Washington Hill was
looking for a way to increase the sales of Pall Mall cigarettes, the brand
having been introduced two years earlier. Hill decided to lengthen the
smokes from 70 to 85 millimeters, making it longer than any other brand
on the market, ads claiming that the longer length "travels the smoke and
makes it mild."

☞ CRIME

On June 7, 1939, a German named Eugen Weidman had the
unhappy distinction of being the last person in France to be publicly
executed, his death being inflicted by the guillotine. Weidman had been
convicted of murder, and his execution took place in the Rue Georges
Clemenceau, next to the Palais de Justice at Versailles. Crowds jammed
the surrounding buildings, and windows offering a good view of the
guillotine were rented for outlandish prices. Newspaper pictures of the
event brought widespread protest against public executions, and they
were soon banned.

☞ BOOKS

Ernest Vincent Wright's novel *Gadsby* was published in Great
Britain in 1939 and was considered highly unusual, although it was not
apparent in the prose, an example of which follows:

> Gadsby was walking back from a visit down to Branton Hills'
> manufacturing district on Saturday night. A busy day's traffic
> had had its noisy run; and with not many folks in sight, His
> Honor got along without having to stop to grasp a hand, or
> talk; for a Mayor out of City Hall is a shining mark for any
> politician. And so, coming to Broadway, a booming bass drum
> and sounds of singing told of a small Salvation Army unit carry-
> ing on amidst Broadway's night-shopping crowds.

227

If one rereads this passage, one will note that it does not contain the most frequently used letter in the English alphabet—the letter *e*—nor does *e* appear anywhere else in the 50,000-word novel.

☛ ENTERTAINMENT

Despite the Depression, Americans averaged one visit a week to their local movie theaters as talking pictures revolutionized Hollywood, bringing a whole new dimension to films. Suddenly there could be intricate plots, and movie moguls paid handsomely to attract the finest writers in the land to the world of the silver screen.

Few could resist the opportunity to make more money in a week than they could in a year away from Hollywood. Screenwriter Herman Mankiewicz wired playwright Ben Hecht in the early 1930s, informing him that "millions are to be grabbed out here and the competition is idiots. Don't let this get around." But it did get around, and they came in droves, Faulkner, Fitzgerald, and just about every other major writer in the country. Hollywood also began buying Broadway plays in large numbers and converting them to film.

When Louis B. Mayer purchased Lillian Hellman's *The Children's Hour,* he was warned that the play had a lesbian theme that would never be acceptable. "Don't worry," said Mayer. "We'll make them Americans." And while their original works and screenplays were often so heavily blue-penciled that they lost their meaning, the authors kept coming to the gold-lined streets of Hollywood. And despite the studios' wholesale editing of their work, films began to improve.

The decade opened with a host of gangster films that glorified toughs and ridiculed law and order. Censorship was nonexistent, and the movies of W. C. Fields and Mae West were packing the cinemas, West going well beyond sexual innuendo with lines such as, "Is that a gun in your pocket, big boy, or are you just glad to see me?" Bluenoses across the United States finally stepped in and forced Hollywood to clean up its act, giving rise to censorship that brought an end to corrupt policemen, sexual innuendo, abundant cleavage, political dissidence, depictions of poverty, and a host of other taboos. America, writes author Frederick Lewis Allen, began to be portrayed as "a country in which almost everybody was rich or about to be rich, and in which the possession of a huge house and a British-accented butler and a private swimming pool not merely raised no embarrassing questions about the distribution of wealth, but was accepted as the normal lot of mankind."

Constance Bennett, whose characters had given birth to illegitimate children in *Common Clay* (1930), *Born to Love* (1931), and *Rockabye*

(1932) would no longer have to bear the public's wrath directed at fallen **1939** women, and crime would no longer pay. Hollywood suddenly began to give forth copious amounts of sweetness and light.

If the first part of the decade belonged to W. C. Fields, Mae West, and gangster heroes like James Cagney, the mid-1930s saw a host of musicals and romantic comedies. Fred Astaire and Ginger Rogers, Nelson Eddy and Jeanette MacDonald, Dick Powell, the Busby Berkeley spectaculars—music was in the air, and people were tapping their feet. Moviegoers were also entranced by the light, romantic banter of Clark Gable and Claudette Colbert, William Powell and Myrna Loy, Gary Cooper and Jean Arthur, and Cary Grant and Katharine Hepburn. Even Greta Garbo tried romantic comedy in the film *Ninotchka*, handling this new medium with surprising skill.

During the 1930s, no actress dispensed more common sense and good cheer than Shirley Temple. She was the top box office draw in 1936 and 1937, to be replaced by another youngster named Mickey Rooney, who played Andy Hardy in a rash of films that brought him tremendous popularity. But no film personality achieved the worldwide acclaim that came to Charlie Chaplin, an actor who did not need sound to communicate and who was as well known in Karachi and Nairobi as he was in the United States.

Born in London in 1889, Chaplin had been brought up by his mother in extreme poverty, spending time in his childhood years in both an orphanage and a workhouse. As a child, he had set his sights on acting and had toiled at a variety of odd jobs while attempting to get work in the theater, eventually becoming a successful child actor and music hall artist before traveling to Hollywood, where his salary for one year reached the then astronomical sum of $670,000.

When he had been told to wear "something funny" to an audition for Mack Sennett, the 5 foot 4 inch, 130-pound actor had borrowed some trousers from the amply padded "Fatty" Arbuckle, put size-14 shoes on the wrong feet, donned a worn tail coat and a small derby, put on a false mustache, and wielded a bamboo cane, a wardrobe that would be his film uniform for over two decades. Chaplin commented, "All my pictures are built around the idea of getting me into trouble and so giving me a chance to be desperately serious in my attempt to appear as a normal little gentleman. That is why, no matter how desperate the predicament is, I am always very much in earnest about clutching my cane, straightening my derby hat and fixing my tie, even though I have just landed on my head."

Chaplin once claimed to be "known in parts of the world by people who had never heard of Jesus Christ," and no one disputed his boast. Upon Chaplin's death, Alden Whitman wrote in the *New York Times*: "No motion picture actor so enthralled the world as did Charles Spencer

1939 Chaplin. . . . He elucidated with stunning accuracy the theme of the little fellow capriciously knocked about by life, but not so utterly battered that he did not pick himself up in the hope that the next encounter would turn out better."

Many film buffs remember 1939 as a vintage year for movie making. Among the films produced that year were *Gunga Din, Beau Geste, Destry Rides Again, Stagecoach, Drums Along the Mohawk* (with dialogue by William Faulkner), *Goodbye, Mr. Chips, Ninotchka, Wuthering Heights, Of Mice and Men, The Wizard of Oz* (voted the "Most Colossal Flop of 1939" by the Harvard *Lampoon*), and the epic to end all epics—*Gone with the Wind*.

Getting *Gone with the Wind* from a novel to a film took two and one-half years. It started before the novel was published when Macmillan hired agent Annie Laurie McWilliams to sell the film rights to the book to a Hollywood studio. Her first stop was MGM, which turned thumbs down on the work, Irving Thalberg saying to Louis B. Mayer, "Forget it, Louis. No Civil War picture ever made a nickel." For various reasons, Warner Brothers, RKO, and Universal followed suit, and the agent's next stop was at the office of Kay Brown, story editor for Selznick International Pictures, who fell in love with the book and urged David O. Selznick to purchase the movie rights. After considerable backing and filling, punctuated by the publication of the book with sensational early sales, he did so, paying $50,000. The largest investor in the film was John Hay "Jock" Whitney, who had been attracted to Hollywood after coming into a vast fortune.

When news of the purchase reached Henry Ginsberg, Selznick's production head, he was fit to be tied, exclaiming, "Good Christ, *we* could never make this picture, it would cost us a fortune." Sobered by Ginsberg's judgment, Selznick attempted without success to find another studio to assume the rights, Paramount's Y. Frank Freeman saying, "What, that white elephant?" But while Selznick was hawking the novel, sales of the book were booming, and speculation as to who would play the roles of Scarlett O'Hara and Rhett Butler was becoming a national preoccupation. Selznick sent out cards to PTA groups across the country asking for suggestions, and the PTA members who responded favored Bette Davis as Scarlett, followed by Katharine Hepburn and Tallulah Bankhead. Davis was not available, and Selznick thought Hepburn and Bankhead not quite right for the role, deciding to launch a search for an unknown to play Scarlett. Debutantes, drama students, and players in amateur theatricals were auditioned, generating publicity that brought letters and photographs from a host of would-be Scarletts. On Christmas Day 1937, a huge gift-wrapped package was delivered to the Selznick house, borne by two uniformed footmen. When it was opened, out popped a young lady dressed in Civil War period garb, yet another candidate for the celluloid Scarlett.

230

While the search for Scarlett continued, Selznick began to run short of funds, having incurred considerable production expenses without having a cast to go before the cameras. Selznick not only went back to Whitney for more capital, but he also struck a deal with his father-in-law, Louis B. Mayer, for additional funds and the loan of Clark Gable, leader in the PTA poll for the role of Rhett, in return for distribution rights and a chunk of the profits. Since his early rejection of the book, sales of the novel and a storm of publicity surrounding the impending movie had convinced Mayer that *Gone with the Wind* would be a movie well worth MGM's participation.

In the summer of 1938, shooting was scheduled to begin in February 1939. Still without his Scarlett, Selznick did have his Rhett, although Gable took the role without enthusiasm, believing it to be a severe test of his skills as an actor. Selznick had also signed up a reluctant Leslie Howard, who believed himself too old for the role of Ashley Wilkes, finally giving in with the words, "Money is the mission here, and who am I to refuse it?" Director George Cukor had been hired early in the proceedings; costumes and sets were in the works, with the film to be shot in Hollywood. The first go at a script totaled over 400 pages, quite enough for a six-hour film, and a host of writers blunted their creative picks on the script, including F. Scott Fitzgerald. When shooting started, there would still be no finished script, and the next day's lines were often written the night before, placing considerable pressure on the actors.

Unsuccessful in finding an unknown to play Scarlett, Selznick finally narrowed the competition to four experienced actresses. They were Paulette Goddard, Joan Bennett, Jean Arthur, and a British actress named Vivien Leigh. Leigh was having an affair with Laurence Olivier, who introduced her to David Selznick's brother, Myron, as the answer to their quest for Scarlett. When she won the screen test and the role of Scarlett, it brought a horrified reaction from movie columnist Hedda Hopper, who proclaimed the selection of a foreigner to be a slap in the face for American actresses. Quite to everyone's surprise, the Daughters of the Confederacy did not protest the choice of a non-Southerner, content that at least no Yankee actress had been chosen for the role. In the end, 1,400 would-be Scarletts had been auditioned, ninety of whom were given screen tests.

As the shooting date drew near, Ben Hecht was hired to rewrite the first half of the film, which he did, virtually without sleep, in a week, receiving $15,000 for his Herculean effort. Selznick had yet again to return to his backers for funds, but at last the time was at hand when the filming could finally begin. When shooting got underway, there was a clash between Cukor and Gable, and the director was sacked. He was replaced by Victor Fleming, a Gable favorite, who later stalked off the set but was coaxed back to finish the film. Out of this incredible mayhem

231

1939 came what the *New York Times* would describe as the "greatest motion picture mural we have seen and the most ambitious filmmaking adventure in Hollywood's spectacular history." The film won ten Academy Awards and broke every attendance record in Hollywood history.

☞ FUN AND GAMES

American college students were impressed when Harvard student Lothrop Withington, Jr., swallowed a live three-inch goldfish to win a ten-dollar bet. Withington shrugged off the accomplishment, saying that he had seen the feat performed many times in Hawaii when at the age of ten he had visited his grandmother there.

If Withington downplayed the event, Boston newspapers did not, sending news of his piscivorous snack across the wires, where it was picked up by other journals from coast to coast. Soon other collegians took to swallowing the colorful little fish in great quantities, and the number consumed at a single sitting rose rapidly; it was not long before a student at Pennsylvania's Kutztown State College downed forty-three, earning him a suspension from that seat of higher learning for "conduct unbecoming a student." The Boston Animal League protested, calling for legislation to stop the "slaughter," while a California professor fanned the flames by saying that at least 100 goldfish could be consumed in a single swallowing session without damaging one's constitution. Turning to a fertile new field of consumption, a University of Chicago student earned accolades for downing two and one-half photograph records, including the songs "Deep Purple" and "Who's Sorry Now?"

• The first goldfish had been brought to the United States from Japan in 1878 by an American sailor.

☞ QUOTES

In the July 12, 1939, edition of *Time*, two pronouncements pertinent to the European war were made:
• "The modern German theory of victory by *Blitzkrieg* . . . is untried and, in the opinion of many experts, unsound."
• "The French Army is still the strongest all-around fighting machine in Europe."

A young woman named Nancy Davis, later to marry actor Ronald Reagan, was appearing in a high school play entitled *First Lady*, in which she had only one line of dialogue to deliver: "They ought to elect the First Lady and then let her husband be President."

232

1940

We really did feel that the war was over now. It looked as if we should not even have to land in England . . . all we had to do was to send in the Luft-waffe to help them make up their minds.

—Baron Tassilo von Bogenhardt, German officer

☛ THE WAR

During the winter of 1940, it was difficult to believe that a state of war existed between Germany and both Great Britain and France. Troops did not exchange fire, and planes dropped only propaganda leaflets. While German U-boats were attacking Allied convoys, the worst ordeal to many Europeans was the particularly severe weather.

This period of relative tranquility was truly the proverbial calm before the storm. The month of April saw Hitler once again launch an offensive, in search of what he believed was the right of the German people to more living space—*Lebensraum,* as the Führer called it.

April 9—German troops occupied Denmark and Norway in order "to protect these countries from the Allies" and "to defend their true neutrality until the end of the war." Soviet Minister Vyacheslav Molotov

233

endorsed the action, wishing "Germany complete success in her defensive measures." The entire operation took less than a day.

May 10—Envoys from Belgium, Holland, and Luxembourg were summoned to the German foreign office in Berlin and told that Nazi forces were attacking their respective homelands at that very moment in order to offer support against a planned invasion of the three countries by Britain and France. On the same day, Britain's Prime Minister Chamberlain was forced to resign, failing to win a vote of confidence in Parliament. A member of that body quoted Oliver Cromwell, saying: "You have stayed too long here. In the name of God, go!"

May 13—Chamberlain was succeeded by Winston Churchill, who spoke the now famous words, "I have nothing to offer but blood, toil, tears, and sweat." In time, Churchill's words would be shortened by many to "blood, sweat, and tears."

May 14—The Dutch army surrendered. When it did, writes author Geoffrey Perret, "The United States moved up to nineteenth place on the scale of world military powers. . . . Most of the planes now in service were too old for combat; even Italy was better equipped in the air."

May 16—Those who expected that France would soon he invaded were heartened by the presence of the Maginot Line, a string of seemingly impregnable fortifications that protected a 200-mile stretch of the Franco-German border from Belgium south to Switzerland. It had been constructed in the early 1930s and was named for France's then minister of war, André Maginot. To the surprise of French leaders, the Germans did not attack the Maginot Line head-on. Nazi panzer divisions drove through the Ardennes Forest, heretofore considered an impenetrable buffer between Belgium and France, swept down from the northeast, and outflanked the Maginot Line, attacking it from the rear and rendering it virtually useless. During the Cold War, it was converted to a bomb shelter.

May 26—To the northwest sped the German tanks, and soon the Nazis had forced British and French troops to the English Channel. Just when it appeared that German forces had stalemated the opposition, the Führer, for reasons that have never been made totally clear, ordered his tanks not to press on to Dunkirk, allowing the British to mount a massive rescue mission called Operation Dynamo. Since he was short of transport ships, Admiral Bertram Ramsay sought the aid of civilian boats, and 861 craft of various sizes, speeds, and levels of seaworthiness crossed the Channel from England. Called the Mosquito Armada, it successfully evacuated over 300,000 troops.

June 4—Too busy to make the radio broadcast himself, Winston Churchill used a stand-in to deliver an address to the British people. His name was Norman Shelley, an actor who had perfected Churchill's voice and intonations so that even his closest friends could not tell the

234

difference between the two. Churchill, or Shelley, captivated Britons with one of the prime minister's most stirring speeches: "We shall fight in France, we shall fight on the seas and oceans, we shall fight with growing confidence and growing strength in the air, we shall defend our island, whatever the cost may be, we shall fight on the beaches, we shall fight on the landing grounds, we shall fight in the fields and in the streets, we shall fight in the hills; we shall never surrender." Commenting on Shelley's rendition, Churchill remarked, "Very nice. He's even got my teeth right."

June 10—Italy had not yet joined the war, but as news of one fresh German triumph after another rolled in, *Il Duce* decided that he had better cast his lot and jump on the Führer's bandwagon *subito* if Italy expected to get a share of the spoils of war. So on June 10, Mussolini announced that Italy was declaring war on both Britain and France.

June 21—France surrendered. In only six weeks, Germany had conquered the Low Countries and France with the loss of just one third the number of men who had fallen in a single engagement in World War I—the Battle of Verdun.

July 16—Hitler's staff received these words from the Führer: "As England, in spite of the hopelessness of her military position, has so far shown herself unwilling to come to any compromise, I have decided to begin to prepare for, and if necessary carry out an invasion of England. . . . This operation is dictated by the necessity of eliminating Great Britain as a base from which the war against Germany can be fought, and if necessary, the island will be occupied." Germany military leaders began working on plans for the invasion called Operation Sea Lion.

July 19—While plans for the invasion were underway, the Führer floated a trial balloon in a speech indicating his willingness to make peace with England. Hitler said, "Mr. Churchill, or perhaps others, for once believe me when I predict a great empire will be destroyed, an empire it was never my intention to harm." The British cabinet did not even bother to meet to discuss the Führer's words, a radio announcer at the BBC taking it upon himself to comment on Hitler's seemingly conciliatory posture: "Let me tell you what we here in Britain think of this appeal to what you are pleased to call our reason and common sense. . . . We hurl it back to you. Right back into your evil-smelling teeth."

July 21—Never one to let grass grow under his boots, Hitler ordered that planning be initiated for the invasion of the Soviet Union. The Führer believed that Britain would either opt for peace or be easily overcome, freeing his armies for further glories to the east. The existence of a nonaggression pact between Germany and the U.S.S.R. did not appear to have given Hitler even a moment's pause.

August 13—The Führer put Operation Eagle into effect, a plan "to wipe out British Air Force from the sky." If successful, the foundation

1940 would be laid for the first invasion of Britain since the Norman Conquest. Hitler had 1,900 bombers and 1,100 fighters to do the sky wiping, opposed by only 350 RAF bombers and 700 fighters. In the early days of the Battle of Britain, the Luftwaffe inflicted heavy damage on Britain's radar stations in the south and east of the country, a severe blow to the RAF, since radar enabled British fighters to be deployed with great precision and in limited numbers, conserving both pilots and planes. But Luftwaffe leader Hermann Goering did not know of the success of his sorties, and on the night of August 15 opted to discontinue attempts to strike directly at British radar installations. Goering conjectured, "It is doubtful whether there is any point in continuing the attacks on radar stations, since not one of those attacked so far has been put out of action."

The British had equipped night fighters with Mark III Airborne Interception units. According to Sir Robert Watson-Hatt, "Nowhere else in the world did there exist in 1940 any airborne radar, a circumstance that gave Britain an inestimable advantage over her foe." Despite the aid of radar, the Luftwaffe's advantage in numbers required RAF fighter pilots to take to the skies three, four, and even five times a day. Although heavy British losses would be sustained, two Luftwaffe planes would be shot down for every RAF plane lost. The Germans lost 4,383 aircraft between August 1, 1940, and March 31, 1941, and Luftwaffe dominance in the air would never be established.

September 10—Edward R. Murrow's radio broadcasts from London told the American people of the tremendous destruction being wrought by the Luftwaffe. "We are told today that the Germans believe Londoners, after a while, will rise up and demand a new government, one that will make peace with Germany. It's more probable that they'll rise up and murder a few German pilots who come down by parachute. . . . I've seen some horrible sights in this city during these days and nights, but not once have I heard man, woman, or child suggest that Britain should throw in her hand. These people are angry. How much they can stand I don't know."

When Churchill later recalled the London blitz, he commented, "Our outlook at this time was that London, except for its strong modern buildings, would gradually be reduced to a rubble heap." But the people could and would take more before Hitler eventually realized that the RAF could not be "wiped from the sky." Just one example of the valor of the people was the king's awarding the Order of the British Empire to Mrs. Norman Cardwell, the wife of a farmer. British newspapers wrote of how Cardwell had qualified for her OBE by quoting the recipient, "I saw a man floating to earth with an enormous white thing like a balloon above him. I saw him walking along by a hedge in the paddock about 150 yards away from me. I went toward him and called to him to put up his hands. He did not understand English, so I showed him what I wanted him to do

236

and he did it. I said to him: 'What the dickens do you think you are doing **1940** here?' but of course he didn't understand me. Then I noticed that he had a revolver and by pointing indicated that I wanted it. He handed it over at once. I just walked down the yard with my prisoner going ahead of me. About half a minute afterwards some soldiers came along the road on motorcycles."

October 12—While the Battle of Britain would continue until the following spring, Hitler sent a top secret memo to his staff on October 12, announcing that plans for the invasion of England had been canceled until the "spring or early summer of 1941."

• Prime Minister Winston Churchill had been a dedicated cigar smoker since his youth, and his cigars were carefully stored in a vault at Dunhill's in London. One night during a Luftwaffe bombing attack, a direct hit leveled that venerable vendor of smoking material. Author David Louis writes, "At two o'clock that morning, the manager journeyed to the still-smoking site of the bombing and rummaged through the debris in the cellar until he found what he had come for. 'Sir,' he reported to the prime minister shortly afterward, 'your cigars are safe.'"

☞ NATIONAL NEWS

In the early part of the year, the November presidential election took a back seat to the war in Europe, what little political interest there was centering on whether FDR would seek an unprecedented third term. Roosevelt did not tip his hand until the late spring of 1940 when the success of Hitler's blitzkrieg convinced him that the escalating European war demanded an experienced internationalist in the White House for the next four years.

Sensitive to Republican charges that he was attempting to establish a long-term dictatorship, FDR did not want to appear too eager to run, hoping to be drafted at the Democratic convention. A White House spokesman said, "The president has never and has not today any desire or purpose to continue in the office of the President, to be a candidate for that office, or to be nominated for that office. He wishes in all earnestness and sincerity to make it clear that all delegates to this convention are free to vote for any candidate."

Democratic delegates paid little heed to Roosevelt's shrinking violet posture, giving him an overwhelming first-ballot victory at their Chicago convention. Not long afterward, Republicans were circulating buttons that read:

1940

"No Third Term"
"Two Times Is Enough for Any Man"
"Force Franklin out at Third"
"Washington Wouldn't—Grant Couldn't—Roosevelt Shouldn't"

And soon this parody of the Twenty-third Psalm was making the rounds of Republican gatherings, containing digs not unlike those that Democrats had directed at Herbert Hoover in the 1932 presidential election:

> Roosevelt is my shepherd. I live in want. He maketh me to lie down on park benches. He leadeth me past still factories. He disturbeth my soul. He crooneth me into paths of destruction for his party's sake. Yeah, though I walk through the shadow of Depression, I anticipate no recovery, for He is with me. His policies and diplomacies they bewilder me. He prepareth a reduction in my salary. He anointeth my small income with tax. His expenses runneth over. Surely unemployment and poverty shall follow me all the days of my life, and I shall dwell in a mortgaged home forever.

At the beginning of 1940, it looked as though the Republican nomination would go either to Ohio's Senator Robert A. Taft or to New York's Thomas E. Dewey, who had gained national acclaim for prosecuting and jailing several notorious racket bosses. But as the possibility of America's involvement in a war increased, Taft's isolationism seemed less and less practical and the youthful Dewey a bit unseasoned for the complexity of the times. Instead, the Republicans chose a man who had never run for office before—forty-eight-year-old Wendell L. Willkie.

Willkie had grown up in Indiana, working his way through the state university. He then practiced law in Akron, Ohio, where his courtroom successes caught the eye of Bernard Capen Cobb, president of Commonwealth and Southern, a utility company. After working for the company's New York law firm for four years, Willkie succeeded Cobb as president of Commonwealth and Southern and proved himself an excellent executive by pruning expenses, thereby enabling the utility to cut the cost of electricity to its customers and expand its services. Willkie soon became an effective spokesman for the industry and a frequent witness before congressional committees concerned with utilities. More important to his political future, he became an increasingly articulate and outspoken supporter of private enterprise, as well as a critic of New Deal business and economic policy, subjects dear to the hearts of many Republicans. When he won the presidential nomination, the Democrats regarded him the most formidable candidate since Theodore Roosevelt.

238

As a German invasion of Britain became a distinct possibility, the war became the key issue of the campaign. "A vote for Willkie is a vote for Hitler!" screamed the internationalists, and Willkie received the unwanted support of pro-Nazis and of the Irish who hated the English. "A vote for Roosevelt is a vote for war!" chanted the isolationists. Willkie labeled the president a warmonger who would have American armed forces in the fray within six months. FDR chose not to respond, staying close to the White House except when he was touring defense plants or military installations. He made a commitment to send some World War I destroyers to Great Britain without consulting Congress, and while Willkie approved of the military aid to Britain, he denounced FDR's failure to seek congressional approval as "the most dictatorial and arbitrary act of any President in the history of the United States."

As the election drew near, a Gallup poll showed that Willkie was closing in on the incumbent, a revelation that finally forced the president to take to the hustings, as well as to the radio, for a series of addresses. In response to the pleas of his aides, FDR tried to play down the war issue, telling the public, "Your boys are not going to be sent into foreign wars."

Despite Roosevelt's calming words, it would later be revealed that FDR had become increasingly committed to the support of Britain. Robert Sherwood, FDR's presidential aide in 1940, later commented, "If the isolationists had known of the secret alliance between the United States and Britain, the demands for the President's impeachment would have rumbled like thunder through the land." But they did not know, and instead of being impeached, he was reelected, his promise to the parents of America helping to defeat Willkie. FDR had won by his narrowest margin, winning 54.8 percent of the popular vote. If many Americans were disappointed, there were very few citizens in the British Isles who were not delighted to hear the good news as they dug in for what could be the first invasion of their territory since 1066.

The first draft ever conducted during peacetime was held in the United States. The Selective Service Act required one year of military service.

• The United States had held a lottery in 1917 to determine the order in which civilians would be drafted. The first number drawn was 258, which was held by, among others, Alden C. Flagg. In 1940, the first number selected was 158, held by Alden C. Flagg, Jr.

• American Indians were included in the draft for the first time, and 25,000 of them would be in uniform during World War II.

• Under the mistaken assumption that married men would receive a deferment, the marriage rate soared, and a well-known manufacturer of wedding rings saw his sales more than double.

1940   On the afternoon of September 27, 1940, German Foreign Minister Joachim von Ribbentrop, Italian Foreign Minister Count Galeazzo Ciano, and Japanese Ambassador Suboro Kurusu signed a ten-year military and economic alliance, forming the Axis powers. For the first time, the United States had to come to grips with a potential foe to the west as well as one to the east.

Hitler's alliance with Japan caused a stir among German professors knowledgeable about the origin of races. They would please the Führer by coming up with documentation that proved that the Japanese were Aryans.

☛ ENTERTAINMENT

During a broadcast of the popular radio show *The Goldbergs*, the program was interrupted for a speech by Adolf Hitler. When the Führer's oration came to an end, the announcer said, "You have just heard the concluding remarks of Chancellor Hitler through the courtesy of the Goldbergs."

Tommy Dorsey agreed in 1940 to participate in an unusual experiment at the Philadelphia Zoo, assisted by eight members of his orchestra. The purpose of the research was to ascertain what effect, if any, music would have on monkey behavior.

The musical publication *Etude* interviewed a zoo employee to see how the simians had reacted to Dorsey's concert: "The monkey's couldn't stand it. The band first played some violent jazz. The chimpanzees were scared to death. They scampered all over the place, seeking the protection of their keepers and hiding under benches. . . . One chimp tried to pull the trombone away from Tommy Dorsey." Misery was widespread: "One old chimp in particular had such a wounded and resentful look on his face that band members couldn't bear to continue."

Then Dorsey tried another tune, his oh-so-sweet-and-poignant theme song, "I'm Getting Sentimental over You." Within seconds, tranquility overcame the animals, and they took to their benches, where they sat calmly "watching the players with interest."

The European war was reflected in two pieces of entertainment in 1940:

• Charlie Chaplin wrote and starred in a film called *The Great Dictator*, which spoofed two world figures whose identities were not heavily disguised. Chaplin played the parts of dictator Adenoid Hynkel of Tomania and of a Jewish barber, while Jack Oakie took the role of a Fascist leader called Benzino Napaloni.

240

☛ FOOD AND DRINK

The staff of the Mars company had been working hard to develop a candy for American troops that could withstand the rigors of being knocked about in their packs and pockets and that would not melt as easily as a chocolate bar. The result was a confection called M&M's which "melts in your mouth, not in your hand"—hands and fingers that had to throw a hand grenade or squeeze off a round of ammunition. The two M's stand for the names of Mars employees Forest E. Mars and Bruce E. Murrie, who collaborated on the tasty invention.

In its November 25, 1940, edition, *Time* magazine reported on the cuisine of home front Germans:

> To a war menu which already included fish-fed poultry, decrepit horses, goats and numerous zoo animals, Germany last week added those of its dogs. A new law, effective January 1, states that dogs, wolves, foxes, bears, badgers and wild hogs have been legalized as meat. . . . Dog meat has been eaten in every major German crisis, at least since the time of Frederick the Great. . . . Of European dog breeds, the German dachshund is considered the most succulent.

☛ MEMORABILIA

Oglethorpe University of Atlanta, Georgia, left reminders of the times for future generations in a sealed crypt that, God willing, was to be opened in the year 8113. Among the items left for posterity were instructions for learning English, a Donald Duck doll, and a quart of beer.

☛ BOOKS

The Publication of an Agatha Christie novel was an event that mystery story lovers particularly looked forward to. In 1940, she had another whodunit published in London called *Ten Little Niggers*. It would be issued in the United States first as *And Then There Were None*, the title later to be changed once more to *Ten Little Indians*.

Also in 1940, Christie wrote *Curtain*, a novel in which Belgian

241

1940 investigator Hercule Poirot died after a distinguished career solving difficult crimes in many of her works. The book was not published until 1975 when Poirot's "death" would rate a front-page obituary in the *New York Times*.

The author would become second only to William Shakespeare in sales by a writer in the English language, and her play, *The Mousetrap*, which opened in London in 1952, is still running in 1987.

A group of self-appointed censors came down hard on a Communist book store in Oklahoma, purging the store of various publications that they faulted for "advocating violence," putting them to the torch in a public demonstration. There were some red faces when it was learned that two of the works that had been turned into ashes were the Declaration of Independence and the Constitution of the United States.

F. Scott Fitzgerald's life had become a sad one. After his triumphs in the golden days of the Jazz Age, an era he had helped to popularize, his books had not sold well during the Depression. The sales of all his works in 1939 had totaled a mere 114 copies, bringing him royalty payments of only $33. He had suffered bouts of alcoholism, and his screenwriting jobs in Hollywood had become few and far between, forcing him to write short stories for magazines to which he would never have submitted his work in his glory days. Fitzgerald's wife Zelda had been treated for schizophrenia from 1936 to 1939, having suffered a nervous breakdown in 1930. Even though the two loved one another, theirs was a bittersweet and often destructive relationship that made it impossible for them to live together. Since 1937, Fitzgerald had been having an affair with a British movie columnist named Sheilah Graham, who lived near him in Hollywood.

In 1939, Fitzgerald had suffered a bout of tuberculosis, which was followed by a heart attack in November 1940. On December 21, 1940, he was with Graham in her apartment. While reading the *Princeton Alumni Weekly* and eating a Hershey bar, he suffered another heart attack, dying before medical assistance arrived.

• "A writer like me must have an utter confidence, an utter faith in his star. . . . I once had it. But through a series of blows, many of them my own fault, something happened to that sense of immunity and I lost my grip." (F. Scott Fitzgerald)

• "Sometimes I don't know whether Zelda and I are real or whether we are characters in one of my novels." (F. Scott Fitzgerald)

242

On the squad of the Daytona Beach Islanders baseball team in 1940 was a young pitcher named Stan Musial. When a shoulder injury ended his pitching career, Musial had no other choice but to try to make the team at another position and gave the outfield a try. His conversion would be a success, and he was soon elevated to the St. Louis Cardinals, where he won seven National League batting titles.

A young Cleveland Indians hurler named Bob Feller became the first major league pitcher to toss a no-hit game on the opening day of the season. Whether or not his mother was there to share his glory is not recorded. She could hardly have been faulted for not attending, for while at a Mother's Day game a year earlier at Comiskey Park, Feller's mother had been rendered unconscious when struck on the head by a foul ball. "Rapid Robert" Feller's blazing fastball would gain him the admiration of the nation's baseball fans and early entry to baseball's Hall of Fame.

Washington Redskins owner George Preston Marshall described the Chicago Bears as "quitters" after the two teams had met in a National Football League game in 1940. The two squads met again in the league's championship game, and what the Bears could not quit doing that day was scoring, humiliating Marshall's Redskins by the score of 73–0.

☞ PEOPLE

California professor S. L. Katzoff brought joy to lovers of all ages when he made a startling announcement regarding the act of kissing. Katzoff said, "A genuine kiss generates so much heat it destroys germs."

It was revealed that Wendell Lewis Willkie, Republican candidate for the presidency, was actually Lewis Wendell Willkie. His given name at birth had been reversed in an error by the U.S. Army during World War I, and his efforts to effect a change within government bureaucracy had been unsuccessful.

Movie theater owners Richard and Maurice McDonald opened a drive-in eatery near Pasadena, California, which would later grow into a national chain that would bear their name.

1940   Congress awarded its Medal of Honor to composer-actor George M. Cohan for his patriotic songs "Over There" and "You're a Grand Old Flag."

Americans were learning about the devastating effectiveness of Hitler's Tiger tanks. They had been conceived of by a man named Porsche, who would later design an expensive automobile bearing his name.

First Lady Eleanor Roosevelt gave her support to a controversial issue of the day: birth control.

Movie star Tom Mix was killed on Columbus Day 1940, in a car crash while driving his high-powered Cord. Nearly as famous as Mix was his horse Tony, which died two years later on the anniversary of Mix's death.

Joseph P. Kennedy, American ambassador to Great Britain, told newsman Louis M. Lyons of the *Boston Globe* that "democracy is finished in England. It's all an economic question. The whole reason for aiding England is to give us time. It isn't that she's fighting for democracy."

John Fitzgerald Kennedy had a book published, entitled *While England Slept*. He donated royalties from English sales to the British city of Plymouth, which had been leveled by Luftwaffe bombs. With his first American royalties, Kennedy purchased a shiny new Buick.

1941

☞ THE WAR

Germany and Japan carried out numerous belligerent acts against the Allied nations during World War II, but two dwarfed all others in terms of their scope. And while they brought initial joy to their expansionist governments, they would contribute to the eventual downfall of their respective countries. The first was Germany's invasion of the Soviet Union; the second was Japan's attack on Pearl Harbor.

As the Axis powers contemplated the expansion of the war to new territories, they were unaware that the Allies already held an advantage that would weigh heavily upon the outcome of the war—the ability to decode German and Japanese secret messages.

• Polish intelligence agents had ambushed a German truck and absconded with an Enigma code machine, leaving evidence that the device had been destroyed by fire. A little larger than a portable typewriter, it was turned over to British agents.

245

1941 • Cryptologist William F. Friedman of U.S. Army Signal Intelligence had built a version of the device that the Japanese used to transmit and receive its secret Purple code. Shortly thereafter, U.S. Navy Lieutenant Francis A. Raven had figured out how the keys to the code were selected by the Japanese.

Thus, the Allies possessed an advantage in 1941 that was of greater value than any weapon that would be used during the remainder of the war with the possible exception of the atomic bomb.

Napoleon's invasion of Russia had been the start of his downfall, and it was a lesson of history that the Führer well remembered but chose to ignore. For in doing battle with the Soviets, Hitler had to defeat and occupy a nation that extended from the Baltic and Black seas to the Pacific Ocean; he would have to do it at a time when Nazi forces were already occupied in Western Europe, Africa, and the Middle East; he would tax his nation's ability to manufacture weapons and supplies for all these engagements while his supply lines extended farther and farther from native soil; and unless he could strike quickly and with great success, he would be forced to fight during the Russian winter when his troops, weapons, and vehicles would be subject to the most exacting conditions.

In mid-November 1940, Soviet Foreign Minister Molotov visited Berlin to discuss the U.S.S.R.'s joining Germany, Italy, and Japan in an alliance. Having plotted the Soviet Union's downfall for over a decade, the Führer was not eager to welcome the Soviets into the Axis, but since he did not feel bound by the peace treaties he signed, he had agreed to his foreign minister's request that the U.S.S.R. be a signatory to a four-power pact.

To the Führer's surprise and intense irritation, Molotov not only failed to jump at the offer but displayed what in Hitler's opinion was immense gall by proposing certain conditions that Germany would have to meet if the Soviet Union were to join the Axis. The quick-tempered Führer decided then and there "to settle accounts with Russia, as soon as fair weather permitted."

Comrade Stalin was displeased to learn that the proposed pact had not been consummated. His purges had reduced Soviet manpower and had left the economy in a shambles; he desperately needed to stall for time as he readied his nation for war. So, two weeks later, Stalin let Berlin know that the U.S.S.R. would join the alliance after all, with few stipulations.

Hitler never even bothered to answer Stalin and initiated plans for the Soviet invasion—Operation Barbarossa. Although Hitler claimed to have "pondered long and anxiously over Napoleon, and his experiences in Russia," he chose to disregard the parallel. He had ruled out an invasion of Britain and saw continuing American aid to England as prolonging that

246

war. If the Soviet Union was to be attacked, and Hitler was determined **1941** that she was, why not get on with it before Stalin could mount serious resistance?

If Hitler's failure to respond to Stalin's message had not hinted at the Führer's intentions, the Soviet leader should have begun to know them when he received a flood of intelligence from all corners of the globe indicating an impending German invasion of his homeland. But Stalin chose to disregard these signals, thinking that they were British tricks to get the U.S.S.R. and Germany to fight one another. Furthermore, Stalin was convinced that Hitler would deal with Britain before contemplating an attack on the Eastern front. And besides, conjectured the Soviet leader, Germany would not be stupid enough to attack the U.S.S.R. when it was already committed in so many other areas.

The following are some key events in Germany's preparation for the invasion:

February 3—Hitler doubted that the Soviet invasion would bring the United States into the war: "When 'Barbarossa' commences, the world will hold its breath and make no comment," said the Führer.

March 20—By intercepting Japanese messages, the United States learned that Germany planned to attack the Soviet Union and passed on the information to the Soviet ambassador.

March 30—Hitler told his senior officers that the invasion would take place on June 22, saying: "The war against Russia will be such that it cannot be fought in knightly fashion! This struggle is one of ideologies and racial differences and will have to be conducted with unprecedented, merciless, and unrelenting harshness."

April 13—Japan and the Soviet Union signed a five-year peace pact, neither wanting to be diverted by a war along their common borders.

May—"This war with Russia is a nonsensical idea, to which I can see no happy ending . . . we must face the fact that it can't be won in a single summer campaign. Just look at the distances involved. We cannot possibly defeat the enemy and occupy the whole of western Russia, from the Baltic to the Black Sea, within a few short months." (German Field Marshal Gerd von Rundstedt)

June 14—A Soviet agent in Tokyo informed the Kremlin that "war begins June 22."

June 17—A German sergeant who feared execution because of insubordination surrendered to the Soviets, informing them that the invasion was to begin on June 22.

June 22—The invasion began on a 900-mile front from the Baltic to the Black seas, Germany blaming the Soviets for being "about to fall on Germany's back." Hitler predicted that the war would be won in four months; Goebbels said eight weeks. Stalin, according to author John

247

Toland, "was so convinced that the Nazi invasion was a mistake . . . that he kept open radio communications with the Wilhelmstrasse while requesting Japan to mediate any political and economic differences between Germany and the Soviet Union." Also, notes Toland, "The Pope's attitude was not at all vague, citing Germany's opposition to Bolshevism as 'high-minded gallantry in defense of the foundations of Christian culture.'"

In the first month of the Russian campaign, German forces won some 720,000 square miles of Soviet territory, duplicating the success of Napoleon's efforts more than 100 years earlier; as the summer wore on, they advanced closer and closer to Moscow. But just when it looked as though the capital was within his grasp, Hitler diverted his armies to take Leningrad and to secure the Ukraine. Not laying siege to Moscow at this time was disputed by some of Hitler's generals, who believed that its occupation would signal the end of serious Soviet resistance.

Nevertheless, the Germans rolled on, encircling Kiev and capturing upward of a half million Russians in mid-September. By October 16, Nazi troops were advancing on Moscow once more, forcing the Soviets to move their government some 500 miles east to Kuybyshev. But the autumn rains were slowing down the Nazi track vehicles, and soon the rain turned to sleet, and the sleet to snow, accompanied by high winds and subzero temperatures. German troops had not yet been supplied with winter uniforms, and frostbite was widespread; fires often had to be lighted under tanks to thaw them sufficiently enough to operate.

Yet, in early December, the Nazi advance came almost within sight of the Kremlin, and it appeared as though Moscow would provide winter quarters for a good portion of the Wehrmacht. But Hitler was to be denied his prize when Soviet General Georgy Zhukov launched a massive counterattack, throwing three armies totaling 1 million men against the fatigued German troops. Slowly the fortunes of war began to change. While the Soviets would come close to defeat again, the Führer would never succeed in bringing them to heel.

• The Russian winter turned out to be the coldest in more than thirty years. Author John May writes, "On the fourth Sunday of Advent 1941, at Ozarovo on the Russian front, a German lance corporal named Teitz spotted an immobile group of Russian troops and their horses. They had been ordered to halt for a rest and had frozen to death, preserved as they stood like a monument. As he tried to photograph the scene. Teitz's tears froze over the viewfinder and the shutter seized up."

In September 1941, American soldiers were carrying out a mock war in Louisiana, divided into forces called the Red and Blue armies. One day, the Blue Army was put under heavy fire from across a river and
248

responded with rifles and machine guns firing blank ammunition. The exchange went on for almost a half hour before both sides were given a "cease fire" by the umpire. Only then was it discovered that over 500 tanks and assorted vehicles had been stopped dead in their tracks by three boys, aged nine, twelve, and fourteen, who had been playing with a toy cannon. The umpire located the boys' mother and asked her help: "Please stop your boys from shooting that cannon. . . . They are holding up the war and most of the Blue Army."

By the summer of 1939, Japan had made serious inroads into Chinese territory, occupying a large number of major cities. Americans were sympathetic to China, and newspapers were calling attention to the fact that Japanese weapons were being made from scrap iron and steel imported from the United States. Increasing anti-Japanese sentiment led Congress to terminate a trade agreement that had existed between the two countries since 1911. From then on, trade was carried out on a day-to-day basis, with the United States gradually specifying more and more types of goods that could not be exported to Japan. When Japan went into Indochina in September 1940, scrap iron and aviation fuel were added to the list; later that month, Japan joined Germany and Italy in the Axis alliance.

In the spring of 1941, Japan and the United States entered negotiations, the Japanese expressing a willingness to evacuate certain territories in exchange for renewed trade with America. But the United States took a hard line, and when the Japanese moved into southern Indochina, FDR froze Japan's assets in the United States on July 26; shortly thereafter, Washington decided to send no more oil to Japan. When Britain and the Dutch East Indies followed suit, writes author Alonzo Hamby, "Japan faced a worldwide embargo on the one item that it had to obtain from foreign powers. The effect was that of an ultimatum. The Imperial Government would have to retreat or push forward; to stand still would be to invite the destruction of the Japanese economy and the empire's military machine."

Meanwhile, the Japanese cabinet was falling increasingly under the influence of military leaders. Premier Fumimaro Konoye, however, was a moderate and hoped to avoid war with the United States. Konoye proposed to Washington that he meet with Roosevelt, but he was turned down. Having failed to find a diplomatic solution to Japan's problem, Konoye resigned on October 16, 1941. Three days later, General Hideki Tojo became prime minister of Japan.

In Cambridge, Massachusetts, a young Harvard student during a debate had pointed out the strategic importance of Pearl Harbor to

1941 America's western defenses. The year was 1902. The student's name was Franklin D. Roosevelt.

Ironically, the man who planned the attack on Pearl Harbor regarded a war with the United States as the utmost folly. He too had studied at Harvard and had spent quite some time in the United States. His name was Isoroku Yamamoto, and in January 1941 he had written this letter:

> Should hostilities break out between Japan and the United States, it would not be enough that we take Guam and the Philippines, nor even Hawaii and San Francisco. To make the victory certain, we would have to march into Washington and dictate terms of peace in the White House. I wonder if our politicians, among whom armchair arguments about war are being glibly bandied about in the name of state politics, have confidence as to the final outcome and are prepared to make the necessary sacrifice.

The countdown to war proceeded as follows:

November 26—The Japanese fleet sailed eastward from Tankan Bay in northern Japan, observing strict radio silence and a nightly blackout, using fuel that was nearly smokeless.

November 29—The program for the Army-Navy football game included a picture of the U.S.S. *Arizona* with the following caption: "It is significant that despite the claims of air enthusiasts no battleship has yet been sunk by bombs." The *Arizona* would be bombed while at anchor in Pearl Harbor and would sink with the loss of 1,102 men.

December 1—"Climb Mount Niitaka" was the message broadcast in Tokyo to the Japanese fleet, setting December 7 as the date for the attack on Pearl Harbor.

December 4—"No matter what happens, the U.S. Navy is not going to be caught napping." (Secretary of the Navy Frank Knox)

December 5—Honolulu FBI agents listened in on a phone call from Tokyo to a Japanese dentist in Honolulu. The positioning of American ships and aircraft in Hawaii was discussed, but the call was judged to be of no particular significance.

December 6—Naval intelligence employee Dorothy Edgers decoded a message that had been intercepted from the Japanese indicating that Hawaii was to be the target for an attack. Her boss told her that there were more important things to be dealt with in the office and that she could finish decoding the message on Monday, two days later.

Also that day, a message from Tokyo to the Japanese embassy in Washington was intercepted, indicating that Japan would not comply with
250

United States requests that might have avoided war. When the message was delivered to President Roosevelt, he said, "This means war."

December 7—At 8:00 A.M. Washington time, another message from Tokyo was intercepted, ordering an official rejection of United States demands at exactly 1:00 P.M. EST. The message was forwarded to General George Marshall's headquarters at Fort Myers, Virginia, but staff members had orders not to disturb the general when he was not on duty, and Marshall was taking his usual Sunday morning horseback ride. When Marshall finally read the message, he realized that the Japanese could be planning an attack to coincide with the rebuff that their envoys would be delivering to the secretary of state in a few hours. Instead of telephoning Hawaiian headquarters immediately, Marshall decided to send a telegram, fearing that even a scrambled telephone call might be intercepted by the Japanese. Since the radio at the War Department had been unable to make contact with Honolulu that morning, the message was sent by Western Union. It arrived in Honolulu at 7:33 A.M., which was considered a bit early by the local Western Union office to teletype to army headquarters.

Just after 7:00 A.M. in Hawaii, two radar stations had picked up some blips indicating the approach of aircraft from the north. At about the same time, a navy destroyer reported that it had sunk two subs at the entrance to Pearl Harbor. None of this information was acted on in time to produce an all-forces alert. At 8:00 A.M., the alert came after the attack had begun, Captain Logan C. Ramsey sending out the message, "Air raid . . . Pearl Harbor. . . . This is no drill." Captain Ramsey knew about such things, having written in 1937 an article entitled, "Aerial Attacks on Fleets at Anchor."

Less than four months before the attack on Pearl Harbor, Congress had debated whether or not to continue the draft. After heated congressional discussion, continuation of the Selective Service Act was approved by one vote.

☛ SPORTS

New Jersey's Plainfield Teachers College football team came out of the blocks in a hurry, romping to easy victories in their first four games, led by a Chinese-American fullback named John Chung, who was averaging 9.3 yards per carry. With each victory, Plainfield information director, Jerry Croyden, found New York's newspapers increasingly eager to get his weekly telephone report on how PTC had fared on the gridiron, including background tidbits such as the fact that the "prowess of Chung

251

1941 may be due to his habit of eating rice between the halves." The *New York Post*, wrote, "If the Jerseyans don't watch out, Chung may pop up in Chiang Kai-shek's offense department one of these days."

The team rolled on to two more easy victories, and an undefeated season seemed within its grasp when a press release from the school brought some sad news: "Due to flunkings in the midterm examinations, Plainfield Teachers College has been forced to call off its last two scheduled games with Appalachian Tech tomorrow and Harmony Teachers on Thanksgiving Day. Among those thrown for a loss was John Chung, who has accounted for 69 of Plainfield's 117 points."

Just when it looked as though sports fans could forget about PTC, the *New York Herald Tribune* published the startling news that there was no John Chung, no PTC football team, not even a school called Plainfield Teachers College. The mythical squad had been the work of a Wall Streeter named Morris Newburger. He and his coworkers at Newburger, Loeb and Company had taken turns pretending to be Jerry Croyden, the fast-talking school representative who made his Saturday evening reports on Plainfield's weekly football fortunes. After the dust had settled, Cas Adams of the *Herald Tribune* wrote this ode to PTC to the tune of "High Above Cayuga's Waters":

> Far above New Jersey's swamplands
> Plainfield Teachers' spires
> Mark a phantom, phony college
> That got on the wires.
> Perfect record made on paper,
> Imaginary team,
> Hail to thee, our ghostly college,
> Product of a dream.

In 1941, Leo Durocher was the manager of the Brooklyn Dodgers. One day, he was sizing up the New York Giants during batting practice at the Polo Grounds while Frank Graham, sportswriter for the *New York Journal American*, listened: "Take a look at them," said Durocher. "All nice guys. They'll finish last. Nice guys . . . finish last. . . . Give me some scratching, diving, hungry ballplayers who come to kill you."

The Brooklyn Dodgers had not won a pennant in twenty-one years. They had a reputation for zaniness that had started the day Ebbets Field opened in 1913. Someone had lost the key to the park, halting the dedication parade; when dignitaries finally made their way to the center field flagpole to hoist the colors, no flag could be found. Fly balls bounced off players' heads, and it was not uncommon to find two, even three, Dodger base runners occupying the same base.

The Dodgers had come by their name because in the early 1900s

252

Brooklyn enjoyed the distinction of being the most dangerous city for **1941**
pedestrians and trolley car riders. Author George Gipe writes,

> Brooklyn trolleys had killed an average of one person a week.
> The motormen, who had learned their trade as horsecar drivers,
> were blamed for the high mortality rate. Not realizing they had
> the power of fifty horses under their control, they tended to
> drive recklessly, so much so that as one newspaper put it, "Ere
> long, the country rang with horror at the holocaust of victims
> sacrificed to the reign of electricity in Brooklyn."

In addition to the speed at which the trolleys were operated, riders
and pedestrians were in further jeopardy because there were dozens of
trolley lines in the borough that constantly crossed one another, making
the potential for collision high. So the Dodgers were not so named
because they dodged baseballs but because the citizens of Brooklyn were
Trolley Dodgers; those who were not agile in the streets were in daily
danger of meeting their Maker.

Durocher's Dodgers won the pennant in 1941, playing in the World
Series against their hated crosstown rivals, the New York Yankees,
producing high drama. The first three games were extremely tight, the
Yankees taking a 2–1 lead. The fourth contest found the Dodgers clinging
to a 4–3 lead as Dodger relief pitcher Hugh Casey faced the Yankees in
the top of the ninth inning. Casey retired the first two Yankees on ground
balls to the infield, and one more out would have evened the series. With
the count three and two on outfielder Tommy Henrich, Casey broke off a
sharp curve ball that Henrich swung at and missed, ending the game. But
wait. The ball bounced off catcher Mickey Owens's glove, and before he
could retrieve it, Henrich was standing on first base. Buoyed by this
reprieve, the Yankees gathered their forces and went on to win the game
and the World Series, forcing Mickey Owens to carry the burden of his
untimely passed ball for the rest of his days.

On May 15, 1941, Yankee centerfielder Joe DiMaggio got one hit in
four times at bat against the Chicago White Sox, hardly an auspicious day
at bat for Joltin' Joe, a slugger much feared by American League pitchers.
But DiMaggio's modest single was followed the next day by two hits, the
day after by three, and he would go on to hit safely in every game over the
next two months until he finally went hitless on July 17, his streak broken
after fifty-six straight games. The previous major league record had been
held by Wee Willie Keeler of the Baltimore Orioles, who had hit safely in
forty-four straight games back in 1897.

On the night of July 17, 1941, 67,468 fans showed up at Cleveland's
Municipal Stadium to see if Joe D. could prolong his streak. But while he

1941 rifled two seemingly sure hits toward third base, Cleveland's Ken Keltner made two spectacular plays to turn them into outs, and DiMaggio had been held hitless after collecting 91 hits in 233 at bats and batting .408 over the fifty-six-game skein.

• "It may be the greatest batting achievement of them all." (Ted Williams)

The man who had endorsed DiMaggio's achievement so heartily was also doing pretty well for himself at the plate in 1941. At season's end, Red Sox outfielder Theodore Samuel Williams became the first player since 1930 to hit .400, finishing with an average of .406. No major league player has been able to hit .400 since.

Before the last day of the season, Williams's average stood at .3996. Since major league batting averages were carried to only three decimal places, his average would have been rounded to .400 if he had chosen to sit out the double header that would end the team's season. But when his manager, Joe Cronin, gave him that option, the Splendid Splinter replied, "I'll play. I never want anybody to say that I got in the back door."

The final day of the season was rainy and cold and only 10,000 hearty folk turned out in Philadelphia to see Williams attempt to equal or best .400. In his first four times at bat, Williams delivered three singles and a home run, lifting his average to .404. In the second game, he had two hits in three times at bat to end the season at .406, and fittingly his last hit was a tremendous smash to right field, which Williams would describe as the hardest hit ball he had ever struck.

☛ MUSIC

Bruce Felton and Mark Fowler tell us that American composer Harry Partch was not every music lover's cup of tea. He had forsaken the twelve-tone scale, inventing his own "forty-three note octave," a revolutionary musical structure that required him to construct new instruments not known to conventional orchestras. Some of Partch's creations were the "Whang Gun, a seventy-two-stringed surrogate cithara, glass bells which he called 'cloud-chamber balls,' a strange marimbalike instrument called a 'boo,' and his most famous creation, the bloboys, consisting of three organ pipes, a bellows, and an automobile exhaust pipe."

Partch had received a series of grants to pursue composition from, among others, the Carnegie and Guggenheim foundations. In 1941, his "Third Construction" made its debut, "scored for rattles, drums, tin cans, claves, cowbells, a lion's roar, cymbal, ratchet, texponaxtle, quijadas, cricket caller, and conch shell." Some other Partch works were "And on the Seventh Day Petals Fell on Petaluma," "Water, Water," "U.S.

254

Highway," "Daphne and the Dunes," and "Visions Fill the Eyes of a Defeated Basketball Team in the Shower Room." Several of his works were recorded by Columbia Records.

RCA Victor wanted to find a way to commemorate a milestone when Glenn Miller's "Chattanooga Choo Choo" went over the 1 million mark in record sales. They sprayed one of the disks with gold paint and presented it to the orchestra leader, starting a trend that endures today.

☛ BOOKS

The cocktail party is an American institution, a means of social intercourse often attended by the affluent and intellectual. It has both its supporters and detractors, and those on the negative side occasionally call to mind a bizarre incident that happened in 1941. Noted author Sherwood Anderson consumed an hors d'oeuvre at a cocktail party, failing to note a toothpick that was lodged therein, dying shortly thereafter of peritonitis and other attendant complications.

☛ MARRIAGE AND COURTSHIP

Actress Joyce Matthews was a glutton for punishment. In 1941, she married comedian Milton Berle, but they were divorced in 1947. The couple were soon reconciled and remarried in 1949, only to have the marriage break up in 1950. Joyce Matthews then turned her attentions to producer Billy Rose, marrying him in 1956, with that union ending in divorce in 1959. But she was persistent if not successful in her bouts of matrimony, and she was wed to Rose again in 1961. In 1963, Matthews went through her fourth divorce, split equally between two husbands.

☛ ENTERTAINMENT

The year 1941 marked the Paris debut of a play by Pablo Picasso called *Desire Caught by the Tail*, starring existentialist authors Jean-Paul Sartre and Simone de Beauvoir, and directed by Albert Camus. The central characters were called Big Foot, Fat Anxiety, and Thin Anguish, and one critic described the play as juxtaposing the "features of medieval morality plays with twentieth-century smut."

When the work was presented in Saint-Tropez in 1967 at the Festival of Free Expression, the town's mayor objected to the scene in which a character named Tart "urinates on stage as a variety of disgusting sound

255

1941 effects play over the loudspeakers." Director Jean-Jacques Lebel refused to continue the play's run in Saint-Tropez, saying, "We're not at liberty to emasculate a work of art in order to pander to bourgeois sentiment."

The following are several lines from the play, with the hope that the English translation does justice to the original French:

• "We sprinkle the rice powder of angels on the soiled bed sheets and turn the mattresses through blackberry bushes."

• "And with all power the pigeon flocks dash into the rifle bullets! And in all bombed houses, the keys turn twice around in the locks."

1942

This is not the end. It is not even the beginning of the end. But it is, perhaps, the end of the beginning.
—British Prime Minister Winston Churchill, commenting on British forces turning the tide of the war in North Africa, November 1942.

☞ THE WAR

During the summer of 1942, it appeared eminently possible that the Japanese and the German armies might soon meet in India. Since their attack on Pearl Harbor, the Japanese had moved quickly to dominate the Pacific and had turned the corner into Asia, securing Hong Kong, Singapore, Malaya, Burma, and Thailand, and were advancing to the Indian Ocean. The invasion of Australia was a realistic objective for the forces of Nippon, for they had conquered islands only a few hundred miles from that country and had already fired on the mainland, including the harbor of Sydney. Their partner in war, Germany, had reversed its losses in the U.S.S.R. and was soon advancing on Stalingrad for a major confrontation with what was left of the Red Army. Should the Nazis prevail, the Soviets would surely fall, freeing up a huge army for work elsewhere. In North Africa, General Erwin Rommel was having his way. German U-boats controlled the North Atlantic, and mines were laid by

1942 the Nazis along the Atlantic Coast, in Chesapeake Bay, and near the harbors of Boston and New York.

Americans saw the Japanese invade the Aleutian Islands, the bombing of Alaska, and German submarines in the St. Lawrence River. For even the most optimistic, these were sobering times indeed.

There had been precious few bits of good news, but several events boosted the morale of Americans:

• On the day the Japanese had attacked Pearl Harbor, Major James Harold Doolittle had said to some friends, "I'm going to get in this thing with both feet. I'm going to Tokyo with a load of bombs." And, just over four months later, he had done exactly that, leading a squadron of sixteen B-25s from the carrier *Hornet* on April 18, 1942, on a raid on the Japanese capital. The planes destined for Tokyo arrived there in full daylight and successfully dropped their bomb loads. Kobe, Nagoya, Osaka, and Yokohama were also bombed, and the squadron continued on toward Chinese airfields according to plan. Unfortunately, they never made it. Bad weather and lack of fuel brought one plane down near Vladivostok (the flyers were interned) and forced the other crews either to crash land or to bail out. But the raid had succeeded, convincing the Japanese that they had to consolidate their newly won territories and venture no farther afield. By late May, Brigadier General Doolittle was back in Washington to receive the Medal of Honor at a White House ceremony.

• In one of the weirdest naval battles in history, the Battle of the Coral Sea was waged in early May. The Japanese and American fleets were almost 200 miles apart and never saw one another, the entire battle being carried out by carrier aircraft. Although the United States fleet lost more ships, it inflicted heavy damage on the Japanese, forcing the cancellation of their plans to carry out the invasion of Australia through New Guinea. For the first time in the war, the U.S. Navy sank a Japanese vessel larger than a destroyer, bagging the aircraft carrier *Shoho*, resulting in the following message from squadron leader Lieutenant Commander Robert Dixon: "Scratch one flattop. Dixon to carrier. Scratch one flattop."

• In the first week of June, Admiral Chester W. Nimitz was ready for another major naval engagement. Intercepted radio messages had told him of the impending assault on Midway, a key American base just over 1,000 miles west of Honolulu. There the Japanese fleet hoped to put the U.S. Navy in the Pacific to rout, and a Japanese force of eight aircraft carriers, eighteen cruisers, eleven battleships, and sixty-five destroyers was assembled to do the job. But Nimitz knew just what Admiral Yamamoto was going to do at every turn and was able to win the day with a far smaller fleet; four Japanese carriers were destroyed, as well as 332 aircraft. The Japanese suffered their first naval defeat since 1592 and would no longer enjoy naval supremacy in the Pacific.

258

• On September 16, 1942, the Germans were on the outskirts of **1942**
Stalingrad, their summer offensive having been a distinct success. But
then the war began to turn around. Before the year was out, Soviet armies
would take the initiative from the Germans, American troops would land
in North Africa, British Field Marshal Bernard Montgomery would have
Rommel's forces on the run, and the U.S. Marines would take control of
the battle for Guadalcanal, the first American offensive of the war, which
had begun on August 7. As 1942 came to an end, it would be only a matter
of time—and lives, millions of lives—before the Axis powers were
defeated.

☛ PEOPLE IN THE WAR

The British Air Ministry notified Lady MacRobert over a three-year
period that three of her sons had died in the service of England. Lady
MacRobert's response was to send a check to Air Minister Sir Archibald
Sinclair, which she hoped would be used to purchase a bomber. She
wrote, "It is my wish to make a mother's immediate reply in a way that I
know would be my boys' reply—attacking, striking sharply, straight to the
mark." In 1942, Lady MacRobert forwarded another check to Sinclair for
the purchase of four fighter planes. She said, "Had I been a man, I, too,
would have flown."

On February 20, 1942, Lieutenant Edward "Butch" O'Hare took off
from the carrier *Lexington*, shot down five Japanese aircraft, and was
eventually awarded the Medal of Honor. He was killed in action in 1944,
but his home town did not forget him. Chicago eventually named its
international airport for the aviator.

As part of the British Empire, Malta had the bad luck to be
positioned near to, or en route to, many areas of interest to the Germans.
Lying south of Sicily, the island underwent some 2,000 air raids. In 1942,
King George VI awarded the George Cross—an award for civilian
gallantry—to the 270,000 people of Malta who had borne these incessant
attacks so nobly and who were the recipients of a medal that was normally
awarded only to an individual.

U.S. Air Corps Captain Fred M. Smith was understandably elated
when he emerged victorious after an encounter with a Japanese
destroyer. Smith radioed, "Saw steamer, strafed same, sank same, some
sight, signed Smith."

During World War I, American troops in Europe had had difficulty
transmitting their messages without the Germans breaking their code. An
259

1942 inventive American officer ruminated about using a little-known language as a code, one that the Germans could not possibly know, and he settled on the language of the Choctaw Indians. The officer turned up eight Choctaws, who provided American forces with a perfect conduit for their secret orders.

In World War II, American Indians were once more heavily involved in the transmission of secret messages. This time it was the Navajos whose language was employed, for it was determined that there were only twenty-eight non-Navajos in the world who could speak the language, none of whom were either German or Japanese. By the end of the war, 420 Navajos would be involved in dispensing messages to American troops.

On November 23, 1942, a torpedo struck an English merchant ship off the west coast of Africa, and a Chinese steward named Poon Lim was thrown overboard. After two hours in the water, he found a life raft among the debris left from the sunken ship and climbed aboard. The raft was approximately eight square feet, and contained some biscuits, water, flares, and a flashlight. After several weeks in which Lim rationed his provisions carefully, his food and water were gone. But Lim was both creative and bent upon survival, and he worked with what he had. He employed his life jacket to gather rain water to drink and removed some wires from the flashlight, making them into fish hooks. When he caught a fish, he used its innards to coax sea gulls to the raft, which he killed with his bare hands and used to nourish himself. On April 5, 1943, 133 days after leaving his ship, Lim had floated to a position just off Brazil, and some fishermen took him aboard. Although he had lost twenty pounds during the ordeal, he went ashore without assistance. When told that he had established a world's record for survival at sea, Lim said, "I hope no one will ever have to break it."

SS General Reinhard Heydrich pulled off quite a deception in 1936 when he had forged papers that made it appear that Soviet military officers were opposed to Stalin. In a resultant purge, Stalin either put to death or exiled some 20,000 officers, severely depleting the leadership of his armed forces.

Heydrich was fiercely opposed to Jews and was a key planner in drafting the Final Solution of the Jewish Question, a blueprint for the systematic extermination of European Jewry. In 1942, when he was the military governor of occupied Czechoslovakia, he was mortally wounded by Czech resistance fighters who attacked his staff car. Hitler eulogized

260

Heydrich at his funeral and ordered severe reprisals that resulted in the death of over 15,000 Czechs. Part of the Führer's vengeance was wreaked upon the small village of Lidice. Every male in the small town was executed, as well as fifty-six females; the rest of the women were sent to concentration camps and the children to "correction schools." Then the Nazis systematically burned down every building in the village and struck Lidice from the rolls of Czech towns.

Mr. and Mrs. Thomas E. Sullivan of Waterloo, Iowa, were notified by the government that their sons Al, Frank, George, Joe, and Matt—all serving in the U.S. Navy—had been killed when the U.S.S. *Juneau* had been sunk in the Battle of Guadalcanal. After that tragedy, the navy would not permit brothers to go on active duty on the same vessel.

Between 1942 and 1944, a group called the WASPs were of tremendous assistance to the war effort. Made up of about 2,000 female civilian pilots, they ferried planes from one destination to another, including the largest bombers made, enabling more U.S. Air Force pilots to fly combat duty. The full name of the organization was the Women's Airforce Service Pilots, and it was commanded by Jacqueline Cochran.

The first American congressman to enlist in the armed forces after the Japanese attack on Pearl Harbor was a Texan named Lyndon Johnson. As a lieutenant commander in the navy, he was sent to the South Pacific, where one day, according to authors Don McCombs and Fred L. Worth, he "went on a bombing mission of New Guinea. A *New York Times* dispatch said the aircraft returned with engine trouble, but Johnson said they were attacked by Japanese aircraft. No one on board had been injured, yet General Douglas MacArthur presented Johnson with the Silver Star. Johnson was the only one on board who received it." Author Doris Kearns writes:

> Details of this mission are ambiguous. Depending on his mood and on the nature of the audience, Johnson told the story in different ways. On some occasions, he tended to deprecate his own role in the mission, insisting that he was not really the one who should have received the Silver Star. Yet, on other occasions, he described, in detail, his courageous behavior when his plane was surrounded by enemies and almost shot down. One fact is clear: Johnson wore the battle ribbon of his Silver Star in the lapel of his jacket for the rest of his life.

Since 1890, the A. N. Wetherbee Company in Lyndon, Vermont, had been making toy tops. It had become the largest manufacturer of that particular item in the world, turning out over 5 million in a good year. In 1942, the War Production Board needed lumber and metal for more important things and closed down the Vermont operation.

"Let no man say it cannot be done. It must be done, and we have undertaken to do it." With these words, President Roosevelt set the following production objectives for 1942:

60,000 airplanes
45,000 tanks
20,000 antiaircraft guns
8 million tons of merchant shipping

Henry John Kaiser was not intimidated by large projects. He had put together a group of construction companies to build the Hoover Dam, a project that was finished two years ahead of schedule; he had then moved on to other challenges like the San Francisco–Oakland Bay Bridge and the Grand Coulee Dam. In World War II, Kaiser applied his talents to shipbuilding and would launch 1,490 ships by the end of the war. In November 1942, the keel of the *Robert E. Peary* was laid; four and a half days later the ship was launched.

"Rosie the Riveter" was a symbol to thousands of American women who took to the factories to help produce weapons to sustain the war effort. "Rosie" was thought to have been named after Rosina B. Bonavita, who, with a fellow employee, purportedly put 3,345 rivets on the wing of a fighter plane in just six hours.

• Women could not be very effective working at a defense plant in skirts. In Boston, Filene's department store saw the trend, opening three Slack Bars, while Hudson's in Detroit inaugurated a trouser shop for women.

• A popular movie actress of the day was Veronica Lake, whose long blonde tresses fell loose in a "peekaboo" style that was considered most fashionable. Production officials in Washington were worried that female factory workers, trying to emulate her hairdo, would get their hair caught in machines, so they asked the movie star to alter her hair style for the good of the war effort.

To conserve copper, the U.S. Mint issued pennies coated with zinc, **1942** the so-called white pennies. By the end of the war, many coins would be made from the casings of spent shells.

When the navy was shopping for a new craft that could travel at high speeds and change directions quickly, a former bootlegger named Andrew Higgins submitted plans for a boat he had designed to evade government agents during Prohibition. It turned out to be just what the navy was looking for, and they decided to call it the PT (patrol torpedo) boat. It was made of plywood and was lightly armed, relying strictly on its speed to evade the enemy. The insignia for the PT boat was the work of cartoonist and animator Walt Disney, picturing a mosquito mounted on a torpedo.

To the surprise of many Americans, one prime example of American manhood was rejected for military service. Yes, Superman flunked his army physical, failing the eye test. Clark Kent's X-ray vision did not work in his favor when he read an eye chart in another room instead of the one in front of him.

How it began, no one knows for sure, but by 1942 the words "Kilroy Was Here" were everywhere, both at home and abroad, sometimes accompanied, according to author Stuart Flexner, by a drawing "showing a wide-eyed, bald-headed face peering over a fence which hid everything below his nose, except for his fingers which were shown gripping the top of the fence."

Civilian defense was the order of the day, and blackouts were initiated in coastal areas. But there was a severe shortage of air raid sirens, and the Office of Civilian Defense put the Bell Telephone Laboratories to work to come up with a siren that could be used in all cities. Author Richard Lingeman writes,

> The result was christened the Victory Siren and could be
> operated by an ordinary automobile engine which powered com-
> pressed air through whirling metal blades. Touted by its desig-
> ners as "the loudest sound in the world," its blast was said to
> be able to break the eardrums of a man standing 100 feet away,
> and the Army considered using it as a weapon for a time. The
> victory siren blanketed an area 10 miles square with its wail,
> but many communities refused to purchase it because it was
> too loud.

Shortages in certain goods are an inevitable result of war, and the United States was not spared this inconvenience. Some items like coffee and

1942 sugar were rationed when there was still plenty to go around because consumer hoarding in anticipation of scarcities depleted the stocks. Because the United States imported all of its rubber, gas rationing was initiated to conserve the use of automobile tires—not because there was a shortage of fuel, although that would soon come to pass. Americans took to their bicycles, but they too would be rationed, so the citizenry began walking to get around. Even this basic mode of transportation would be curtailed when shoe rationing was begun in 1943, and by 1944 civilians could purchase only two pairs of leather shoes a year. Fabric shoes, which could be had in limitless quantities, became popular with women.

Liquor fell into short supply, canned beer availability was limited because of a shortage of tin, and, particularly later in the war, cigarettes were hard to come by. When meat and butter were rationed, Americans took to downing eggs in large quantities, blissfully ignorant of something that would later become a household word—cholesterol. Canned vegetables were soon rationed to conserve tin, and many Americans used their backyards to grow Victory Gardens, some 20 million of which would be turning out 40 percent of the nation's vegetables by the end of the war. Home canning spread to three out of every four American families, which put up an average of 165 jars per family each year during the war. Those who could not do without "luxury" goods risked the scorn of their neighbors by buying on the black market at high prices. And for the first time in what seemed like eons, there was money to spend as the war economy boomed, turning unemployment into a thing of the past. The war had finally brought the Depression to an end.

One day in American history that must be regarded as a low point was February 19, 1942, when President Roosevelt put his signature to an executive order providing for the incarceration of Japanese-Americans living on the West Coast. Many were citizens, many had sons in the U.S. Army, but they were treated as enemies. Their businesses were confiscated, homes disposed of, assets seized, and they were shipped to remote areas of the Far West, where they lived in camps surrounded by high wire fences. Despite these indignities, most of these Japanese-Americans remained loyal to their country. In a strange about-face, Washington would, in January 1943, offer to accept qualified Japanese-Americans who wanted to enlist in the U.S. Army. Despite the treatment they had received, they came in large numbers. Cartoonist Bill Mauldin wrote, "To my knowledge and the knowledge of numerous others who had the opportunity of watching a lot of different outfits overseas, no combat unit in the Army could exceed them in loyalty, hard work, courage, and sacrifice. Hardly a man of them hadn't been decorated at least twice, and their casualty rates were appalling."

One of the reasons Japanese-Americans were treated so badly was

264

the very real fear that in 1942 Japan would attack the United States and that the Japanese living in America must be heavily infiltrated with spies who would come to the aid of the invaders. People living on the West and East coasts were particularly worried about attacks upon their shores. And though no invasions were mounted, there were enough incidents in American coastal areas to keep the possibility of foreign attack strongly in mind.

• At a February press conference, Franklin Roosevelt said, "Enemy ships could swoop in and shell New York; enemy planes could drop bombs on war plants in Detroit; enemy troops could attack Alaska." When a reporter asked the president if our military forces were not of sufficient strength to preclude such strikes, FDR replied, "Certainly not." Shortly thereafter, a Japanese submarine shelled a Santa Barbara, California, oil refinery.

• On June 12, a German submarine delivered to the coast of Long Island four would-be saboteurs, each of whom was either captured by the U.S. Coast Guard or turned himself in to the FBI within weeks. Other German saboteurs were captured on the coast of Florida.

• On June 22, a Japanese submarine rained fire on a military installation at Fort Stevens, Oregon.

• In July, a German U-boat mined the approaches to the Mississippi River.

• In September, a Japanese aircraft bombed Oregon twice in an effort to start forest fires.

▬ SPORTS

World War II saw the beginning of a tradition that endures to this day—the playing of "The Star-Spangled Banner" before sporting events. The national anthem had previously been sung at contests only when a band was present.

There was a severe shortage of scrap metal, and several major league teams offered free admission to certain games in return for a specified amount of that precious commodity.

The Boston College football team had enjoyed a sensational football season, winning eight games while outscoring their opponents by a margin of 249 to 19. They were 4–1 favorites to trounce a mediocre Holy Cross eleven in their final game, after which they had reservations at a Boston nightclub for a victory celebration. However, they were not only upset by Holy Cross, they were totally humiliated by a score of 55–12. Despondent after their loss, the team canceled their plans for a festive

1942 night at the Cocoanut Grove, being mercifully absent when a tragic fire took place at the nightclub on the evening of November 18, 1942, leaving 491 dead.

🖝 ENTERTAINMENT

Actress Tallulah Bankhead volunteered to give blood to the Japanese. Bankhead said, "I told them that I was so damned anemic, my blood would kill a good American soldier."

Since most of their mothers lived too far away to make the trip, soldiers at California's Camp Callan selected a "proxy mother" to visit them on Mother's Day. Their choice to fill in for their moms was movie star Rita Hayworth.

The Allied invasion of North Africa could not have been better timed as far as the people at Warner Brothers in Hollywood were concerned. It brought some free publicity for their new film, *Casablanca*, starring Humphrey Bogart as the owner of Rick's Cafe, Paul Henreid, who played Laszlo, an underground leader who had escaped from the Germans, and Ingrid Bergman, Laszlo's wife, who had fallen in love with Rick when she thought her husband had died. Others in the cast were Peter Lorre, Sydney Greenstreet, and Claude Rains.

Such was the popularity of the film that Warner Brothers made plans for a sequel that never found its way to the screen. The sequel was to be called *Brazzaville* and was to star Bogart, Geraldine Fitzgerald, and Sydney Greenstreet.

• Before Bogart and Bergman were selected, Warner Brothers had earmarked the key roles for Ronald Reagan and Ann Sheridan.

• "Play it again, Sam," a line that is part of the Bogart legend, was not spoken by him or by anyone else in the film. When Ingrid Bergman drops in at Rick's Cafe, she exhorts Sam, the pianist (played by Dooley Wilson), to play "As Time Goes By," saying, "Play it, Sam." When Bogart hears the song that reminds the couple of their earlier love, he asks Sam to play it once again, saying, "You played it for her, you can play it for me. If she can stand it, I can! Play it!"

Two child stars growing up in 1942 were Shirley Temple and Mickey Rooney.

• In the film *Miss Annie Rooney*, Shirley Temple received her first on-screen kiss given in a romantic fashion, an assortment of doting adults having bussed her before platonically. The perpetrator was actor Dickie Moore.

266

• Diminutive Mickey Rooney married a young woman named Lucy Johnson, whose screen name was Ava Gardner.

London-born actress Elizabeth Taylor, ten, came to the screen for the first time in a film called *There's One Born Every Minute*. In 1943, she would continue her film career in the movie *Lassie Come Home*.

☛ ACTS OF GOD

Roy C. Sullivan, a park ranger in the Shenandoah National Park, was struck by lightning, not an everyday occurrence, even for a man of the outdoors. He survived but was struck again, and again and again and again and again and again—seven times, in total, between 1942 and 1977. Sullivan could not explain his attraction to electricity, and it says much about his fortitude that he went out of the house at all. His bouts with lightning would leave him with a number of scars, severe burns, several "cremated" ranger hats, and the loss of a big toenail; and, on one occasion, lightning set fire to his hair and eyebrows.

☛ MEDIA

The Associated Press sent a memorandum to its sportswriters, proclaiming: "There should be a ban on flowery, overenthusiastic lyrical sports writing for the duration [of the war]. Remembering the exploits of military heroes, it does not seem appropriate to overdo the use of such words as 'courageous,' 'gallant,' 'fighting.' . . . It doesn't take much 'courage' to overcome a two-run lead in the ninth."

☛ FOOD AND DRINK

Hoping to capitalize on the food shortages that the war had brought about, a book came on to the market in 1942 entitled *How to Cook a Wolf*, by M. F. K. Fisher—eventually to be one of the nation's most revered food writers.

☛ MEDICINE

In September 1942, American submariner Darrell Dean Rector developed acute appendicitis, but his submarine was in the Pacific Ocean,

1942 far from a hospital. There was no doctor on board, and it became obvious that if Rector's appendix were not removed soon, he would die.

Into the breech stepped Pharmacist's Mate Wheeler B. Lippes, whose credentials were not great but were better than anyone else's on board; at least he had observed an appendectomy during his brief medical career. Lippes turned out to be an inspired innovator, fashioning a scalpel from the blade of a knife and an ether cone from a tea strainer. His crude instruments were sterilized by alcohol from a torpedo. Lippes removed the diseased organ, and two weeks later Rector was out of sick bay and back at his job.

The incident was used in the 1943 war thriller *Destination Tokyo* with Robert Hutton playing the Rector role and William Prince the Lippes one. Cary Grant, the star, administered the anesthetic.

 **EPITAPHS**

In a cemetery not far from Albany, New York, the death of Harry Edsel Smith in 1942 resulted in the following gravestone inscription:

> Harry Edsel Smith
> Born 1903—Died 1942
> Looked up the elevator shaft
> to see if the car was on the
> way down. It was.

1943

We shall attack and attack until we are exhausted, and then we shall attack again.

—General George S. Patton

☞ THE WAR

When Franklin Roosevelt took off from Miami on the *Dixie Clipper* on January 11, 1943, he became the first American president to fly in an airplane while in office and to leave the country during a war. He also became the first American chief executive since Abraham Lincoln to go to a battlefront.

As Roosevelt headed to Casablanca to meet with Winston Churchill, Hitler's Sixth Army was starving in below-zero weather at Stalingrad, surrounded by the Red Army. In three weeks, the Germans would surrender and would not mount a major offensive in the U.S.S.R. again. Meanwhile, Japanese forces were falling back in New Guinea, and General Douglas MacArthur would soon embark on a plan to recapture Japanese occupied islands in the South Pacific that would be known as leapfrogging. It called for American forces to advance north through the islands while avoiding conflict with the most formidable Japanese

269

1943 defenses, simply by bypassing them for easier prey. As more and more American bases were established, those enemy forces that had not been engaged would gradually be cut off from receiving supplies from the Japanese mainland as the Americans took over control of the seas and the skies. And in North Africa, Axis forces would surrender in just four months and one day, with 250,000 German and Italian troops taken prisoner.

Roosevelt first flew to Trinidad, chugging along in a Pan American clipper at 146 mph, in a trip that took ten hours. From there, he flew to an airfield on the northern coast of Brazil, a nine-hour flight, before crossing the Atlantic Ocean to British Gambia on the west coast of Africa, some nineteen hours away. He then boarded a C-54 and flew the final eight-hour leg of the trip to Casablanca.

The four-leg, forty-six-hour flight must have been an ordeal for Roosevelt, whose health was already on the decline. Later in the year, he began to lose weight and suffer a loss of appetite and, in March 1944, was diagnosed as having hypertension, hardening of the arteries, and congestive heart failure—and his blood pressure was at an alarming 186/100.

Roosevelt had made the long journey because he and Churchill had to determine major strategy for the European war, specifically where Allied troops should make their next major attack. Not at the conference was Stalin, who was resentful that Great Britain and the United States were not pulling their weight in the battle against Germany by failing to open a western front in 1942, leaving the Soviets to battle Hitler alone from the east. Despite pressure from Stalin, Roosevelt and Churchill agreed to delay an attack on France until 1944. Instead, they agreed to launch an assault on Sicily, coming up on Europe from the south.

Another momentous decision that would prolong the war was made at Casablanca. Roosevelt proposed, and Churchill accepted, "unconditional surrender" as the only terms under which the Allies should accept the capitulation of their enemies. By not accepting compromise, Roosevelt hoped that a true victory would be achieved, one that would preclude future squabbles over territory that could lead to another war. But in making this decision, Roosevelt and Churchill gave up the opportunity of getting Germany and Japan to lay down their arms before their fanatic military leaders had totally depleted their forces and resources. They had committed their armies not only to fighting all the way to Berlin but also to a military operation that would perhaps result in more casualties than in any other in the war—the invasion of Japan, where the honor of the people, it was said, could be upheld only by their deaths. In the name of the emperor, virtually every man, woman, and child was supposedly prepared to die in an attempt to keep Yankee invaders from their soil.

Three other key events of the war in 1943 were as follows:

270

• The Allies practiced one of the most effective deceptions of World War II, which began when a body was recovered in the nets of some fishermen one day in April 1943 near the Mediterranean port of Huelva, Spain. The body of an Englishman who had died of pneumonia had been given the false identity of a Royal Marine traveling by air as a courier to Allied Headquarters in North Africa, one Captain William Martin. The fake documents he was carrying were intended to convince the Germans that the Allies were planning an invasion of Greece instead of the actual target—Sicily—a next step the Allies thought was so obvious that Winston Churchill had said that "anybody but a damn fool" would realize that a Sicilian invasion was soon to be in the cards.

The corpse had been taken by submarine to the Spanish coast and released. After the fishermen brought it to shore, it was anticipated that the officer's papers would be handed over to the pro-German Franco government, which would see that they were passed on to the German embassy in Madrid. The officer's death was reported to the British embassy, and feigning huge concern, the British frantically requested the officer's papers, which were turned over to them. Sophisticated tests showed that the papers had indeed been looked through, and it was learned after the war that their contents had reached the top of Nazi officialdom.

When the Allies did attack Sicily, they found themselves opposed by only three divisions—two German and one Italian. Not only had the ruse worked, but it would also turn out to have double value. When a German spy copied the actual plans for the Normandy invasion and sent them to Berlin, they were considered just another Allied ruse and filed under the category of misleading information.

• On November 14, President Roosevelt was on the battleship *Iowa* en route to a conference with Churchill and Chiang Kai-shek. With him during the Atlantic crossing were top brass representatives Generals George Marshall and "Hap" Arnold, and Admirals William Leahy and Ernest King, the cream of American military leadership. Three hundred and fifty miles east of Bermuda, the American destroyer *William D. Porter* was conducting a drill and fired what was thought to be an unarmed torpedo at the *Iowa*. When it became apparent that the torpedo was a live one, the *Iowa's* helmsman attempted to turn the ship out of the line of fire, and the torpedo exploded in the *Iowa's* wake, detonated by the turbulence.

The president's log carried the following entry: "Had that torpedo hit the *Iowa* in the right spot with her passenger list of distinguished statesmen, military, naval, and aerial strategists and planners, it could have had untold effect on the outcome of the war and the destiny of the country."

Air Corps General Arnold said to Admiral King following the incident, "Tell me, Ernest, does this happen often in your navy?"

1943 • Mussolini and his cabinet resigned after the Fascist Grand Council had voted to return the king to power. Italy surrendered in early September, and Italian forces soon changed sides.

☛ PEOPLE IN THE WAR

When a torpedo struck the tanker he was in, Roy Dikkers found himself in deep trouble: The blast had wedged shut the door of his cabin, making it impossible for him to get out. As he debated what to do, a second torpedo hit the ship; its impact broke down the door, allowing him to make his way topside. When he came on deck, he saw that the ship was encircled by burning fuel, making a jump for safety certain suicide. Again, as Dikkers debated his next move, it was taken care of by higher powers: A third torpedo smashed into the vessel, sending him airborne; his body arced over the flames and into the clear water beyond, where he providentially surfaced right next to a life raft. Plainly, Dikkers was not destined to perish at sea. Sure enough, three days later, he was picked up by a passing ship.

Desmond T. Doss had a moral aversion to killing his fellowman and was designated a conscientious objector. Assigned to the U.S. Army as a corpsman, Private Doss's numerous acts of bravery under fire won him the Medal of Honor, the country's highest award for valor, the first time it had ever been awarded to a conscientious objector.

Author A. A. Milne's son, Christopher Robin, the engaging child whom Milne had written about in *When We Were Very Young*, was fighting for the British in Italy in 1943.

In North Africa, some GIs came upon a group of Italian prisoners of war, and a few Yanks who could speak their language could not resist letting loose a few verbal gibes. One of the prisoners finally became fed up with the abuse and said, "All right, laugh, but we're going to America. You're only going to Italy."

Soviet lieutenant and air force pilot Lilya Litvak had shot down twelve German planes and had been awarded the Order of the Red Banner and the Order of the Patriotic War. She was killed in action in September 1943.

Lieutenant (junior grade) John F. Kennedy was at the helm of a PT boat in the Solomon Islands one moonless night in 1943, on a mission to intercept Japanese vessels harassing American supply ships trying to restock American bases in the area. Kennedy had tried to enlist in the army but had been rejected because of an old football back injury. After an exercise program had strengthened his back sufficiently to gain acceptance in the navy, he had volunteered for PT boat duty.

The young lieutenant was not having an easy time of it that night because visibility was virtually zero. Only one of the four boats in his section had radar, and it had become separated from the other PT boats, leaving Kennedy's and the other two remaining boats with little idea of what lay ahead.

Suddenly, he saw that a Japanese destroyer was nearly on top of his boat, traveling at some forty knots. Kennedy turned hard right, but before he could fire his torpedoes, the *Amigiri* smashed into PT 109, cutting it in two. Japanese Commander Kohei Hanami did not even bother to stop, certain that the PT boat was headed for Davy Jones's locker with no survivors.

Miraculously, only two of the thirteen-man crew had been killed in the collision, and one half of the craft was still afloat. Machinist Mate Patrick H. McMahon had been the only crew member below decks, and he had been badly burned. Kennedy started swimming toward land, pulling McMahon behind, his teeth holding the strap of the wounded man's lifejacket. The other men followed, and it took the group four hours to swim to an island three miles distant.

It was a week before the men were rescued, and Kennedy moved the group to another island three days later, attracted by some coconut palms that offered nourishment; once again, he had McMahon in tow by the same method. At last, the men came upon two friendly natives, who took this message—scratched on a coconut shell—from Kennedy to the PT base at Rendova: "Eleven alive native knows posit and reefs Nauru Island Kennedy." After they were picked up, Kennedy was hospitalized for four weeks, his old back injury aggravated by the ordeal, and he had also contracted malaria. When his back failed to respond to treatment, he was sent to the Chelsea Naval Hospital in Boston, where he was operated on, a damaged vertebra replaced with a metal disk. For his heroic conduct, Kennedy was awarded both the Navy Medal and the Marine Corps Medal.

Not long after John Kennedy returned to the United States, his older brother Joe had finished his second tour of combat duty as a U.S. Navy lieutenant on antisubmarine duty with the British Coastal Command. Nevertheless, Joe volunteered for an extremely hazardous mission called Operation Aphrodite, in which he was to fly a B-24 packed with explosives to a point close to a German submarine base on the French Coast; he then had instructions to bail out while the bomber was guided to its target by another plane using remote control. Kennedy brought the aircraft into position, and when he activated the explosives, the plane blew up.

• Joseph P. Kennedy, Jr., was awarded the Navy Cross posthumously, and a destroyer was named in his honor.

• Not long afterward, Robert F. Kennedy, younger brother of both Joe and John, left college for the U.S. Navy, to serve on the destroyer *Joseph P. Kennedy, Jr.*

British troops who had just fought their way into the Italian village of Colvi Vecchi were in desperate straits. They had just learned from another newly arrived English unit that it had called for an Allied bomber attack on the same village, in the belief that the German positions were impregnable. None of their radios had survived the action. How could they tell the Allied base twenty miles away to call off the attack?

This was a job for GI Joe, an American carrier pigeon assigned to one of the units. Bearing the crucial message, off the pigeon went to the airfield twenty miles away, covering the distance in the Supermanlike time of just twenty minutes, arriving in the nick of time to halt the bombers before they took to the air.

• At a ceremony in London in 1946, GI Joe would receive the Dickin Medal for gallantry, an award presented by the British to animals acting with particular heroism, the first time the medal had been given to a recipient not from the British Isles.

The following excerpts are translations from letters written by three German soldiers at Stalingrad in early 1943:

• "Until Christmas 1942 the daily bread ration issued to every man was a hundred grammes [about 3.5 pounds]. After Christmas the ration was reduced to fifty grammes per head. Later on only those in the forward line received fifty grammes per day. No bread was issued to men in regimental headquarters and upwards. The others were given watery soup which we tried to improve by use of bones obtained from horses we dug up. As a Christmas treat the Army allowed the slaughtering of four thousand of the available horses."

• "I was horrified when I saw the map. We're quite alone, without any help from the outside. Hitler has left us in the lurch. . . . Hannes and I have no intention of going into captivity; yesterday I saw four men who'd been captured before our infantry re-occupied a strong-point. No, we're not going to be captured. When Stalingrad falls you will hear and read about it. Then you will know that I shall not return."

• "All we have left are two machine-guns and four hundred rounds. And then a mortar and ten bombs. Except for that all we have are hunger

274

and fatigue. B. has broken out with twenty men on his own initiative. Better to know in three days than in three weeks what the end looks like. Can't say I blame him."

☛ THE HOME FRONT

A man in Poinsett County, Arkansas, was unwittingly volunteered for duty when he showed up at his draft board bearing a letter that read as follows:

> Dear United States Army: My husband asked me to write a recommend that he supports his family. He cannot read, so don't tell him. Just take him. He ain't no good to me. He ain't done nothing but raise hell and drink lemon essence since I married him eight years ago, and I got to feed seven kids of his. Maybe you can get him to carry a gun. He's good on squirrels and eating. Take him and welcome. I need the grub and his bed for the kids. Don't tell him this, but just take him.

The Supreme Court overturned a West Virginia law calling for the expulsion of students from the public school system who chose not to salute the American flag.

Future president James Earl Carter, a plebe at the U.S. Naval Academy, stood 5 feet 1.5 inches tall when he arrived at Annapolis from Georgia. However, he would grow three inches in his first year, another four before graduation; he would finish the curriculum in just three years. Nicknamed Johnny Reb because of his pronounced Southern accent, Carter, like all plebes, was hazed unmercifully by upperclassmen, but there was one request that he steadfastly refused to comply with: He would not sing the song "Marching Through Georgia."

The United States was highly dependent on rubber imported from Brazil to make tires for military vehicles. To keep workers on the rubber plantations happy, Washington was willing to comply with just about any reasonable request. And so it was with great alacrity that a supply of fishhooks was sent to the Amazon Valley in response to the following telegram from Brazilian rubber workers: "NO FISHHOOKS, NO FISH; NO FISH, NO EAT; NO EAT, NO RUBBER."

Time magazine, in its April 5, 1943, edition, reported:

> Britian last week lifted a ban on the railway transport of spring flowers. From Scotland the first box of snow drops went

275

1943

south. London's Hyde Park was carpeted with purple crocuses which lovers crushed, unmindful of passersby, and botanists haunted bomb cavities for London rocket (*Sisymbrium irio*), which flourished after the great fire of 1666. Already 95 types of flowers and shrubs unknown for decades before the blitz have been found in holes where nitrates from burning bombs have enriched the soil.

In order to improve the cash flow of the United States government, a means of taking in income tax revenues more quickly was initiated in 1943: the federal withholding tax. This means of taking in dollars to finance the war effort had also been used between 1913 and 1916. Taxes were removed from paychecks by employers instead of being paid by the taxpayer after the tax year had ended.

On September 31, 1943, singer Kate Smith put in a long day raising money for the war effort, delivering about sixty-five messages over the radio exhorting listeners to purchase war bonds. Americans responded generously to the much-loved singer, buying just under $40 million worth of bonds on that one day.

In their book, *The Homefront*, Mark Jonathan Harris, Franklin Mitchell, and Steven Schecter have assembled the recollections of an assortment of people who were on the home front during World War II. Three recollections are as follows:

> • Three months after the war started, my boyfriend came home to West Virginia on emergency leave, we were married, and I came back to the West Coast with him. My husband was with the Seventh Fleet, on the U.S.S. *Chicago*, and their home port was San Francisco.
> The men wanted their wives and families on the West Coast because they were never sure when they would come back into port and they didn't always get a long enough furlough to travel where their families were. Ship movements were secret, too, so no one knew when they would dock or when they would leave again. The men wanted to have a feeling of home when they got back. If they didn't have someone in San Francisco, then they would have to live on the ship, or on the base. And, naturally, they wanted a little loving and a little caring when they came home.
> I had never traveled farther than Pittsburgh before, and here I was suddenly, three thousand miles from home, in San Francisco. Almost as soon as we got there, my husband shipped

276

out and I was on my own, living in a city I didn't know and
where I knew very few people. It was like being an orphan.
I felt completely alone.

I got a job as a keypunch operator for Standard Oil, and I
found a furnished room because it was impossible to find an
apartment or housing of any kind. There was a waiting list of at
least a year, and military men and families were given priority.
During the day I worked at Standard Oil and at night I'd return to my room. I learned to knit at that time and spent many
nights knitting socks for my husband and listening to the radio
for war news. I lived alone for four years during the war, and
they were the most painful, lonely years I think I will ever
spend. I look back and wonder how I ever got through those
years, but when you're young you can do a lot of things that
you can't do as you grow older. I spent many nights by myself
in my room, crying because I was so lonely.

The occasional times my husband would come on leave, we
would talk about the future. "As soon as the war is over," he
would say, "I'm going to leave the Navy, and we'll go back to
the East Coast, buy a home, raise a family." We had the house
all built in our minds. It was a two-story brick home, with a
beautiful entrance hall. There was a lovely winding stairway
leading upstairs and bedrooms enough for five children. I just
loved that house and carried those plans around in my mind
for years and years.

• I remember having to read a "Dear John" letter for one of
the soldiers. He was a Southerner and his reaction was complete silence. He got up and walked away, came back and asked
me to read the letter again, then folded it, put it in his pocket
and walked away. I could see the lines of grief in his face, the
total disbelief. Then it spread to all the men throughout the
company. We understood how he felt, and it made us all very
insecure. Most men were insecure about how their wives would
act while they were thousands of miles away.

Still, having a wife at home was very sustaining. I did a lot
of dreaming about coming home to her. I wanted to buy a
house and have a family, and I spent many hours thinking about
exactly the kind of house I'd like to have. A very smart man I
know said once that anticipation was sixty percent of life. There
was this anticipation of returning to this beautiful girl. And fantasies of kids and jobs. It was absolutely sustaining.

• The doorbell rang and a very old man delivered the telegram. On the envelope were two or three stars. I saw the stars
and my blood turned cold. I knew immediately that my brother

277

had been killed. We ripped open the telegram. I can't remember the wording, but it was from the Adjutant General, somebody I'd never heard of before, who regretted to tell me that my brother had been killed. It was one of the most horrible moments in my life.

I kept saying, "I don't believe it; this did not happen," and I laughed, because it was ludicrous. Part of me knew that I was simply anesthetized, that I was numb with shock, and that when the numbness wore off I would have to face the fact that my brother was dead, that he had been killed on a training mission right here in the United States. The waste, I thought, the terrible waste.

He was a trained pilot—he knew what the hell he was doing—and they stuck him up in a C-47, a flying boxcar (so safe they could fly themselves), and they said, Fly up a thousand feet and drop these supplies. It was a night flight and one of the planes got lost and ended up directly over my brother's plane. When they got the order to drop, they dropped the supplies right through the wing of my brother's plane. At a thousand feet, they couldn't recover. One man bailed out, but my brother was killed along with everybody else on the plane. He had just turned twenty-one and had never even voted.

At the funeral, the rabbi who gave the service said how wonderful it was that a Jew, in this country, could give his life helping the Jews all over the world. My sister said, "Isn't that a beautiful thought, isn't that comforting." And I said, "That's bullshit."

In June 1943, the Los Angeles Zoot Suit Riots took place, starting innocently enough with a fistfight between a sailor and a group of Mexican civilians wearing zoot suits—long double-breasted coats and pegged pants, which was the uniform of the day for trendy young urban males not serving in the armed forces. This skirmish erupted into a full-scale riot when soldiers and marines joined the sailors in broadening their field of battle, carousing through the streets, assaulting anyone dressed in a zoot suit, and later extending their antagonism by attacking dark-skinned males in any garb. After several days of fighting, servicemen were restricted from visiting Los Angeles while on pass.

☞ MEDICINE

An operation on the mentally ill that became popular in the 1940s was the prefrontal lobotomy, in which sections of the front part of the brain were removed. During the decade, fifty thousand people received this operation, and in 1949, Antonio de Egas Moniz received the Nobel Prize for having conceived of this unique form of surgery.

By the mid-1950s, however, this radical surgery would be frowned upon by the medical profession because it rendered many patients lethargic and infantile in their behavior.

When a Swiss chemist named Albert Hoffmann was conducting an experiment, he began to have hallucinations after some of the chemical substance that he had been working with had penetrated his skin. Further experimentation with the chemical would lead to the development of LSD.

🖝BOOKS

Religious books were big sellers during World War II, the sales of the Bible having increased more than 25 percent since the United States had entered the world conflict. Other top-sellers were *The Robe* and *The Song of Bernadette*.

Pocketbook sales had quadrupled since 1941, and 40 million were sold in America in 1943, these low-cost editions helping significantly to increase reading in the United States during the war. Prior to 1939, the average book consumption per person was approximately one half a book per year. The government was doing its part by distributing paperbacks to servicemen that were small enough to fit into uniform pockets. About 1,324 separate works appeared in Armed Forces Editions, and other books carried a label urging the buyer to pass it along when read "to a boy in the armed forces anywhere in the U.S. . . . only 4¢."

Little fiction of critical acclaim appeared during World War II. The best war novel came from a 1943 Harvard graduate in aeronautical engineering who was stationed in the Pacific theater until 1946, and his book, *The Naked and the Dead*, would establish Norman Mailer as a new force in American literature after its publication in 1948, author George Orwell describing Mailer's work as "the only war novel of any distinction to appear hitherto."

🖝SPORTS

Baseball stars had gone to war, leaving the young, the old, and those unfit for military service to fill out the rosters of the major league teams.

1943 Diamond stars in the military services were often put to work at their craft to entertain the troops, making teams like the Great Lakes Naval Training Station formidable powers. In an exhibition game against the 1942 World Series winners, the St. Louis Cardinals, Great Lakes took the major league champs by 5–2.

In order to leave public transportation for those with higher priorities, major league baseball teams trained close to home between 1943 and 1945, conducting their spring practice sessions in weather that was often better suited for cross-country skiing. The New York Giants were in nearby Lakewood, New Jersey, saving fuel by commuting to their daily practice sessions by horse and buggy.

Short on players, Pennsylvania's two professional football teams joined forces, the Pittsburgh Steelers and the Philadelphia Eagles playing under the name "Steagles."

Along with the American college football bowl games, there were football bowls for servicemen as well, held in the following locations in one or more years during World War II:

BOWL	LOCATION
Spaghetti Bowl	Florence, Italy
Tea Bowl	London, England
Riviera Bowl	Marseilles, France
Lily Bowl	Bermuda
Potato Bowl	Ireland
Arab Bowl	Oran, Algeria

☛ ENTERTAINMENT

Scantily clad movie stars whose pictures hung just about everywhere in the world where there were American servicemen were called pinup girls. Betty Grable and Rita Hayworth were among the young women whose pictures were most frequently displayed.

Actor Leslie Howard was flying from Lisbon to London in the spring of 1943 when his KLM flight was attacked by German planes and shot down, Howard losing his life. Perishing with Howard was a portly, cigar-smoking Britisher named Alfred Chenhalls. Winston Churchill, in *The Hinge of Fate*, published in 1950, wrote:

280

The daily commercial aircraft was about to start from the Lisbon airfield when a thickset man smoking a cigar walked up and was thought to be a passenger on it. The German agents therefore signalled that I was on board. Although these neutral passenger planes had plied unmolested for many months between Portugal and England and had carried only civilian traffic, a German war plane was instantly ordered out, and the defenseless aircraft was ruthlessly shot down. Fourteen civilian passengers perished, among them the well-known British film actor, Leslie Howard, whose grace and gifts are still preserved for us by the records of the many delightful films in which he took part. The brutality of the Germans was only matched by the stupidity of their agents. It is difficult to understand how anyone could imagine that with all the resources of Great Britain at my disposal I should have booked passage in a neutral plane from Lisbon and flown home in broad daylight.

Actor Errol Flynn had gained quite a reputation as a womanizer, and the expression "in like Flynn" became a popular phrase among American servicemen to denote easy success—sexual or otherwise. When Flynn was tried for the statutory rape of two teenage girls in early 1943, sympathetic American youngsters started an organization called ABCD EF—American Boys Club for the Defense of Errol Flynn.

Actress Lucille Ball reported a strange occurrence to authorities: When she happened to be in a certain area of Hollywood, she would pick up broadcast in a language that sounded like Japanese coming from the fillings of her teeth. Thanks to Ball's alert incisors, an investigation uncovered several Japanese spies and the radio they used to transmit intelligence.

☛ OBITUARIES

Humorist and critic Alexander Woollcott was participating in a radio panel show called *The People's Platform* when he suffered a heart attack followed by a cerebral hemorrhage, dying before an ambulance could get him to New York's Roosevelt Hospital. In a bizarre finale that would have amused Woollcott, his ashes, destined for burial at Hamilton College in Clinton, New York, from which institution Woollcott had graduated, were sent by mistake to Colgate University in Hamilton, New York. When the mistake was discovered, the ashes were sent on to Clinton, arriving with 67 cents postage due.

1943 George Bernard Shaw's wife died in 1943. Irish-born Charlotte Payne-Townsend Shaw's will left $263,000 "to polish the manners of the Irish," a bequest that left her trustees somewhat baffled as to exactly how these funds should be put to use, leading to the proposal "of various cultural institutions as legatees."

1944

"Oh, God," he sobs, looking down at the queer, unattached leg lying beside his face and realizing it is his. "Oh, God," as the ramp goes down and the twelve men in front of him pile up in the cold two feet of water, with the machine-gun bullets inside them.
—Irwin Shaw

☛ THE WAR

As the European winter faded and turned to spring, both the Allied and Axis forces knew that an invasion of France would shortly be launched from England, an undertaking that would be the largest amphibious assault since mankind had learned the art of war. If it were successful, Germany's fate would be sealed, as the vise—represented by the Soviets on the eastern front and the Allies to the west—inexorably closed until the Third Reich was crushed between the two powers. If the Germans could concentrate their forces on the point of attack, the Allies' efforts would either fail or perhaps result in the highest casualties ever sustained in an invasion. If the German forces could be taken by surprise, however, the odds for success would be dramatically increased.

One could say with much justification that to carry out an operation of this size and to surprise one's enemy seems contradictory. How can anyone hide 600 ships, 9,500 aircraft, and nearly 200,000 men, as they are

1944 moved across the water from England to France? Such an undertaking would require skillful deception, if it were at least to confuse and at best totally mislead the enemy, causing the Germans not to concentrate overwhelming strength against the invasion area.

German problems within their armed forces would act in favor of the Allies, as would a lack of high-grade information from air reconnaissance and intelligence sources, as indicated by the following:

• The German armed forces had no centralized chain of command because Hitler was constantly injecting himself into military planning, making it difficult for his senior officers to know whether or not they could or should make certain decisions on their own. Confusion as to who had the authority to direct the movement of forces would result in some crack German divisions not getting to Normandy on D-Day.

• Unbeknownst to the Germans, virtually every Nazi agent in the United Kingdom had been "turned" and was under the control of British intelligence.

• Casualties had taken their toll on the Wehrmacht. One third of its soldiers were thirty-four years old or older; many of the units were heavily represented by foreign troops, 30,000 in the Normandy area alone. When the British landed at Gold, Juno, and Sword beaches, they would find many Russians in German uniforms, who would quickly remove themselves from the scene, leaving their Nazi commanders to fight alone.

• The Luftwaffe lacked the air reconnaissance capability to gather good intelligence on Allied troop movements in England.

• In early May 1944, German army intelligence called the invasion target right on the money, predicting that it would take place on the Normandy coast. However, by mid-May, they changed the target to the Pas de Calais. They reasoned that it was closer to England as well as to Germany, shortening supply lines and the distance the Allies had to fight across France. Pas de Calais also had several excellent ports to accommodate large supply ships.

All of these factors favored the Allies in their decision to invade Normandy, but they would have been of little value if Hitler's instincts had told him that Normandy was the area where the Allies would strike. Actually, Hitler did believe that an attack would take place on the Normandy coast, but he thought it would be only the precursor of a larger assault that would follow in the Pas de Calais area. What the Allies want me to do, reasoned the Führer, is to react to the Normandy invasion by sending all my divisions there, severely reducing forces that could be used in the subsequent attack on the Pas de Calais beaches.

To lend support to the Führer's reasoning, Operation Chattanooga Choo-Choo was initiated, a series of air strikes, 60 percent of which were carried out in the Pas de Calais area. The targets were key bridges and rail

284

lines, and there was an additional motive beyond appearing to be softening up the region in advance of an invasion. The air attacks also had the mission of crippling transportation routes to the extent that German units would have a more difficult time getting out of the area should they be summoned to Normandy.

In the meantime, the Allies had gone to great extremes to build a staging area near Dover, cross-Channel from the Pas de Calais, that appeared to be a large force of troops readying for an invasion. Allied set designers and camouflage artists built what looked from the air like a huge base complete with an oil refinery. Every detail was perfect, right down to the vehicles, which were actually rubber inflatables.

As D-Day approached, several occurrences added to the nervousness of Allied leaders:

• In April, an American general was stripped of his command, demoted, and sent stateside for revealing at a London cocktail party that Europe would be put under attack prior to June 15.

• Also in April 1944, an English officer was being more explicit, suggesting to friends that the Normandy coast appeared to be the likely invasion locale.

• In May and June, the *London Daily Telegraph* crossword puzzle's answers included a disturbing number of D-Day codewords, including Mulberry, Neptune, Omaha, Overlord, and Utah, a happening that, upon investigation, turned out to be just a strange coincidence.

As commander of the Allied forces in Europe, General Dwight David Eisenhower, at his British headquarters, was understandably nervous on the eve of D-Day, jingling the lucky coins in his pocket that had worked in the favor of his troops at both the North African and Sicilian invasions. Having postponed the invasion for one day because of bad weather, he had committed himself to June 6, although the forecast had not vastly improved, since an additional delay would have put off the attack for two weeks in order to get the favorable early morning tides again at Normandy.

Eisenhower is a German name that Hitler probably would have wished for one of his own generals, for it means "one who forges shields and swords." Eisenhower had been born in Dennison, Texas, one of seven boys in a family of limited means. His mother was a pacifist who was often heard to say, "He who conquereth his own soul is greater than he who taketh a city." The Eisenhowers had moved to Abilene, Kansas, where Dwight took the examinations for both Annapolis and West Point at the same time, in quest of a free college education. He was found to be too old for Annapolis but was admitted to West Point when the young man who had finished ahead of him in the examinations failed to pass the physical. At the military academy, Eisenhower had been an average student and had enjoyed some success on the football team until, legend has it, he sustained an injury attempting to tackle Jim Thorpe.

1944   After graduation in 1915, he had been given training assignments during World War I that had kept him out of combat, bad luck for a career army officer trying to advance in the officer ranks. His army days proceeded without opportunities for particular distinction until he was befriended by General Fox Conner, who arranged for Eisenhower to attend the two schools where officers could catch the attention of their superiors, Command and General Staff, where he performed with great distinction. After a stint serving under General Douglas MacArthur in the Philippines, he returned to the United States. Shortly thereafter, he participated in the Louisiana Maneuvers in 1941, where he performed brilliantly, bringing himself to the attention of General George C. Marshall, army chief of staff. After Pearl Harbor, Marshall brought Eisenhower to Washington, assigning him to the War Plans Division of the War Department, where he began working on plans for what he would shortly undertake—a Northern European invasion. Winning Marshall's trust, he had been appointed commanding general of the European Theater of Operations in 1942 while only a major general, having been elevated over a host of officers senior to him in rank. The invasions of North Africa and Sicily had come under his direction, and on Christmas Eve 1943, Dwight Eisenhower had been appointed supreme commander of the Allied Expeditionary Force, with the responsibility for engaging the Germans on the western front, an officer who had never commanded troops during wartime in his entire army career. In the event the invasion failed, Eisenhower had prepared a message that fortunately he never had to transmit: "Our landings in the Cherbourg-Havre area have failed to gain a satisfactory foothold and I have withdrawn the troops. . . . If there is any blame or fault attached to the attempt, it is mine alone."

On the night before the invasion, something happened that, had he known of it, would have ruined what precious little rest Eisenhower would manage before hostilities began. On June 1 and 2, a line of a poem by French poet Paul Verlaine had been inserted in a BBC broadcast—*Les sanglots longs des violons de l'automne* ("The long sobs of the violins of autumn"). It was a signal to members of the French resistance to stay close to their radios, for the second half of the message would mean that D-Day would take place within forty-eight hours. On the eve of D-Day, the second half of the message was broadcast four times—*Blessent mon coeur d'une langeur monotone* ("Wound my heart with a monotonous languor"). What Eisenhower did not know was that, through an agent, German intelligence had learned of the significance of that message and immediately passed on the news to Field Marshals Rommel and von Rundstedt that the invasion was imminent. Both men chose to disregard the intelligence because the weather in the English Channel was so poor, and Rommel, Germany's most effective general, decided that he would **1944** take advantage of the invasion-proof weather, heading home to pay a short visit to his wife on her birthday. He would miss the first hours of the invasion, hours he knew would be critical to its outcome. He had remarked to an aide just two months earlier, "Believe me, Lang, the first twenty-four hours of the invasion will be decisive . . . for the Allies as well as Germany it will be the longest day."

As Allied ships headed for Normandy, other vessels proceeded toward the Pas de Calais area, using special instruments that caused German radar screens to be filled with blips, simulating a giant fleet. Dummy paratroopers made of rubber were dropped on the beaches, equipped with recordings of weapons fire and soldiers' voices, while overhead Allied aircraft dropped bits of metal foil that affected German radar so as to give the appearance of squadrons of planes headed toward the bogus invasion site.

When dawn came to Normandy, Major Werner Pluskat, commander of gun emplacements overlooking the beaches, called division headquarters to report that ships were off what the Allies called Omaha Beach. When headquarters asked in which direction the ships were headed, Major Pluskat answered, "Right for me."

• Only one panzer division of the ten that could have been made available was pressed into service on D-Day. Military expert B. H. Liddell Hart later gave the opinion that the employment of just three of the ten divisions would have prevented the Allies from consolidating their positions.

• A highly trusted German spy under British control kept sending bogus reports to German intelligence after the landings, indicating a second invasion. It would be well into the summer before it dawned on the German command that Allied troops would probably not attempt to storm the beaches of Pas de Calais.

The following is a chronology of some other events in the war:

January 22—Allied forces landed at Anzio on the central Italian coast, just thirty-five miles from Rome. (The first man out of his landing craft was a 6-foot 7-inch GI named James Arness, who later starred in the long-running television series *Gunsmoke*. Arness had been selected to go first because his commanding officer wanted to see how deep the water was.) After initial success, the Allied troops did not press their advantage over the Germans, enabling them to dig in, turning Anzio into an unnecessarily long and bloody battle before the Nazis were subdued, delaying the capture of Rome until June 5. Major General John P. Lucas was relieved of his command two days after the battle started.

February 2—For the first time during the war, Allied troops attacked

1944 Japanese territory, assaulting areas of the Marshall Islands that had been under Japanese mandate before the war started. All previous engagements had been fought on lands that had been seized from Allied countries by Japan.

March—American intelligence agents were shocked, according to Irving Wallace, when they saw a short story in the March issue of *Astounding Science Fiction* magazine describing a weapon that was a dead ringer for the atomic bomb under development in the United States. "Made of an isotope of uranium, U-235," it packed the power to lay waste an entire planet, and the hero of the story described the inner workings of the weapon, how it was activated, and the resulting detonation, all of which were astonishingly similar to what the Manhattan Project expected from its own efforts. When agents looked into the origin of author Cleve Cartmill's short story, they were even more nonplussed. He had done his research at the public library, using scientific sources readily available to anyone who asked for them.

March 10—Ireland refused to send home German and Japanese diplomats posted to their shores as requested by the United States.

April 24—The U.S. War Department forecast that "the collapse of Japan can only be assured by the invasion of Japan proper."

June 4—The U.S.S. *Pillsbury* captured a Nazi U-boat, the first time that an enemy vessel had been taken on the high seas since 1815.

June 10—SS troops attempting to reach the Normandy front from Toulouse had been hampered by French resistance, and they had also had one of their officers kidnapped by partisans. To pay the penalty for these crimes, the SS chose the village of Oradour-sur-Glâne not far from Limoges, although none of its inhabitants had taken part in either action against the Nazis. Nearly 600 men, women, and children were put to death.

June 13—Germany began the use of a devastating weapon called the *Vergeltungswaffe-1*, or Reprisal Weapon-1, which would be known by the Britons as the V-1. The 25-foot-long rocket bomb built by Volkswagen cost only $600 to manufacture and was launched from the French coast of the English Channel, arriving over the target area with a buzzing sound, followed by a terrifying screeching noise as the weapon hurtled downward. It was followed in the fall by the V-2, which had a 2,000-pound warhead and made its descent at over 2,000 miles per hour, fueled by alcohol and liquid oxygen. If Hitler had come into the possession of these unmanned weapons earlier, the war might well have had a different outcome. The weapons would kill 10,000 Britons and injure 28,000 more, chiefly civilians, and would cause approximately 13,000 casualties in the Antwerp area.

• The V-2 rocket had been designed by an engineer named Wernher von Braun, whose invention would pioneer missile development. He
288

would come to the United States following the war to lend his expertise to America's rocket program.

• The British called the German weapons "Bob Hopes"—"Bob down, and hope for the best."

July 9—The island of Saipan fell to American forces in a bloody battle that accounted for nearly 4,000 army and over 10,000 marine casualties.

• En route to Saipan, a sergeant was giving his men an orientation of the island: "Saipan is covered with dense jungle, quicksand, steep hills and cliffs hiding batteries of huge coastal guns, and strongholds of reinforced concrete. Insects bear lethal poisons. Crocodiles and snakes infest the streams. The waters around it are thick with sharks. The population will be hostile towards us." After a lengthy pause, a corporal popped up, "Sarge, why don't we just let the Japs keep it?"

August—Tipped off by informers as to their whereabouts, the Nazis found seven Jews hiding in an attic in Amsterdam. Teenager Anne Frank was one of those apprehended, and she and her mother and sister later died in concentration camps. Her father survived and returned to their Amsterdam hiding place to find Anne's diary of her two years there, which later would be published as *The Diary of a Young Girl*.

October 23—*Time* magazine reported the death of Germany's youngest and most brilliant field marshal, Erwin Eugen Rommel, in an automobile accident when his staff car was strafed by an Allied fighter on July 17. Actually Rommel was very much alive on July 17. But when an assassination attempt on the Führer failed on July 20, he was suspected of being sympathetic to its intent. On October 14, two generals arrived at Rommel's house, saying that he was suspected of being a part of the plot to kill Hitler, offering him the choice of committing suicide or of being put on trial. Frau Rommel recalls:

> As he entered the room there was so strange and terrible an expression on his face that I exclaimed at once, "What is the matter with you? What has happened? Are you ill?" He looked at me and replied: "I have come to say good-bye. In a quarter of an hour I shall be dead. . . . They suspect me of having taken part in the attempt to kill Hitler. It seems that my name was on Goerdeler's list to be President of the Reich. . . . I have never seen Goerdeler in my life. . . . The Führer has given me the choice of taking poison or being dragged before the People's Court. They have brought the poison. They say it will only take three seconds to act. . . . I would not be afraid to be tried in public, for I can defend everything I have done. But I know that I should never see Berlin alive."

1944

• "The fact that your husband, Field Marshal Rommel, has died a hero's death as the result of his wounds, after we had all hoped that he would remain to the German people, has deeply touched me. I send you, my dear Frau Rommel, the heartfelt sympathy of myself and the German Luftwaffe. In silent compassion, Yours, Göring, *Reichsmarschall des Grossdeutschen Reiches*."

☛ PEOPLE IN THE WAR

In 1913, Theodore Roosevelt had said, "I had always felt that if there was a serious war I wished to be in a position to explain my position to my children why I did take part in it and not why I did not take part in it."

His own military service is well known. As to his four sons, each served in World War I, during which Theodore Roosevelt, Jr., was awarded the Purple Heart, the U.S. Distinguished Service Medal, and the Distinguished Service Cross; Archibald was severely wounded, awarded the Croix de Guerre, and discharged as disabled; Kermit served first in the British army and later, with the United States' entry into the war, with the American army; and Quentin was shot down and killed by German fighters over France.

The surviving three sons each served again in World War II. Theodore Roosevelt, Jr., was part of the first assault wave to land on Normandy on D-Day and was awarded the Congressional Medal of Honor posthumously (he died soon after the landing, of natural causes). Kermit, too, died of natural causes while on duty, in Alaska. Archibald was again severely wounded, this time fighting in the Pacific, and was again discharged as disabled.

A Connecticut boy named George Bush had enlisted in the navy's flight training program on his eighteenth birthday and, when he won his wings, had become the youngest pilot in the U.S. Navy. On September 24, 1944, Lieutenant (junior grade) Bush, having reached the ripe old age of twenty, took off from the carrier *San Jacinto* in a torpedo bomber on a mission to knock out a Japanese radio transmitter on a small island north of Iwo Jima called Chi Chi Jima. As he moved in on the target, his aircraft was hit by Japanese antiaircraft fire, killing one of his two crew members and setting the plane on fire. Nevertheless, Bush continued his dive and, before bailing out, let loose his bombs, several of which hit the target. The other crewman died when his parachute failed to open properly, but Bush landed safely in the ocean, inflated a raft, and began paddling away from shore. Witnessing Bush's descent, a Japanese boat headed out from the island to pick up the aviator, but one of his fellow pilots spotted him and the pursuing craft and managed to halt the vessel with his fire. Not long afterward, an American submarine that had been alerted to Bush's position surfaced nearby and took him aboard.

Since the submarine was on patrol duty, Bush spent the next month aboard, during which time the U.S.S. *Finback* underwent several depth charge attacks, as well as a surface assault from a Japanese bomber. The *Finback* finally dropped Bush off at Midway, and he was later awarded the Distinguished Flying Cross and three Air Medals for heroism.

Second Subaltern Elizabeth Alexander Mary Windsor, eighteen, was an automobile mechanic in the British Auxiliary Territorial Service, and the future queen of England successfully passed her course in heavy mechanics.

☛ NATIONAL NEWS

The *New York Times* summed up the first presidential election during a war year since 1864 as follows:

Franklin D. Roosevelt has been re-elected in a war year as a war President who could promise the country victory in the war and on the basis of victory, a lasting peace. If a majority of the American people were willing to accept the hazardous precedent of a fourth term, it seems clearly because they were convinced that in this extraordinary crisis the Republican party offered them no satisfactory substitute for Mr. Roosevelt's experience in military affairs and foreign policy, and no equally good assurance that under Republican leadership the country could achieve a lasting peace.

Defeating Thomas E. Dewey, Roosevelt tallied 432 electoral votes and a popular vote victory of over 3.5 million votes.

☛ MEDICINE

Polio cases totaled about 20,000, the largest number since 1916 when 27,621 had been reported.

American manufacturers of artificial limbs were running way behind on orders and were unable to accept a Soviet request for 2 million artificial legs.

☞ SCIENCE

The first "automatic digital computer" was constructed at Harvard with a grant of $5 million from IBM. The machine had 760,000 parts and 500 miles of wire, and took a sprightly four seconds to deliver simple multiplication, eleven for simple division, although it was frequently idled by mechanical problems.

☞ BOOKS

Kathleen Winsor wanted to write a novel on British kings of the late seventeenth century and read 400 books on the subject, keeping notes that began to fill some very hefty notebooks. It took her five years to write a manuscript of approximately 2.5 million words that came to 971 pages when it was published in 1944, weighing in at two pounds. *Forever Amber* contained abundant amounts of sex, which may have helped the novel sell more than 1 million copies in its first year of publication.

☞ FASHION

Wartime shortages dictated many styles. Skirts were up to the knee and supplied with a single kick pleat for roominess. Suit jackets lost their collars and cuffs. Stylish women were urged to rely on the "good little black dress," which they could "vary" with accessories. A favorite with less wealthy women was the dirndl, a simple gathered skirt which could be run up from two yards of cotton in an hour or two. The boxy, broad-shouldered look was in, achieved with shoulder pads and, in summer, cap sleeves. Someone invented the shirtwaist dress, which has never altogether gone out of fashion since. Someone else came up with leg makeup to replace scarce silk and unobtainable nylon hose; it went out of fashion almost immediately.

Millinery went skimpy too. For formal occasions, women wore off-the-face hats, decorated with eye veils, but by far the most common head covering was a large square scarf, folded into a triangle and tied under the chin.

☞ THE HOME FRONT

Fuel supplies in the eastern United States were bolstered by the completion of the world's longest petroleum pipeline, which stretched from Texas to eastern Pennsylvania. Called the Big Inch, the pipeline had been built across thirty rivers and 200 streams.

Office of Price Administration head Chester A. Bowles put consumer purchases of black market items during 1943 at over $1 billion.

Americans had become extremely productive savers and gatherers of items that the government had asked civilians to salvage for use in the war effort. Drives in 1944 produced 18.5 million tons of scrap iron and steel, 185,676 tons of tin cans, 7 million tons of wastepaper, and 84,807 tons of fat.

☛ ANIMALS

A German shepherd was awarded the Distinguished Service Medal for attacking a machine gun nest in the Sicilian invasion, and seven dogs were commended posthumously for their action in the South Pacific.

☛ ENTERTAINMENT

The Ringling Brothers and Barnum & Bailey circus was giving a matinee performance in Hartford when the big top burst into flames, dropping burning canvas on the crowd. One hundred sixty-eight persons died, 487 were injured, and one of the people who died was a young girl whom no one identified. Because her face had not been burned, her photograph was displayed across the United States in the hope that some relative or friend might come forth to identify her, but the girl's identity has never been discovered.

One of the extras in the 1944 film *Bathing Beauty* was a young Latin who would later have a baseball tryout with the Washington Senators. His name was Fidel Castro.

One of the youngest majors in the U.S. Army was Howard Cosell, who had joined as a private. He saw his rank rapidly improve at his post at the New York Port of Embarkation.

Turned down for the draft because, at 140 pounds, he was underweight for his height, 6-feet 2.5 inch actor Jimmy Stewart fattened himself up by 10 pounds and was accepted in the U.S. Army Air Corps prior to Pearl Harbor. In 1944, he was awarded the Distinguished Flying Cross and also came home with the Croix de Guerre and the Air Medal.

1944   Actor Clark Gable had flown missions over Germany in B-17s while filming material for a training film. When Luftwaffe head Goering heard that Gable was taking to the air, he offered $5,000, a promotion, and a long rest to the pilot who could manage to blast the movie star out of the skies. The award was never claimed, and Major Gable was discharged in 1944 with the Distinguished Flying Cross, his discharge papers signed by a Captain Ronald Reagan, who had been kept stateside because of poor eyesight.

☛ PRODUCTS

The Federal Trade Commission, with broad duties to monitor deceptive claims, filed suit against Wallace Laboratories seeking removal of the word "liver" from its Carter's Little Liver Pills product. Before the suit was settled in the government's favor, 11,000 pages of testimony were recorded and the case was carried to the Supreme Court.

The United Fruit Company believed that it could increase the sales of its bananas if it created a brand name that would set its fruit apart from unbranded bananas. And so Chiquita Banana was introduced with a musical radio jingle that was soon familiar to millions of Americans:

> I'm Chiquita Banana
> And I've come to say
> Bananas have to ripen in a certain way.
> When they are flecked with brown and have a golden hue
> Bananas taste the best and are the best for you.
> You can put them in a salad
> You can put them in a pie-aye.
> Any way you want to eat them
> It's impossible to beat them.
> But bananas love the climate of the very, very tropical equator
> So you should never put bananas in the refrigerator.

☛ RELIGION

Four chaplains who served on the same troop transport received the Distinguished Service Cross, awarded posthumously. All four had served on the *Dorchester* when it was struck by a torpedo off the coast of **1944** Greenland. *Time* magazine wrote, "Together they passed out life jackets, encouraged panicky soldiers to jump. When all other life jackets were gone, the four chaplains gave away their own. Survivors last saw them standing together on the deck, arms linked, praying, as the ship went down." The four men who were honored were George L. Fox and Clark V. Poling, Protestants, John P. Washington, Catholic, and Alexander D. Goode, a Jew.

1945

This war, like the next war, is a war to end war.

—David Lloyd George

Sometime they'll give a war and nobody will come.

—Carl Sandburg

☛ THE HOME FRONT

While Allied forces were winning one victory after another in Europe and in the Pacific, the preoccupation of those at home was on one simple question: How soon would the war be over? Subsections of that question were expressed in other questions: Would Hitler surrender? Would America have to invade Japan? Would the troops who had fought in Europe have to go to the Pacific? And there were many permutations to the subsection questions as well.

Life in the United States, as it has a way of doing, also proceeded on more mundane levels in 1945:

• Considerably ahead of their time, the citizens of Grand Rapids, Michigan, agreed to have fluoride added to the town's water supply in order to combat tooth decay.

• An ex-coast guardsman named Arthur Michael Godfrey took to the

296

airwaves of the CBS radio network, where he would remain for twenty-
seven years.

• A fourteen-year-old boy named Merrill Kenneth Wolf received a B.A. degree in music from Yale.

• Unhappily, the final year of the war was marked by a low point in marital fidelity. The divorce rate peaked in the United States at 3.5 per thousand, up from 0.9 in 1910. After the war, it would move steadily downward until 1963.

• Sugar reserves had been severely depleted, resulting in a 25 percent cut in rations. Better news was the lifting of shoe rationing.

• The dominance of the Allies in world skies resulted in a 30 percent cut in the production of military aircraft.

• The Federal Communications Commission specified the use of thirteen channels for the fledgling commercial television industry, although channel 1 was later reclaimed for noncommercial use.

• A New York City woman named Bess Myerson, twenty-one, was crowned Miss America at Atlantic City, New Jersey.

☛ AMERICAN GENERALS

No American soldier contributed more to the success of the European War than a general named George Smith Patton, Jr., a West Point graduate who had led one of first American tank units into battle in World War I, winning the Distinguished Service Cross and the Distinguished Service Medal for his efforts. A career soldier who truly loved his profession, Patton was a flamboyant man who once said, "The leader must be an actor. He is unconvincing unless he lives the part." And Patton played his role in the theater of warfare to the hilt, donning his pearl-handled pistols, working, berating, driving, inspiring, and praising his men until they were among the elite fighting groups in the world. Nicknamed Old Blood and Guts, Patton so often volunteered himself and his troops for difficult campaigns that his men's response to the general's nickname was summed up as follows: "His guts, our blood."

In 1943, Patton had been severely censured for verbally and physically abusing two hospitalized soldiers for malingering when they were truly ill, resulting in considerable negative publicity on the home front. Patton's anti-Soviet sentiments also received attention, as did his admiration for some characteristics of the German character. Patton often had his boot-shod foot in his mouth, causing his commanding officer a myriad of problems. Yet Ike well knew Patton's abundant gifts for military command. When contemplating who should command American forces in the Normandy invasion, Eisenhower wrote General George Marshall that "Patton certainly deserved consideration. His rehabilitation of the II

Corps in Tunisia had been 'quickly and magnificently done,' and his leadership in Sicily was 'close to the best of our classic examples.'"

When Patton reached the Rhine River, some say that he urinated into that body of water as a symbolic gesture of his disdain for the Nazis, although other sources say that he had relieved himself in the Seine. Whether or not the Rhine story is true is unimportant. It is totally consistent with his personality—tough, defiant, irreverent. Show the enemy no sympathy; let him know your disdain and hatred for him. These were truisms for Patton. But even more important to Patton's military credo was attack, attack, attack, always move forward as quickly as possible, and when you encountered the enemy face to face, as Patton once told a group of trainees, "Rip their belly buttons; spill their guts around."

• "To be a successful soldier, you must know history. . . . What you must know is how a man reacts. Weapons change but a man who uses them changes not at all. To win battles you do not beat weapons—you beat the soul of man, of the enemy man." (General George S. Patton, Jr.)

Halfway around the world, General Douglas MacArthur was also advancing toward his ultimate goal. If Patton's goal was the capture of Berlin, MacArthur's was the conquest of Tokyo. He was a brilliant general whom Generals Marshall and Montgomery would acknowledge as the finest strategist in World War II. He also had a first-rate mind, and many would call him a genius. And he was a man who dared death, who had become the youngest divisional commander in World War I, earning, like Patton, the Distinguished Service Cross and the Distinguished Service Medal.

MacArthur had been born on an army post, the son of General Arthur MacArthur, who had won the Medal of Honor for actions during the Civil War. He had graduated from West Point with the highest marks seen at the academy in a quarter of a century. During World War I, MacArthur had been wounded twice, received thirteen decorations, and was cited for bravery under fire no fewer than thirteen times. Following the war, he had taken command of West Point. No American fighting man came to World War II with a better background, and MacArthur was given command of military forces in the Far East. Forced to evacuate the Philippines, he had promised to return and had fulfilled that promise in October 1944.

Despite his impeccable credentials, MacArthur had managed to incur the wrath of a host of American leaders because of his incredible ego and a drive for self-aggrandizement that was all-consuming. In the mid-1930s, Franklin Roosevelt had described the general as the second most dangerous man in the United States, topped only by Huey Long. Harold Ickes described him as "the type of man who thinks that when he gets to heaven, God will step down from the great white throne and bow him into His vacated seat." Dwight Eisenhower, a man well known for his lack of rancor toward his fellowman, spoke of his pre-World War II days serving under MacArthur as follows: "I studied dramatics under him for five years in Washington and four years in the Philippines." And Harry Truman, not one to hold back his true feelings, remarked, "There was never anybody around him to keep him in line. He didn't have anybody on his staff that wasn't an ass kisser. He just wouldn't let anybody near him who wouldn't kiss his ass. So . . . there were times when he was . . . I think out of his head and didn't know what he was doing."

But in the spring of 1945, MacArthur knew exactly what he was doing and was doing it well, restoring lands spread across half an ocean with fertile imagination and with amazing speed.

NATIONAL NEWS

Franklin Delano Roosevelt was relaxing at his cottage in Warm Springs, Georgia, at about one o'clock on the afternoon of April 12, 1945, having his portrait painted while he chatted with two cousins and his love of days gone by, Lucy Rutherford. Suddenly, he put his hand to his forehead and fell back in his chair, saying, "I have a terrific headache," the last words he ever spoke.

When the president's doctor arrived, he found FDR's blood pressure at 300/190 and diagnosed the patient as having "suffered a massive cerebral hemorrhage," administering papaverine and amyl nitrate. Failing to respond to treatment, Roosevelt died at 3:31 P.M. Author John Gunther writes, "A cloud of grief . . . descended on the country and world. Citizens saw the headlines and burst into tears."

Roosevelt would have chuckled at Gunther's report, knowing that many who had disagreed with his policies would be dry-eyed upon his death. But even his detractors felt that the timing of his death was unfair. For a man who, in ill health, had literally given his life for his country by presiding over the nation during the war, it seemed only proper that he be allowed to see the fruits of his efforts that would come so shortly— peace.

PEOPLE IN THE WAR

Of all the sung and unsung heroes of World War II, one bears special mention. Audie Leon Murphy had joined the army as a private in 1942 at sixteen, claiming to be a year older. By the winter of 1945, the nineteen-year-old Murphy had received numerous battlefield promotions and was a second lieutenant. He had also received twenty-four decorations, more

1945 than any other soldier in the war, including the Medal of Honor, the Distinguished Service Cross, the French Legion of Honor, the Croix de Guerre, three Silver Stars, the Bronze Star, three Purple Hearts, and the Legion of Merit. Murphy had killed or captured 240 German soldiers, and his Medal of Honor citation reads as follows:

> Near Holtzwihr, France, 26 January 1945 . . . Second Lieutenant Murphy commanded Company B, which was attacked by six tanks and waves of infantry . . . ordered his men to withdraw . . . while he remained forward at his command post and continued to give fire directions to the artillery by telephone. Behind him, to his right, one of our tank destroyers received a direct hit and began to burn. Its crew withdrew. . . . With the enemy tanks abreast of his position, [he] climbed on the burning tank destroyer, which was in danger of blowing up at any moment, and employed its .50 caliber machine gun against the enemy. He was alone and exposed to German fire from three sides, but his deadly fire killed dozens of Germans and caused their infantry attack to waver. . . . For an hour, the Germans tried every available weapon to eliminate [him], but he continued to hold his position and wiped out a squad which was trying to creep up unnoticed on his right flank. Germans reached as close as ten yards, only to be mowed down by his fire. He received a leg wound, but ignored it and continued the single-handed fight until his ammunition was exhausted. He then made his way to his company, refused medical attention, and organized the company in a counterattack which forced the Germans to withdraw.

☛ THE EUROPEAN WAR

January 16—Hitler took up quarters in a bunker under the Reichs Chancellery in Berlin, moving there from his command post in East Prussia.

February 13–14—In a raid that would be highly criticized for humanitarian reasons, Allied bombers attacked Dresden, believed to be a key German communications center for the eastern front, raining tons of incendiary bombs on the city.

It was later determined that Dresden was packed with refugees. Else Wendel, a German housewife writes:

> There were two hundred thousand refugees in Dresden when,
> on the night of 13 February 1945, the firestorms fell on the

town. There are no figures of the numbers who perished that night in Dresden, for the simple fact that the chaos was so complete no one knew who was in town and who was not. Identification being impossible, and a decent burial out of the question, petrol was poured over the corpses, and all of them were set alight. Officially it was reported by the German authorities that the casualties were four hundred thousand. The British gave the numbers as two hundred and fifty thousand. No one will ever know the truth.

• Author Kurt Vonnegut, Jr., was a prisoner of war in Dresden during the raid and escaped death by being in an underground slaughterhouse. *Slaughterhouse Five* is, in part, based on his recollections of the bombing.

March 14—Nazi official Adolf Eichmann, sensing that the days of the Third Reich were numbered, stated that he "could go to his grave happy knowing that he had helped kill six million Jews." In the late winter of 1945, Allied armies moving toward Berlin began liberating concentration camps, and the world began to know the full dimension of the horrors that had taken place in Hitler's efforts to exterminate European Jewry.

• When General Patton visited the Ohrdruf Nord Camp, that hardened soldier vomited while touring the facilities. He was so horrified at the conditions that he summoned the mayor of the town and his wife and personally conducted them through the buildings so that they could see with their own eyes what gross crimes against mankind had been practiced in their town. When the couple returned home, they hanged themselves.

April 28—Caught by Italian partisans as he was attempting to flee to Switzerland, Benito Mussolini was killed by a firing squad with his mistress, Claretta Petacci.
April 30—Adolf Hitler and Eva Braun, his wife of one day, committed suicide in the bunker under the Riechs Chancellery in Berlin as Russian troops closed in.

• "German men and women, soldiers of the German Armed Forces. Our Führer, Adolf Hitler, is dead. The German people bow in deepest sorrow and respect. Early he had recognized the terrible danger of Bolshevism and had dedicated his life to the fight against it. His fight having ended, he died a hero's death in the capital of the German Reich, after having led an unmistakably straight and steady life." (Gross Admiral Karl Doenitz)

1945 ☛ THE PACIFIC WAR

February 19—The bloodiest battles involving American troops in the Pacific, unlike the European war, were reserved for the finale. Moving closer and closer to the Japanese mainland, the U.S. Marines attacked Iwo Jima, an island of only eight square miles, deemed to be an ideal location for an airbase, to assist in attacks on Japan. It took almost a month to overcome Japanese troops burrowed in caves and hillside bunkers, and American casualties were extremely high.

March 9–10—The most devastating air raid of the war in the Pacific was carried out not on Hiroshima, not on Nagasaki, but on Tokyo on the night of March 9 by 279 American B-29s. High-level pinpoint bombing had failed to curtail Japanese war production, especially since it was heavily diversified into small factories and home machine shops; it was decided instead to resort to low-level incendiary bombing of the slum district Shitamachi, where much of this scattered industry was located. The airmen were to fly in low and drop bombs filled with a relatively new fire-inducing substance called napalm. This brought about incredible devastation, creating a firestorm that consumed thousands of homes and buildings, and heat that brought lakes and rivers to a boil. An estimated 100,000 people died.

April 1—Sixty thousand American soldiers and marines attacked Okinawa, only 360 miles south of Japan. Okinawa was eventually taken, but with the highest casualty rate ever sustained by American troops, one regiment losing nearly 2,900 of its 3,500 men.

May 24—American military leaders set November 1 as the date for the invasion of Japan.

July 16—A secret message was sent to Washington from rural New Mexico, which read, "Operated on this morning. Diagnosis not yet complete but results seem satisfactory and already exceed expectations." The first atomic bomb had been detonated just before sunrise at Alamogordo, New Mexico. Author Peter Wyden writes, "At 5:29:45, suddenly, noiselessly, the sky ignited. A yellow-reddish fireball infinitely brighter than the sun, its temperature 10,000 times greater, began an eight-mile ascent . . . turning night into day for more than a hundred miles . . . scientists were 'shaking hands, slapping each other on the back, laughing like happy children.'" But, according to Wyden, scientist Isadore Rabi had a different reaction: "At first I was thrilled. It was a vision. Then, a few minutes afterward, I had gooseflesh all over me when I realized what this meant for the future of humanity."

July 27—The USS *Indianapolis* delivered "essential components" of the atomic bomb to an American airbase at Tinian Island. Three days later, the ship sank in the Indian Ocean after being hit by a torpedo.

302

July—Kamikaze attacks in World War II accounted for the destruction of forty-five American ships and inflicted heavy damage on many others, including ten aircraft carriers and fifteen battleships. As Japan was pushed back to its home islands, the attacks became more numerous.

• "The Empire stands at the crossroads between victory and defeat. The first suicide unit determined to triumph through the power of the spirit will inspire, by its success, one unit after another to follow its example. It is absolutely out of the question for you to return alive. Your mission involves certain death. Your bodies will be dead, but not your spirits. The death of a single one of you will be the birth of a million others. Neglect nothing that may affect your training or your health. You must not leave behind you any cause for regret, which would follow you into eternity. And, lastly: do not be in too much of a hurry to die. If you cannot find your target, turn back; next time you may find a more favorable opportunity. Choose a death which brings about the maximum result." (First order to the Kamikazes)

• "I leave for the attack with a smile on my face. The moon will be full tonight. As I fly over the open sea . . . I will choose the enemy ship that is to be my target . . . I will show you that I know how to die bravely." (A Kamikaze pilot)

August 5—Shortly after Harry Truman assumed the presidency, he was briefed on the development of the atomic bomb by Henry L. Stimson, secretary of war. At Stimson's urging, the president formed a committee to, in Truman's words, "study with great care the implications the new weapon might have for us." The committee included James F. Byrnes, secretary of state; Ralph A. Bard, undersecretary of state; George L. Harrison, special assistant to the secretary of state; Dr. James B. Conant, president of Harvard and chairman of the National Defense Research Committee; Dr. Vannevar Bush, director of the Office of Scientific Research and Development; and Dr. Karl T. Compton, president of M.I.T.

Offering technical assistance to the committee were four scientists who were key figures in the development of the bomb: Dr. Arthur H. Compton, Dr. Enrico Fermi, Dr. E. O. Lawrence, and Dr. J. Robert Oppenheimer.

After due deliberation, the committee recommended that the bomb be deployed against the enemy at the earliest possible date; further, according to Truman, that it "be used without specific warning against a target which would show its devastating strength."

In his memoirs, Truman states that the scientists advising the committee ruled out a "technical demonstration" of the weapon in a remote, uninhabited area as a means of convincing the Japanese of the destruction that such a weapon might render if deployed against their homeland.

In the end, of course, the decision to use the weapon was Truman's alone. It was typical of the man that he did not vacillate despite the grave consequences involved. He later repeatedly stated that the decision was obvious, that no other alternative existed, and that debating whether or not to use this new means of inflicting inestimable destruction and loss of life had not caused him the loss of a moment's sleep. That is because Truman was convinced, according to author Merle Miller, that "if we had to invade Japan, half a million soldiers of both sides would have been killed and a million more 'would have been maimed for life.' It was a simple as that. That was all there was to it."

However, Truman commented, "I wanted to make sure it [the bomb] would be used as a weapon of war in the manner prescribed in the laws of war. That meant that I wanted it dropped on a military target . . . a war production center of prime military importance."

On the night of August 5, the president was crossing the Atlantic on the U.S.S. *Augusta*, returning from a meeting at Potsdam with Premier Stalin and two British prime ministers, Churchill and Atlee (Churchill had been removed from office in mid-conference when the Conservative Party had been decisively defeated in parliamentary elections, forcing his resignation). As the ship steamed towards Norfolk, Truman did not know the exact date of the bombing. Nor did the president know exactly what target would be bombed, four having been selected in order of priority, with the understanding that weather conditions over the target could alter the order of preference. But there was one thing that the president knew for sure. Within the next few days, horrendous destruction would be wrought upon either Hiroshima, Kokura, Niigata, or Nagasaki by the most cataclysmic force ever conceived by man.

August 6—A Japanese journalist writes:

> The town was not much damaged. It had suffered little from bombing. There were only two minor raids, one on 19 March last by a squadron of American naval planes, and one on 30 April by a Flying Fortress.
>
> On 6 August there wasn't a cloud in the sky above Hiroshima, and a mild, hardly perceptible wind blew from the south. Visibility was almost perfect for ten or twelve miles.
>
> At nine minutes past seven in the morning an air-raid warning sounded and four American B-29 planes appeared. To the north of the town two of them turned and made off to the south and disappeared in the direction of the Shoho Sea. The

other two, after having circled the neighborhood of Shukai, flew off at high speed southwards in the direction of the Bingo Sea.

At 7:31 the all-clear was given. Feeling themselves in safety, people came out of their shelters and went about their affairs and the work of the day began.

Suddenly a glaring whitish pinkish light appeared in the sky accompanied by an unnatural tremor which was followed almost immediately by a wave of suffocating heat and a wind which swept away everything in its path.

Within a few seconds the thousands of people in the streets and the gardens in the center of town were scorched by a wave of searing heat. Many were killed instantly, others lay writhing on the ground screaming in agony from the intolerable pain of their burns. Everything standing upright in the way of the blast—walls, houses, factories and other buildings—was annihilated and the debris spun round in a whirlwind and was carried up in the air. Trams were picked up and tossed aside as though they had neither weight nor solidity. Trains were flung off the rails as though they were toys. Horses, dogs and cattle suffered the same fate as human begins. Every living thing was petrified in an attitude of indescribable suffering.

Even the vegetation did not escape. Trees went up in flames, the rice plants lost their greenness, the grass burned on the ground like dry straw.

Beyond the zone of utter death in which nothing remained alive houses collapsed in a whirl of beams, bricks and girders. Up to about three miles from the center of the Explosion lightly built houses were flattened as though they had been built of cardboard. Those who were inside were either killed or wounded. Those who managed to extricate themselves by some miracle found themselves surrounded by a ring of fire. And the few who succeeded in making their way to safety generally died twenty or thirty days later from the delayed effects of the deadly gamma rays. Some of the reinforced concrete or stone buildings remained standing, but their interiors were completely gutted by the blast.

About half an hour after the explosion, whilst the sky all around Hiroshima was still cloudless, a fine rain began to fall on the town and went on for about five minutes. It was caused by the sudden rise of over-heated air to a great height, where it condensed and fell back as rain. Then a violent wind rose

1945 and the fires extended with terrible rapidity, because most Japanese houses are built only of timber and straw.

By the evening the fire began to die down and then it went out. There was nothing left to burn. Hiroshima had ceased to exist.

• "A single demand on you, comrades. Provide us with atomic weapons in the shortest possible time. You know that Hiroshima has shaken the whole world. The balance has been destroyed. Provide the bomb—it will remove a great danger to us." (Joseph Stalin)

• "If I would be a young man again and had to decide how to make my living, I would not try to become a scientist or scholar or teacher. I would rather choose to be a plumber. . . ." (Albert Einstein)

INDEX

309

INDEX

311

318